AN ENDURING ...

*The History of Troy Annual Conference
1982-2010*

with

*The Story of Troy Conference Camps
1805-2010*

by

Ralph A. Marino

*Published by
The United Methodist Church
Troy Annual Conference
Commission on Archives and History*

Troy, NY

ISBN 978-0-615-37019-4

Printed in the United States of America

5 4 3 2 1

Contents

Acknowledgments

As the primary author of a history covering a time period I saw unfolding through the years, I am very conscious that making history is easier than writing about it. I've discovered that some things I remembered didn't happen and many things happened that I didn't remember. This trip down memory lane has been challenging, exciting, and even comforting as the Troy Conference I knew and loved goes out of existence.

Fortunately, I did not have to make this trip alone. My wife Jackie readily agreed to serve as copy editor, even knowing that she would be reading everything at least twice while postponing things as important as anniversary celebrations and visits with our grandchildren. Her guidance, organizational skills, and careful eye brought us, without untoward incident, from early draft to the finished product you have in your hands. Thanks to her also for fixing several excellent lunches when the editorial team met around our dining table. My long-time friend, Bill Pattison, whose collaboration with me goes back to the days when video was done in black and white on reel-to-reel recorders, was quick to sign on as photography editor. Beyond selecting, preparing, and placing the pictures, he also spent considerable time searching them out from books, boxes, and a variety of digital formats. He was also our dependable and high-tech link to all things computer related in the book creation process. They have both done their very excellent best to keep me from egregious errors. I'm sure some mistakes have slipped through anyway, but the responsibility for that is mine. The polished prose is due to their patient diligence.

Many others were willing to prepare materials for me

and then allow me the freedom to edit and adjust as I saw fit. I have not deliberately violated their trust. See the Other Voices on page v for the names of those who so fully supported my efforts to tell the human side of the story. I appreciate the time Julius Archibald, Bill Lasher, David Murphy, Harold Shippey, and Patricia Thompson spent in reading parts of the manuscript and raising red flags where I went astray. Their friendship and support give me confidence that the parts of the text under their scrutiny are a faithful record of our past.

Additional thanks go to Karen Staulters, conference archivist, both for permission to use materials she previously prepared and for other details she researched as the project moved along. The major sources of this work are the conference journals, so I thank the editors for their patiently created records of the daily proceedings, as well as the report writers who year by year did their best to keep track of how the old transitioned to the new.

I am grateful to the Conference Commission on Archives and History for choosing me to write this account and for the confidence they showed in my decisions throughout the project.

And finally, thank you to all the congregations, pastors, and bishops of Troy Conference from its beginning to the present day. I found great pleasure, through the writing of this history, in this opportunity to know you better.

Ralph A. Marino
Valley Falls, NY
2010

Other Voices

Foreword

Troy Annual Conference held its first session at State Street Methodist Church in Troy, NY, on August 28, 1833. The adventure of Methodism in upstate New York and Vermont from its pre-conference days of the late 1700s through its mature functioning in 1981 is more than ably recounted in *A Flame of Fire: The Story of Troy Annual Conference*, written by the Rev. Charles and Ouida Schwartz. Their supplemental volume, *A Spreading Flame: The Story of the Churches of Troy Annual Conference*, presents some vivid details about Methodists and Methodist work that help to personalize the drama of Wesleyan faith in action.

The present writers, though not the skilled historians who preceded us, intend to bring the earlier history up to date—from 1982 through the end of Troy Annual Conference. At the time of this writing, the final session of conference is scheduled for May 22, 2010 at Christ Church United Methodist in Glens Falls, NY. For the rest of the book we shall assume that events scheduled between this writing and that session will take place as planned, always including the sincere but unwritten proviso, "the good Lord willing."

A book many church leaders are presently reading is *Five Practices of Fruitful Congregations* by Robert Schnase, bishop of the Missouri Area of The United Methodist Church. The practices Bishop Schnase identifies are:
- radical hospitality
- passionate worship
- intentional faith development
- risk-taking mission service, and
- extravagant generosity.

It strikes us that these practices might well describe at least some of the ways Troy Conference lived out the Gospel from 1982 to 2010. Not everything we feel needs saying fits comfortably into these categories, but the ideas provide a useful starting place.

In addition, we want to expand on the history of Troy Conference camping. The roots of camping, anchored in the camp meeting experience, are laid out in *A Flame of Fire*. But in the late 1930s a new style of church camping began to flourish in Troy Conference. It still flourishes and we trust will continue to do so in the years ahead. At present, those who can tell us about the early days of Skye Farm and the transition from Missisquoi to Covenant Hills are still with us. Theirs is the camping history we want to tell while memories of Troy Conference and those days are fresh.

The primary sources for most of this book are the official Journals of Troy Annual Conference. We have cited the year of each source but not page numbers, as it is fairly easy to navigate the journals should more information be required. Other primary sources are people who, like the authors, lived through the decades of interest and who recalled their experiences for us and for future readers.

Rev. Ralph A. Marino
Jacqueline L. Marino, Ph.D
Rev. G. William Pattison

Chapter 1

Historic Highlights 1760–1982

Yea, I have a goodly heritage. Psalm 16:6

Early Preachers

Through no fault or virtue of its own, the territory covered by the modern Troy Conference has been home to many of the central happenings in early Methodist history. For details of these events and the people involved, *A Flame of Fire* is the central resource. However, to set the stage for the coming chapters, we will recap some of the highlights here.

Philip Embury and his cousin, Barbara Heck, came to New York in 1760. Embury held a local preacher's license in Ireland and began a modest preaching ministry in the New World in 1766. In 1770, he and his family moved upstate to the Cambridge-Ashgrove area, where he helped form the first Methodist Society north of New York City.

Captain Thomas Webb

Captain Thomas Webb of the 48th Regiment of Foot, after an extensive tour of duty in America, returned to England for leave. While there, he was deeply touched by Methodist preaching. He came back to America in 1765 and engaged in powerful evangelistic efforts in Albany and Schenectady.

James Dempster, John Wesley's last missionary to

America, arrived in New York in 1774. Through the years he preached in, among other places, Sacandaga, Mayfield, Canajoharie, Galway, Underhill, Schaghticoke, Fort Edward, Johnstown, Saratoga, Scotia, and the Mohawk Valley. His Bible is still to be seen in Amsterdam UMC.

Margaret Appleton Peckett, formerly John Wesley's housekeeper, immigrated to America in 1773. In 1780 she moved to Bradford, VT, where she organized an informal Methodist class and did considerable teaching and exhorting. Her other claim to fame is that she mentored many young men of faith, including her own son William, and encouraged their entry into the ministry. Several of them became important figures in early Methodism: John Langdon, Laban Clark, and Martin Ruter. These, and others, were "children" of Mother Peckett, as she was called.

Freeborn Garretson, Jason Lee, and Lorenzo Dow are all numbered among the early preachers with roots and connections in Troy Conference.

Early Churches and Circuits

Many present-day congregations owe their start to the work of early organizers and circuit riders. The Ashgrove meeting house was erected in Cambridge in 1788. The following year, the Grooms Methodist Society was organized in Clifton Park. Other early buildings and societies were:

North Hartland

- 1790 North Hartland, NY
- 1791 Saratoga circuit and Johnstown church
- 1792 Wells and Danby, VT churches
- 1793 Vershire, VT church
- 1796 Societies in West Camden, NY and Arlington and Shaftsbury, VT
- 1796 Vershire circuit, divided into Vershire and Barnard,

with the Vergennes and Windsor circuits following shortly afterward

1799   Plattsburgh, Essex, and Whitingham circuits
1800   Appointment of twenty-two itinerant preachers to the Albany, NY and Pittsfield, MA circuits
1802   Adams, MA and Grand Isle, VT circuits.

To give some idea of the vigor of the work in this part of the country, note that in 1803 the New York Conference was held at Ashgrove, NY. That same year the Albany district had 927 members, more than all of New York City.

While the Methodists were organizing, the predecessor churches of the Evangelical United Brethren were also active. When the Methodist Church and the Evangelical United Brethren became one denomination in 1968, there were four active EUB congregations in Troy Conference territory: West Sand Lake, Amsterdam, Calvary on Delaware Avenue in Albany, and East Stone Arabia.

Vermont Conference 1796–1940

The work in Vermont began early. Vermonters made major contributions to the growing Methodist denomination despite the frequent changes in their relationship to the larger structure of the church. In 1796, General Conference created annual conferences for the first time. All of Vermont and New York east of the Hudson River were part of the New England Conference. In 1800, the New York Conference was created, and Vermont and a portion of New Hampshire became part of that conference. In 1804, New Hampshire and Vermont east of the Green Mountains were transferred back to the New England Conference. Indeed, New England Conference actually was held in Barnard, VT, in 1811. In 1829, New Hampshire and parts of Vermont became a conference of their own. This state of affairs lasted until 1845, when the Vermont Conference was created with three districts: Montpelier, Springfield, and Danville.

In 1834, Newbury Seminary opened. Betsy Dow was the first teacher of ministerial students in that institution.

The school became the first Methodist seminary in America, the Newbury Bible Institute. Eventually the institute became the first school of Boston University.

Other items of interest from our Vermont heritage include:

1850 revivals held by Phoebe Palmer, a holiness evange-list, in Saint Johnsbury and Lyndon Center

1855 "Great Debate" over which conference would contain the Burlington District (settled in 1884 when, after several relocations, it went to the Troy Conference)

1855 founding of a church in Wolcott by George S. Brown, a black Methodist preacher

1900 consecration of Millie Martin Dodge as the first Vermont Conference deaconess

1912 establishment of the North Barre mission for Italian marble cutters

1915 appointment of Lillian Rember as the first woman supply pastor in the conference

1920 resolution to General Conference seeking eventual "complete ministerial equality of the sexes"

1925 ordination of Ruth G. Barr, the first woman in the conference to be ordained a deacon serving as a local pastor.

Troy Conference 1832–1940

Troy Conference came into being in 1832 when it was set apart from the New York Conference. At that time, 98 preachers were spread across the Saratoga, Troy, and Middlebury, VT, Districts. The conference first met in 1833, and among its items of business was the passage of a resolution calling for churches to provide parsonages for their preachers. The Ashgrove congregation built the first parsonage in the conference that same year. Also that year, George S. Brown, the first African American pastor in Troy Conference, received his license to preach. In 1836, the Troy Conference Academy, later to become Green Mountain College, opened in Poultney, VT. In 1868, a ten-day camp meeting was held at the newly purchased property in Round Lake.

Other significant dates and events include:

1921 Eight women in the conference were licensed to preach

1923 Saint Timothy's organized in Schenectady to serve the Italian population

1926 Georgia Harkness and Eliza Duffield became local deacons

1928 Eliza Duffield became the first woman local pastor in the conference to be ordained as elder

1939 Georgia Harkness became an elder and a Professor of Applied Theology at Garrett Biblical Institute, the first woman to hold such a position at a major seminary.

A United Conference 1940–1982

In 1939, the Methodist Episcopal Church became The Methodist Church. By action of the Northeast Jurisdictional Conference, Troy Conference and the Vermont Conference were to be united by 1942. The Vermont Conference held a special session on November 7, 1940, to deal with closing business. The first session of the new united Troy Conference was held in Saratoga Springs, April 17, 1941, with Bishop Francis J. McConnell presiding.

Skye Farm Camp was established on Sherman Lake in 1942, and in 1950 Riverside Campground on the Missisquoi began its transition to Camp Missisquoi. In 1955 Dr. Dorothy Brown, whose education had been strongly subsidized by the women of Troy Conference, became the first African-American member of the American College of Surgeons. Doris Hartman, a missionary to Japan, in 1959 became the first woman admitted on trial to Troy Conference. She came into full connection in 1963. Philip Embury's grave and monument became a Methodist historical landmark by action of the Northeastern Jurisdiction Association of

Methodist Historical Societies in 1967. The Woman's Society of Christian Service began the Summer Learning Fellowship in 1970. Embury Apartments opened in 1972. In 1978, Ruth Harlow became the first woman to serve as conference lay leader. And in May of 1981, the Conference Commission on Archives and History hosted the annual meeting of the Jurisdictional Commission in Barre, VT—while eagerly awaiting the 1982 publication of *A Flame of Fire* by the Rev. Charles and Ouida Schwartz.

Chapter 2

Radical Hospitality

This is my commandment, that you love one another
as I have loved you. John 15:12

Radical hospitality insists upon inclusiveness. It implies going beyond ordinary courtesy to reach out to others who may be on the margins or whose worth is minimized by society.

Troy Annual Conference has shown an intention to extend that kind of hospitality from its earliest years. The conference struggle to think through and respond to the issue of slavery is outlined in *A Flame of Fire*. One positive expression of radical hospitality was shown by the support given to the Rev. George S. Brown, a Methodist black preacher-missionary of the early 1800s. Although racism was widespread, history suggests that Brown was able to overcome significant obstacles and achieve an effective cross-racial ministry in Troy Conference.

During the period of present interest, Troy Conference made clear efforts to offer radical hospitality in its commitment to:

· dismantling racism
· developing ministries with ethnic minorities
· aiding refugee resettlement
· supporting the "reconciling movement" around the issue of homosexuality in the church, and
· affirming women in leadership positions.

Each of these efforts reveals something different about the dynamic of Troy Conference and its people.

Dismantling Racism

One key problem with white privilege is that those who have it can unconsciously harbor racist attitudes. The Vermont Conference and Troy Conference, both before and after their union in 1940, frequently took strong stands in opposition to overt racism nationally and locally. However, active efforts to dismantle internal racist attitudes began in the 1980s.

Roy Calvin Nichols was the first African-American to be elected bishop following the formation of The United Methodist Church in 1968. After serving 12 years in the Pittsburgh area, Bishop Nichols received his assignment to the New York Area in 1980. In 1981, the same year that the Ethnic Minority Local Church became a missional priority, Bishop Nichols and his wife Ruth were warmly received at annual conference. Many found out then for the first time what it was like to have a black leader. Bishop Nichols was fond of talking about "when the rubber hits the road" and nearly thirty years later, when we get serious about moving the church forward, his catch phrase still resonates with those members of conference who had the chance to work with him.

The desire to overthrow racism shows itself in a variety of resolutions passed at annual conference through the years. In 1982, two Ku Klux Klan rallies within the bounds of conference stimulated a resolution calling Klan ideology abhorrent and urging churches to find non-violent ways of responding. That same year conference resolved to do better in meeting the Black College Fund apportionment from the general church and called for additional funding for the Ethnic Minority Scholarship Incentive program. A report also noted a seed grant of nearly $1,400 to support Grace UMC in Ravena as they began a day care program for Hispanic migrant farm workers.

The official structure of the conference at that time called for a Commission on Religion and Race. This

The Life and Ministry of the Rev. George S. Brown

George S. Brown was born on July 25, 1801, in Newport, RI, the son of an elder in the Baptist church. Brown himself was converted in Kingsbury, NY, in 1828 and came under the influence of a Methodist circuit rider, William Ryder.

Brown became active in the Sanford's Ridge Methodist Episcopal Church. In 1831 he received his exhorter's license and two years later was granted a license to preach—the first given to an African-American in Troy Conference. During these years he made his living by building stone walls in the area. His pay was a dollar for every 16 feet of wall he laid, plus a night's room and board.

Brown soon experienced a call to missionary work in Liberia. He was first a teacher and then a preacher among the African-Americans who chose to make that nation their new homeland. The Liberia Missionary Conference received him as a probationary member and elected him to both deacon's and elder's orders in 1838. He had to return to New York for ordination.

Back in Liberia, he got caught in a conflict between the white superintendent, John Seys, and the Liberian government. Brown was suspended from duties in 1843 and expelled by Seys in 1844 for refusing to take sides. Brown returned to America to plead his case before the Methodist Missionary Board. It took until 1848 before Brown won his back pay from the board, and it was not until 1853, following civil lawsuits and struggles against racist attitudes, that Troy Conference restored his credentials.

Brown moved to northern Vermont and worked with an ally within the conference, the Rev. Henry Taylor. In 1855, Brown moved to Wolcott and began Methodist class meetings. The following year he supervised the commission was duly constituted and had a substantial number of minority members, even though it took nearly all the active minority members of conference to fill those leadership positions. The commission's 1987 report noted that conference support went to Hispanic work in Amsterdam (continuing an active interest reaching back to at least 1975), Korean work in Newtonville, and to a growing ministry among Pakistanis at Calvary-Saint Luke's in Albany. That same year, conference also committed itself to a multi-year Comprehensive Plan for Racial and Ethnic Inclusiveness.

One outcome of that plan involved devoting a major portion of the 1989 Annual Conference agenda to issues of racism. Workshop training was designed to help people confront an uncomfortable reality: that it is possible to reject racism on the conscious level while still acting in racist ways. Major leadership came from visiting Bishop Leontine T. C. Kelly, a black woman recently retired from the San Francisco area. In her opening message, she sounded themes that would need much repetition before the reality of racism could sink in and serious dismantling could begin: "Racism is part of the political system of our country ... Any religion concerned about souls and not about the economics in the slums is a religion awaiting burial...How would your life be affected if you were black? Where would you live in your community? Where would you work?"

Also in 1989, conference took a stand specifically affirming General Conference's resolution of the previous year opposing a constitutional amendment making English the official language of the United States. The resolution states the concern very directly: "We are convinced that the movement to declare constitutionally English as the official language of the nation is not based on any real need. ... We condemn the English-only movement as a manifestation of the sin of racism..." The Board of Church and Society also put forward a similar resolution that urged the writing of letters to the President, senators and congressional building of the present Wolcott UMC and served as pastor in charge.

Due to severe illness Brown had to leave Wolcott soon afterward. He returned to the Glens Falls area and reconnected with the Sanford's Ridge congregation. Interestingly enough, in 1863 the relative of a Glens Falls businessman hired Brown, whose health was now apparently restored, to relocate to Jackson, MI, to build a one-mile-long stone wall. Brown was now getting $1.50 a day plus board and didn't have to lay stone on stormy days. The wall took Brown and his crew two years to build, and the landowner won a silver medallion for the wall's artistic design and construction in 1869.

George S. Brown then returned to the Glens Falls area. He died there on April 10, 1886, and is buried in the Friends Cemetery in Queensbury. Many of the stone walls that Brown built still stand, with the Wolcott UMC, as monuments to the first African-American pastor of Troy Conference.

(Special thanks go to the Rev. Patricia Thompson for her wide-ranging research on George Brown and her thoughtful description of his life and ministry.)

Shirley Readdean remembers

I came into the Methodist church around 1963. My husband and I lived in a white neighborhood with our twin three year old girls. I was going to a church some distance away and the travel was a problem. Then, going past Broadway, Schenectady, I saw a sign offering nursery care on Sunday morning and thought, "What an opportunity for at least an hour of peace and quiet." So, I started going there. I received a neutral welcome, nothing negative but no real enthusiasm either.

After a while the pastor, Rev. Roland Kelly, came to call and asked if we were interested in joining. Now representatives making the position of conference known.

The 1994 Long Range Plan for Racial and Ethnic Inclusiveness addressed the issue of radical hospitality in several ways. It called for extending ministry to the unchurched on an ethnically inclusive basis. Cross-racial appointments were urged as well as intentional recruitment of ethnic minority pastors. Specifically, the plan called for reaching out to the Asian, Afro-American, Hispanic and Native American communities and to be welcoming to all individuals and groups regardless of their ethnicity. Of course, work of this sort had been undertaken previously by the conference, but the plan called for a much more proactive stance.

In 1999, the Diversity Concerns Group brought forward a petition to hold anti-racism training, and the conference approved. One key issue was concern over the "hidden racism we harbor." A related petition called for monitoring and reporting on discriminatory language in order to help the conference overcome the endemic racism in society and the church. An additional petition called for African American inclusiveness in the conference. Another petition, "Strengthening the Black Church for the Twenty-first Century," was approved and forwarded to the General Conference for action.

The 2000 Executive Session, which handles all matters of clergy conference relationships, gave major attention to racial diversity and white privilege. The whole conference heard a report on the recently concluded General Conference. Shirley Readdean, one of our black ethnic minority members, described the General Conference Act of Repentance for the denomination's racist acts against people of color for over 200 years. The Journal for that year also notes that Christ Church, Troy was the venue for the African Methodist Episcopal Zion's Western/Genesee Conference. The official greetings we sent from one Wesleyan conference to another symbolized our repentance and reconciliation.

this was the time of the civil rights movement, with sit-ins, and racial tension in some places, so I gave him credit for breaking ground by extending that invitation. Because I had been abandoned as a child, I grew up as a ward of the state and had experienced many different denominations through the years. The wonderful thing was, as I began to study Methodism in preparation for joining the church I realized, "This is what I believe." So it was like coming home to a place where I had never actually been before.

Once I got connected there, we all got more comfortable. Marian O'Neal, another African-American woman, put it to me very directly, "You need to be more involved." And as it turned out this was not difficult. I am a risk-taker and a joiner. My attitude usually is, "It's your problem if you don't want me." As people in the church got more comfortable with me, the invitations and opportunities began to come: to teach Sunday school, join UMW, be a UMW officer, to take on youth work and district and conference responsibilities. As there were, and are, few of us people of color, the issue came to be not was I invited to serve, but the risk of burn-out because I was serving in too many places at once.

Within the church—local, district, Troy conference, and beyond, I've been loved, nurtured, and given many opportunities to grow and serve. But the reality of racism continues to be present outside the church. At times my friends have been shocked at the treatment I received when we've gone out together. They thought perhaps I was overly sensitive until they saw it for themselves. One day we walked from annual conference to an antique shop. They wandered freely around the store, but the owner trailed me closely the whole time I was there.

Some of the early attempts at growing diversity were not handled well. We had a retreat at Silver Bay where the outside presenters were attacking and abrasive.

The 2001 report of the Commission on Religion and Race stressed how "white privilege is regularly experienced in systems, no matter the particular people involved." This was understood to be a time for conference to learn about those systems that might be "perpetuating racism in our midst." A number of media resources were later purchased to help churches and individuals understand how to address racism and achieve diversity across the conference.

In 2002, a group of those who took anti-racism training formed the River Community. This group was a positive outgrowth of the work and discussions that began in 1998. The challenge of radical hospitality was to go beyond good thoughts and words in order to understand the factors that keep racism going even where it is unwelcome.

The 2003 Journal lists the thirty-three members of the River Community. The Rev. Barbara Lemmel, Conference Minister and a member of the community, gave the keynote address on racial reconciliation. Other members of the group spoke from their personal perspectives on how racism continues as a problem that diminishes all persons. Not by chance, the music leader for our conference sessions that year was Dr. Francois Clemmons, a well-known black singer who for a long time appeared on the television show *Mr. Roger's Neighborhood* as Officer Clemmons.

Dr. Francois Clemmons, music leader for the 2003 session.

A substantial portion of the report of the 2004 General Conference delegation was devoted to issues of racism. Examples of blatant racism, both active and passive, were presented to show how far society and the church still had to go. At various times during the annual conference session the River Community presented short videos illustrating

They condemned the whites present as racist. Then the presenters went away without doing any reconciling or re-connecting. That experience made people gun-shy of diversity training. We had a few pastors of color come into the conference, but those experiments did not work out well. They typically were put in rural parishes without support or preparation. They felt isolated and tended not to stay long.

On the other hand, Troy Conference has recognized my leadership qualities and those of other people of color. Our General and Jurisdictional Conference delegates in 2000 were one-third minorities, and that from what is probably the whitest conference in the United Methodist Church. This was not patronizing or token representation but appreciation and affirmation of us as individuals committed to the church.

The issue ahead of us is finding ways to work at growing diversity. This is not "our grandparents' society." The General Conference is struggling with the concept of a global church. Annual Conferences must recognize the ethnic changes in local communities, seeing these changes as an opportunity to understand that while Wesley saw the "world as his parish," that "parish has reached our doorstep." That is one thing the new conference alignment will help, as there will be more opportunities for interaction in all parts of the old Troy Conference. One of the keys is getting more local churches to work at attracting diversity. In some ways it's like making the church handicapped accessible. The well-meaning excuse for not proceeding is, "Look at our congregation; we don't have the need." But attracting diverse people is essential. We are called to do that, and the future of our church depends on our doing that. I know people are pleased when diversity appears, yet often we don't try to bring it about. We are not trained to live together. We do fine when we mix, but then we go our separate racism as it appeared within our own communities.

Following a retreat on "Healing the Wounds of Racism," a number of members wore prayer scarves as symbols of racism awareness at the 2005 conference session. All members of conference were encouraged to sign a letter to the Governor of Vermont pointing out the lack of racial diversity on the Vermont Human Rights Commission. The River Community noted that Troy Conference postponed holding an Act of Repentance for racism as requested by General Conference so that the act would be that of a people prepared. Shirley Readdean, one of the active persons of color in the conference said, in support of the desire to dismantle racism, "The journey is not either/or. It is OUR journey...The prayer is that we might be made whole in the eyes of God."

The slow, patient monitoring and reporting work of the Commission on Religion and Race continued at the next session of annual conference. The River Community stressed the need for all to be educated about racism. Sandy Allen, an attorney, spoke particularly to the issues of white privilege and systemic racism. One resolution, A Plan for the Recruitment and Retention of Clergy of Color, noted sadly that in Troy Conference, "legislation of 1975, 1987, 1994 and 1999 notwithstanding, there is no discernable progress to report." Conference accepted the need both for more emphasis on cross-racial appointments and for additional monitoring training for members of conference agencies.

A major problem facing those who worked to recruit and retain ethnic clergy was the lack of suitable additional appointments. Thus, a pastor who fit a church well when first coming to Troy Conference might have no good options for a move a few years later. A number of our minority clergy thus had only one appointment here before moving on to other conferences with more minority congregations. The Cabinet also used cross-racial appointments in several instances. While the ministries typically were successful, the lack of an ethnic support group frequently took ways and don't make the progress that otherwise would be possible. The more we do in local churches, the better the outcome will be.

Mildred S. Mason remembers

Becoming chairperson of the Troy Annual Conference Commission On Religion and Race (CCORR) was an extension of my journey for racial justice and inclusiveness. This role has been an honor and a privilege due to the small number of people of color in Troy Conference.

Our collaboration with the sessions and worship committees on the Act of Repentance and the Service of Reconciliation for the 175th Annual Conference, May 2-5, 2007 resulted in a historical and spiritually moving event, a tribute to the progress of Troy Annual Conference. The journey toward change continues with our conference moving forward into the 21st century. The number of female clergy and female laity in leadership positions and people of color indicates how our conference has progressed. The boundaries change means moving from a small entity to a larger body. God is ready for us to do something new. Having built a firm foundation, whatever our conference and committee is named, we will continue to promote racial justice. For as in Amos 5:24, "... let justice roll on like a river, righteousness like a never-failing stream!"

Our Experiences in the Troy Annual Conference

Julius A. Archibald, Jr.

It was on a Sunday morning in June 1956, when Anola and I visited Trinity Methodist Church (now Faith United Methodist Church) in Schenectady, NY for the first time, thereby beginning an extended relationship with the Troy Annual Conference. The historical context was a toll on the pastor and the pastor's family. So promising pastors spent only a short time in our churches. The issue was a frustrating one for our bishops and Cabinet members through the years.

The 2007 session of conference had more youth of color serving as pages, which helped to express the desire to be an inclusive conference. The Service of Repentance and Call to Holiness, held as recommended by the 2000 General Conference, included leadership by several local clergy members of the African Methodist Episcopal Zion Church who represented the Pan-Methodist family of denominations. A Religion and Race monitoring report noted that white privilege appeared in a presentation on boundary issues. This critique was accepted in the spirit offered, and the confessions of inappropriateness were appreciated. District Superintendent Henry Frueh, presenting the report on boundary issues, noted with embarrassment that the 17-minute video featured only white faces. "I know that many have asked, concerning this evening's Act of Repentance, 'Of what do I need to repent?' Though I have been through the anti-racism training offered by our conference, though I'm part of the River Community, and though that has been an acutely important issue for me, I know what's first on my repentance list." On the positive side, the efforts at diversity were affirmed, as was the election of two African American women and a Native American clergywoman as delegates to the Northeastern Jurisdictional Conference.

Continuing the efforts already made, conference called for cultural sensitivity training for the volunteer in mission teams. A petition to General Conference called for including in the historic list of bishops in *The Book of Discipline* the names of the founding bishops of the African Methodist Episcopal Church and the Christian Methodist Episcopal Church, because bishops of The United Methodist Church or its predecessor churches consecrated those leaders.

The struggle to recognize and grow inclusive diversity

important: the Montgomery bus boycott, under the leadership of Dr. Martin Luther King, had just begun. We had been married for just over two years. We had been, for almost one year, living in Schenectady, where I was employed at the Knolls Atomic Power Laboratory following my separation from the United States Air Force. Anola had been a lifelong member of the Simpson Methodist Church in Steubenville, OH, which was a part of the Louisville Annual Conference of the Central Jurisdiction. I had been a lifelong Episcopalian and was a member of St. Luke's Episcopal Church in New York City. We had begun to search for a church where we could both worship comfortably and raise our family. Anola was pregnant at the time. The decision to visit Trinity that morning was made less than one hour before we arrived there; it was based more upon the fact that worship began at 11 a.m. than upon anything else. I knew where the church was located, having driven past it many times on the way to and from work, but had not previously thought of going there.

We were extremely warmly greeted and welcomed at Trinity that morning and made to feel comfortable and at home. We remember in particular Floyd Taylor, who was the head usher and who (we later learned) had an outstanding reputation for being outgoing to visitors, for his graciousness. Dr. Ted Ogden, who was near the end of his tenure as pastor at Trinity, came to visit us on the Thursday following our initial visit and again one week later with his wife, Selma. There really was no further contest. Our search for a church home had come to a happy end, and we began to attend the church regularly, always with the same warm welcoming response from the congregation. We were formally received into Trinity the following October, one week after our son was baptized. We had an active role in the fiftieth anniversary celebration during the following spring and became fully involved continued. One monitoring report at the 2008 session noted with approval the use of sign language during the opening worship service. Another report noted the diversity of gender, age and ethnicity in the communion servers. On the other hand, the video report of General Conference showed no people of color even though three such persons from Troy Conference alone were present. The General Conference team affirmed that they would work to edit the video to correct the omissions before it was distributed to local churches.

And again in 2009, the Rev. Joy Lowenthal, one of the session monitors for the Commission on Religion and Race noted, "Saying 'sorry' is not good enough. We've got to do better next time."

All in all, the effort to dismantle racism continues to be a slow march, encouraged by the faithful leadership of people of color and the clear desire of lay and clergy alike to translate the inclusive Gospel into loving, helpful, and practical terms.

A Partial Listing of Minority Clergy: Past and Present

Brown, George S.	Kim, Chung Yong	Pak, David
Cho, Byung Woo	Kim, Hak Soo	Reyes, Sergio
Chun, Yohang	Kim, Moon Ho	Rodriguez, Mariana
Dozier, L'Yon	Kim, Tae Kun	Rush, Adrianne
Ezekiel, Olive	Lee, Esther	Shand, Wesley
Ford, Pearle E.	Matthews, Marcus	Thompson, Nehemiah
Goings, Carolyn	Moore-Colgan, Marion	Uriu, Miyeko
Greer, H. Ward	Morrison, Joseph	Yang, Chel-Hee
Hahn, Sang-Hyun	Mourice, Camillius J.	Yoon, Tae-Hun
James, Henry	Nichols, Roy C.	
Jhun, Youngstone	Nugent, Randolph W.	

in the life of the church. The appointment of Dr. Dow Clute as pastor the next year did not change any of our relationships with the church. We both became active in the church school program, and during the years that followed, I served for three years as a member of the Commission on Education, two years as a member of the Commission on Missions, and three years as Chair of the Commission on Missions.

This was also a significant period in the life of Trinity Church. Trinity had always had a strong missions program, providing support through the Board of Missions for missionaries serving in places like Zimbabwe, India, and Japan; supporting "Advance Special" programs both nationally and internationally; and earmarking our entire Christmas offering to a mission cause, often within Schenectady itself. Under Dow's leadership, we decided that the church should have an associate pastor who would serve part time as our missionary to the inner city of Schenectady itself. The church was prepared to receive whatever pastor would be appointed to fill this role, and the Rev. Joseph Morrison, a pastor of color, was appointed to come to Trinity in this capacity. Joe came in 1967, the year before we left. Joe stayed for four years, two years with Dow until he retired, and two years with Dr. Paul Hydon. When the time came for a change of appointment for Joe, he left Troy Conference, due in part to the unavailability of a suitable appointment for him within the conference. Joe went on to an outstanding career as a pastor in the New York Annual Conference.

I was actually in my fourth year as Chair of Missions when a General Electric transfer took us away from Schenectady and Trinity Church in 1968. I also completed my lay speaking course during this last year at Trinity. It was not easy to leave Trinity.

During our time at Trinity, we purchased our home in a "nice" residential neighborhood near the church. We learned, some years later, that there had been an attempt by some members of the community to resist, in unspecified ways, our moving into the neighborhood. One member of Trinity whom we knew was approached by this group and asked what he would do to prevent our coming into the neighborhood. His answer was, "Nothing." Indeed, we had a very good, very positive, living experience with wonderful neighbors on Central Parkway. The neighborhood was also not easy to leave.

In 1968, The Methodist Church merged with the Evangelical United Brethren to become The United Methodist Church. This was the year that we moved to Maryland and transferred our membership to The Faith United Methodist Church of Rockville, where the Rev. Kenneth Jones, a former missionary to Zaire, was pastor. Based upon my experience at Trinity, I very quickly became Chair of Missions there. We stayed until 1970, when I accepted an invitation to join the faculty of the State University of New York, College of Arts and Science at Plattsburgh. We were happy to return to the Troy Annual Conference and to transfer our membership to Plattsburgh UMC, where Dr. Robert Klein was serving as Pastor.

In a very real sense, we were "back home" at Plattsburgh UMC, our second Troy Conference Church, and picked up from where we had left off at Trinity in Schenectady. I was back to being a Chair of the Commission on Missions (along with Social Concerns and Ecumenical Affairs), and was elected a lay member of Troy Annual Conference in 1973. During the years since 1973, I have had the privilege of serving both the annual conference and the general church in a number of different capacities, including those of conference lay leader (8 years) and president of the Association of Annual Conference Lay Leaders (2 years).

During these years, I have also had the opportunity

of experiencing and viewing racism in the church from many perspectives. On the personal, micro level, and specifically as a layman, the experiences with the church and conference have been highly positive. I cannot recall ever having been overtly hindered because of my race. This is not to say that everything is fine, or that I have not seen, or otherwise been aware of, evidence of racism at the group or macro level within the Troy Annual Conference!

There is, indeed, a disturbing lack of racial diversity and inclusiveness within Troy Annual Conference! The worst aspect of this is the fact that few persons recognize either the existence or the seriousness of the problem. I suspect that were I a clergy person, my foregoing statements would not be nearly as positive. It is far too easy for us to blame the racial demographics within our geographic boundaries for having enabled and encouraged a "sweeping of the problem under the rug." I would cite, as evidence for the existence of this problem, that the diversity of our congregations in urban areas across the conference does not reflect the diversity of the communities in which our churches are located, that our relationships with other Methodist denominations (specifically African Methodist Episcopal and African Methodist Episcopal Zion, where these denominations have local churches) are less than they should be for effective community witness, and that we have failed to develop the kind of challenging career opportunities for clergy of color that would encourage such clergy to come and stay within our conference. I would suggest that some of the causes are the following: a general denial among our people that there is such a problem; a general failure on the part of many of our local churches (clergy and congregations) to be involved in their communities in other than a condescending manner; a general lack of collegiality among pastors and bishops of various

Methodist denominations; and the lack of a holistic, conferencewide program for the recruitment, retention, and encouragement of diversity among the clergy! It is not to say that we have not tried a variety of things, but rather that our attempts have consisted of "half-way" measures, involving some of our local churches, but never on an effective conferencewide basis. As examples, we have all witnessed clergy of color come to Troy Conference; we have seen very few clergy of color reach retirement age while serving Troy Conference.

Ethnic Minorities

In the early eighties, ethnic minorities were definitely minorities in nearly every Troy Conference community. Nevertheless, efforts at being in ministry with minorities appeared regularly in the vision, reports, and financial commitments displayed in the historical record. Radical hospitality required interest in sharing the good news with people who were not part of our mostly white congregations.

The Ethnic Minority Local Church became a quadrennial denominational missional priority in 1981. Troy Conference is far from the population centers that attracted substantial ethnic minorities and spurred the creation of the priority. Even so, the opportunity to work with various groups appeared within the bounds of conference.

The black populations in Albany and Schenectady were already in the mind and ministry of Troy Conference. Additional opportunities arose for radical hospitality toward Native American, Hispanic, Korean, and Pakistani populations.

Methodist activity in Korea began at least as early as the 1920s, with churches making substantial gifts to the ministry there. Troy Conference had two missionary couples active in Korea in the 1980s, when Korean immigration to the United States surfaced as an issue requiring the response of radical hospitality.

The Albany United Methodist Society, demonstrating a substantial concern for blacks and others of the downtown population, had come into being in 1961 and had been a strongly affirmed ministry of the conference ever since then. *A Flame of Fire* notes that the Ganienkah Indian Community, located north of Plattsburgh, NY, received funding as an advance special of The United Methodist Church in the late 1970s. The work with Hispanics and the Pakistani population came rather later, but no less significantly, to the attention of the conference.

Harbingers of things to come are found in the 1983 reports from the Conference Board of Global Ministries and the Commission on Religion and Race. Global Ministries noted, "We have been working ... to determine whether it is feasible to extend our ministry by starting two new congregations. One possibility is a Black church in the Clinton Avenue area of Albany. The other is a Korean congregation in Latham." The hope for beginning a new black church stimulated a proposed budget of $18,000 and outlined the leadership criteria. Religion and Race spent just $16 for Hispanic work in Amsterdam but urged the continuation of Hispanic work in both Amsterdam and Ravena. They noted, "We will need a Spanish-speaking minister or community developer."

These hopes and expectations took some time to mature in Troy Conference. But in 1985, the Rev. William Lasher, Director of the Conference Council on Ministries, noted in the report of the Enlarged Cabinet, "The mood is changing!" The Rev. Henry E. Johnson, a community organizer from the East Ohio Conference, reported on his work on development of the Freedom Way black church in the Arbor Hill/West Hill section of Albany.

Meanwhile, the Korean UMC of Albany held their organizational service on October 13, 1985 in the Newtonville

UMC, under the leadership of their pastor, the Rev. Tae-Hun Yoon. These were the first new church starts in Troy Conference in nearly two decades. Hispanic work in Amsterdam was renewed as well.

Korean choir

An unanticipated ethnic ministry in Albany appeared as Pakistani and Philippino groups began to find an active home at Calvary-Saint Luke's. The influence of these immigrant people soon came to have a major energizing effect on that congregation.

The 1987 Journal records both frustration and progress. The Ethnic Minority Local Church Missional Priority ended, but the work in Troy Conference was just getting started. The efforts to develop a worshiping congregation at Freedom Way in Albany came to a halt. Over $2,000 in conference funds went to support the ongoing Hispanic work in Amsterdam. Meanwhile, the Korean UMC continued to thrive and develop from its already strong beginning. The situation at Calvary-Saint Luke's drew attention as the Pakistani minority there continued to grow toward majority status within the congregation. Parts of the church newsletter came to be printed in English while other parts were in a Pakistani native language. The Missional Priority Coordinating Committee, under the leadership of Julius Archibald, noted that help might be needed to assist the congregation "through a difficult transition."

At the 1989 session of annual conference, members voted to invest $5,000 to support an independent Chinese Christian fellowship in Albany. The group needed both a pastor and a place to worship. Some hoped that the congregation might become a local United Methodist Church.

Meanwhile, the issue of the sovereignty of the Ganien-kah Native American Community arose again. In 1977, when the community was working to establish itself, the Rev. Richard Campbell, then pastor of Plattsburgh UMC, was instrumental in involving the church in significant supportive efforts. He tells the story of those days in his book, *The People of the Land of Flint.* This led to a lasting feeling of connection between at least some members of the conference and the community. Now, as tensions increased, the Conference Council on Ministries urged New York State to respect the treaty of 1794. The Rev. Donald Washburn, then serving at Mechanicville UMC, became a key intermediary between the state and the Ganienkah community. A 1990 resolution of conference affirms his role as a builder of trust and his commitment to a peaceful solution to the tension. In 1991, the Rev. Washburn introduced a representative from the Ganienkah community to annual conference. The speaker brought, and spoke to, the simple but powerful symbolism of the "Two Row" wampum belt that illustrated and, to the Native Americans, embodied the treaty of 1794 which anticipated a separate, parallel, friendly future between them and the citizens of New York State. Conference also called for a major emphasis on Native American spirituality at its next annual session. Noting that 1992 marked 500 years since the first voyage of Christopher Columbus, conference passed a pair of resolutions that called for a serious recognition of the tragedy inflicted on Native Americans by that event.

Also in 1991 came the recognition that despite nearly two decades of conference support of Centro-Civico, the Hispanic ministry in Amsterdam, no local United Methodist churches had become involved in the ministry there. Funds were set aside for a part-time community worker to explore the opportunity for greater efforts in Amsterdam, Schenectady and Albany.

The 1992 Journal notes support in the amount of

$8,000 to the Korean Church, $2,000 to the Hispanic ministry and $5,000 to the Pakistani ministry in Albany. The larger emphasis that year, however, was on Native American issues. the Rev. Don Washburn won the Howard and Reba Stimmel Award for Social Justice for his ongoing work with the people of Ganienkah. Conference affirmed a resolution from the Board of Church and Society that objected to the Hydro-Quebec plan to dam rivers running into Hudson Bay because, among other reasons, the Grand Council of the Cree saw the dams as destructive of their traditional ways of life. The conference lecturer was Thom White Wolf Fassett, a Native American, General Secretary of the General Board of Church and Society. He commented that the Native Americans, a fourth world people, saw themselves as "a part of nature" rather than "apart from nature." One worship service used the Native American themes of East, North, West and South, and the pouring of water as an image for life.

United Methodist Women's Day at Conference 1993 highlighted Native American spirituality. The keynote speaker was Sue Ellen Hearn, a young Mohawk United Methodist. She used the image of the parallels from the "Two Row" wampum belt to suggest that while each has value separately, there is additional value in allowing the cultures to interact respectfully. Dancers

Native American dancers

from the Onondaga Council also interpreted the theme of unity and diversity. Conference took the further step of creating a standing committee on Native American Ministries under the leadership of the Rev. Marion Moore-Colgan, herself a Native American.

Reports to conference noted ongoing work with Korean and Pakistani people and a new attempt at a Hispanic ministry at Trinity UMC in Albany, under the leadership of the Rev. Jose Vasquez. Additionally, lacking local United Methodist churches within the Afro-American Community, conference affirmed instead a Pan-Methodist ministry which would reach out to the two African Methodist Episcopal and five African Methodist Episcopal Zion congregations within the bounds of Troy Conference.

In 1995, conference ministry with Native Americans continued. Betsy Thompson, Council Director of the Oklahoma Indian Missionary Conference addressed the conference session and noted that those who undertook the forced march called the "Trail of Tears" brought the church with them to Oklahoma. The Native American Ministries report pointed out that money sent to Kanatsiohareke, the Mohawk Valley Project, was used to buy 10,000 strawberry plants to assist moving the community to economic self-sufficiency. The following year Troy Conference nominated Thom White Wolf Fassett as "our candidate" for election to the episcopacy.

The year 1996 saw major steps forward in support of ministry within the Korean community. At that time, the Korean UMC of Albany moved from sharing space at Newtonville to a place of its own at the former Calvary UMC on Balltown Road in Schenectady. Also, a new Korean congregation began to form at Essex Junction UMC in the Green Mountain District.

Native American Ministries came to the attention of the conference in 1997. We celebrated the fact that a Native American youth from our conference was chosen to be trained for peer support leadership in areas of drug abuse and peer pressure, to help break the "Circle of Death" that causes the loss of so many young people. Additionally, conference designated a Native American Advance to raise additional funds to support relevant work within Troy Conference. Conference also voted support for the New York Governor's Program bill that affirmed the sovereignty of Native American nations to manage gasoline and cigarette enterprises on their own with the intention of bringing a swift and peaceful resolution to the conflicts over these issues. There was also a call to recognize the importance of hands-on, cooperative ministry with Native Americans in addition to offering financial support.

The conference session of 1999 revisited the 1994 Plan for Racial and Ethnic Inclusiveness. One major outcome was passage of a Plan for African American Inclusiveness and a related but separate Hispanic Ministry Comprehensive Plan. Conference also established a Coordinator of Hispanic Ministries as a half-time position. Mariana Rodriguez was chosen for that role in February 2000 and became a Local Pastor in furtherance of the leadership she had already provided. In 2003 conference committed itself to $60,000 in funding for this phase of the Hispanic ministry, by then known as the Emmanuel Faith Community.

Also in 1999, the Diversity Concerns Group petitions encouraging Anti-Racism Training and Monitoring Wholeness were approved. In addition, conference endorsed a petition to General Conference entitled "Strengthening the Black Church for the 21st Century," which called for a continued and expanded effort supporting the already established emphasis in the coming 2001–2004 quadrennium. In August 1999, Emmaus UMC hosted a multiracial, multicultural Gospel Singing and Preaching Convention for over 400 persons. Praise and worship were offered there in English, Urdu and Punjabi.

The 2002 session of conference, held in Burlington, VT, celebrated the establishment and chartering of the Vermont Korean-American Church in Essex Junction. Korean flags, costumes and drums were all part of the festivities.

Meanwhile, the conference maintained relationships with three nearby Native American Communities: Keepers of the Circle in Rotterdam Junction, the Ganienkah territory near Plattsburgh, and the Mohawk community near Canajoharie.

In 2004, conference recognized First Church, Rensselaer for inviting the Hispanic ministry, Emmanuel Faith Community, to share their facility. The invitation was accepted so now that ministry extends across the Hudson River. Ministries of the community included weekly services in Spanish, after school programs for children, a music ministry in conjunction with the Salvation Army, a six-week summer camp program, outreach to other United Methodist churches, assistance to Hispanic families moving into the Albany area, a food and clothing pantry and a prison ministry offering a monthly service in Spanish at Mount McGregor Correctional facility in Wilton. The report of the Task Force on Hispanic Ministries noted in 2006 that five families from the Emmanuel Faith Community lost their homes one night in a single fire. After an appeal went out to nearby United Methodist churches, the families received lodging, clothing, household goods, and a new beginning. One church member commented that after experiencing that generous response, she better understood what it means to be a United Methodist. In 2008 the community received the Kinmouth Jefferson Northeastern Jurisdiction Urban Ministry Award, which Pastor Mariana Rodrigues accepted on behalf of the congregation. Also in 2008, the Task Force on Hispanic Ministries was made part of the formal organization of the conference.

The Journal for 2007 notes that conference has ongoing involvement with several Native American communities and supports deliberate efforts to build and maintain good relationships. The laity memoirs thoughtfully record the death of Sara King Blais, a lay member of annual conference and a Native American of the Mohawk tribe. Sara did not learn to speak English until she went to school. She was one of the conference's major contacts with the Fonda Mohawk community and represented Troy Conference at several meetings of the Native American International Caucus.

Work with ethnic minorities had the general support of conference and attracted the specific interests of many. These efforts were marked by confusion and many small, tentative steps—yet they were steps forward as Troy Conference responded to the demands of newcomers to the community with radical hospitality.

Refugee Resettlement

Concern for the refugee is a fundamental part of our faith tradition harking back as far as the story of Abraham and Sarah. The need for a contemporary response to those uprooted and trying to survive in a new land was recognized by the people of Troy Conference. Radical hospitality urged a helpful and supportive reaction.

In fact, concern over refugees was generally a low profile issue for Troy Conference, mostly because of being well away from typical areas where action could be taken. At the same time, local churches often mobilized directly in support of those in need.

In 1982, though far from the center of action, the Lake Placid Cluster presented, and conference approved, a resolution expressing deep concern over the plight of Haitian refugees.

A decade later, the Conference Board of Global Ministries created a Division of Refugee Concerns. Judy Ayers was named as chairperson.

At the 1995 session of conference, four congregations received certificates honoring their work with refugees: Trinidad in Albany, NY, meeting under the sponsorship of Trinity United Methodist Church, and Williston Federated, Grace UMC in Essex Junction, and Essex UMC in Vermont.

In 1998, seven local churches (Voorheesville,

Slingerlands, Delmar, Trinity in Albany, and First, Faith, and Eastern Parkway in Schenectady) were recognized for their efforts in refugee resettlement. Numerous other local churches were also intimately involved in these same efforts.

In more recent years, work with refugees has become less hands-on and more focused on legal issues. Since 2000, the post of chair of refugee concerns on the Board of Global Ministries has been empty. In 2004, the report of the board highlighted the work of Vermont Refugee Assistance, which took on new dimensions when the laws of both the United States and Canada changed leaving a number of persons in a void. The report of the board in 2006 noted that churches could apply for funds from the Golden Cross offering to support a variety of programs, including those that helped provide refugee relief. Emmaus UMC in Albany did work with refugees in 2008 as part of a broader effort that included outreach to youth, as well as after-school and English as a Second Language programs. In 2010, the congregation received an Ethnic Minority Ministry Grant from the General Board of Church and Society in support of their language programs. At that time, the congregation included persons from Pakistan, Iraq, Afghanistan, the Philippines, Myanmar, the Democratic Republic of the Congo, Tanzania, Rwanda, Ghana, and Gabon.

In general, refugee work was a very small part of the overall activity of conference. At the same time, for churches and individuals in a position to interact with those seeking to make their way in a new country, the opportunities were challenging and rewarding.

Refugee Ministry

Judy Ayers

In 1990, I started working with refugees in Vermont through my job as a visiting nurse in the Burlington area. The Refugee Resettlement Program in our area has drawn many of their volunteers from a variety of denominations. I was also connected with a group working as advocates for immigrants and asylum seekers. At that time, county jails without adequate facilities were used to house detained persons until they were able to make progress in the court system. Over the years I had contact with persons from Vietnam, Bosnia, Albania, Rwanda, Congo, Sudan and other African countries, and the former Soviet Union. Through this work, I often felt as if I were receiving more than I was giving and always learning more about other cultures.

Perhaps my greatest joy was recently attending the high school graduation of three young men whose families I visited after they were born in Burlington soon after their families arrived here from Vietnam.

Assisting the Stankovic Family

Susan Hill

At a meeting of our Church Council, Pastor Bill Pattison told us he had been approached about our sponsoring a refugee family from Bosnia. After a short discussion of the needs of refugee families and our responsibilities as sponsors, the council embraced this call to mission.

The family selected for us had lived in a resettlement camp for a lengthy period and were now seeking a new home in the United States. The Stankovic family consisted of Dad Dagon, Mom Sonata, teenage daughter Maya and pre-teen son, Zolton. Because they were of mixed religion, one parent Muslim and one Christian, they were not being accepted by relatives who might otherwise have been able to assist them in their move. In fact, they spent their first night in an empty parsonage as they were unwelcome at the home of Sonata's brother in Albany.

On the night they arrived at the Albany airport, a group of Valley Falls UMC members and supporters of this project gathered to welcome the Stankovics. They arrived exhausted, not speaking English and looking thoroughly confused by this group of strangers clapping and cheering as they entered the airport. They each carried one piece of luggage, a sort of large gym bag, containing their entire belongings. Imagine starting a new life in a new country by squeezing a lifetime of memories, clothing and necessities into a space that size. Add to that wondering where you would live and how you would be able to feed and support your family, all while trying to erase the horrific mind-etched pictures of war and struggling to be safe. I remember us trying to overcome the language barrier and communicate our welcome. One in our group brought a small bouquet of flowers and gave it to Sonata. She bent her head, almost burying her face in the blossoms, to deeply inhale their scent.

Prior to that night, we had much to do to prepare for their arrival. With the assistance of the resettlement advisor, and much to our relief, we found a compact but comfortable and bright three-bedroom apartment on a nice urban street. A request to the congregation for furnishings and related items soon produced beds, mattresses, bedding, linens, tables, chairs, sofa, TV, dishes, pots and pans, lamps, pictures for the walls, and a dust ruffle for the bed. After that our responsibility was financial support for utilities, rent and food. Some of us took the family grocery shopping and to government offices to check out residential requirements, language classes, school enrollment, and job opportunities. Our pastor often brought them to these appointments.

As winter approached, so did the need for warmer clothing. With funds from our UMW, I took Sonata and Maya shopping. Like all teenage girls, Maya had definite ideas of what was most fashionable, not necessarily what was most warm. I recall the slight frown and unspoken look of disapproval on Sonata's face—the same look that had crossed my face when shopping with my own teenage daughter. Mothers and teenage daughters face similar issues no matter where they are from!

The Stankovic family became self-supporting within a year of settling here and continue to be part of our lives. They visit our church on occasion, have worshiped with us and worked at dinners, always thanking us for helping them start their new lives. The parents have jobs and have advanced in them; the children have graduated from high school and attend college. They have bought cars and a home and entertained us there.

Supporting the Stankovic family was a true blessing to the congregation. It began a path of mission work that is now deeply embedded in us all. We continue to thank God for the opportunity to do this work and to experience the reward of helping others. We also thank Pastor Bill for all he did to help this family and for showing us how to open our hearts and live our faith in a meaningful way.

Reconciling Conference

The current expression of church teaching on the issue of homosexuality (Par. 161F, 2008 edition of *The Discipline of The United Methodist Church*) is: "We affirm that all persons are individuals of sacred worth, created in the image of God...The United Methodist Church does not condone the practice of homosexuality and considers this practice incompatible with Christian teaching."

The words are slightly changed from their initial appearance in the *Discipline* of 1972, but the concepts are very much the same. The affirmation of sacred worth was readily accepted, but the judgment of incompatibility was a highly contentious matter in Troy Conference. No time was lost in raising an objection. That same year, while affirming that "all persons are entitled to have their human and civil rights ensured," at the urging of the Board of Christian Social Concerns conference voted (118 for and 99 against) to dissent from these words of General Conference: 'though we do not condone the practice of homosexuality and consider the practice incompatible with Christian teaching.' The ongoing concern for radical hospitality meant the matter was frequently under discussion, and that hospitality had to be offered in two very different ways. First, a majority (frequently a very slim majority) extended frequent efforts to remove the denial of compatibility from the *Discipline* with the aim of making the church more welcoming and inclusive. Second, amid the sometimes highly divergent views about what the Gospel demands, there was a strong focus on remaining in good space together despite the tension and potential divisions.

These early stages of discussion occurred when homosexuals were just "coming out of the closet." The very language itself, with a suggestion of bringing to light what was previously hidden, implied that something was wrong with homosexuality. For many in Troy Conference, knowledge of homosexuality was limited to what they read in the papers. What they read in the papers regularly linked homosexuality with casual sex, predatory interests, and destructive behaviors. The usual suggestion at this time was that people chose to act in these "unnatural" ways. This was, we now believe, far from reality, but that misunderstanding represented at the time the limits of what most of us knew. From that perspective, affirming the sacred worth of homosexuals, even with the added qualifications, was radical hospitality.

Others, however, had a different perspective. They recognized that homosexuals were present in many places in society and in the church. It seemed to them that homosexuals functioned as well as, as faithfully as, heterosexuals and so were not a threat to Christian values. Radical hospitality for them meant homosexuals deserved nothing less than an unambiguous welcome in the church. Radical hospitality meant full equality for all and total indifference to sexual orientation and the choice of a life partner.

So Troy Conference found itself united in wanting to be welcoming and divided over the nature of that welcome. One chief tool of debate was the Wesleyan quadrilateral, which understands "the living core of the Christian faith [to be] revealed in Scripture, illuminated by tradition, vivified in personal experience and confirmed by reason." Those who might be called traditionalists tended to affirm the overwhelming primacy of scripture and tradition. The non-traditionalists tended to interpret the scriptures and tradition from a different point of view and to make more use of experience and reason. The traditional values were put in a new light. The tension between these traditional and non-traditional points of view played out through the years.

The Methodist Federation for Social Action brought two petitions directly bearing on the matter of homosexuality to the 1987 Annual Conference session.

The first was a proposed addition to the disciplinary paragraph that insisted no United Methodist funds were to be used to promote the acceptance of homosexuality in any way. The proposal would have added that there "is diversity of responsible positions" and made explicit the possibility of lawful discussion, debate and education about homosexuality at all levels of the church. The effect of affirming this petition was to send it on to General Conference for further discussion and action.

The petition that had greater direct impact on Troy Conference was the second, titled "Reconciling Conference and Congregation." Noting that the Social Principles read in part, "Homosexual persons are individuals of sacred worth," the petition went on to say that the ban on spending money to promote acceptance of homosexuality is different from a ban on the participation of homosexuals in the life of the church. Therefore, Troy Annual Conference declared

Homosexuality as an Issue in The United Methodist Church

Rev. Steven Clunn

On June 28, 1969, at the Stonewall Inn in the Greenwich Village neighborhood of New York City, the police conducted a raid on this popular nightclub where the homosexual community gathered. The gay community fought back against what was believed to be another incident in a government-sponsored system that persecuted sexual minorities, and a series of violent clashes with police ensued. These events of the summer of 1969, known as the "Stonewall Riots," became the defining event that marked the start of the gay rights movement in the United States and around the world.

The church was also impacted by the Stonewall events. At the General Conference of 1972, a handful of openly gay men offered delegates and visitors the opportunity for conversation about homosexuality. Few responded positively. Instead, in the waning hours of the conference, delegates amended a paragraph in the new Social Principles to hold, "We do not condone the practice of homosexuality and consider this practice to be incompatible with Christian teaching."

In July of 1975, the United Methodist Gay Caucus organized in Evanston, Illinois. Later renamed Gay United Methodists (GUM), the caucus formed to insist that our lives and loving are gifts of God, not rebellion against divine will. About a year after making a powerful presence at the 1976 General Conference, GUM took a new name: Affirmation.

In 1984 at General Conference in Baltimore, delegates voted to amend the Book of Discipline to state that "no self-avowed, practicing homosexual shall be ordained or appointed in The United Methodist Church." In the early morning following the vote on the ordination itself a "Reconciling Conference." The full participation of homosexuals in the life of the conference was affirmed. Local churches were urged to become "Reconciling Congregations" to support the full participation of all persons, regardless of sexual identity, in the life of the congregation. Traditional and non-traditional arguments were made with great passion. The vote was close.

Now, while at the time there was a definition of a reconciling congregation, there was no definition of a reconciling conference. So in 1988 conference approved a resolution from the Board of Church and Society calling for a two–year study and final report on the relevant issues.

The board's report in the 1990 Journal is surprisingly short considering the issues involved. Basically it notes a desire to accept both the liberties and the limits of the *Book of Discipline*, affirms that conference ought to be in ministry for and with all persons, and urges continued study, discussion and prayer on the issue while awaiting the results of a General Conference study due in 1992.

In 1991, the Reconciling Congregation Task Force of the Board of Church and Society presented additional resolutions that, after serious debate, were affirmed by annual conference. One sought a change in the *Discipline's* language that condoned sexual relations only within the marriage bond. New language suggested, "We affirm sexual relations within the context of human caring and covenantal faithfulness." Another called for the deletion of language describing the practice of homosexuality as incompatible with Christian teaching. A third resolution called for eliminating the ban on financial support of efforts to promote the acceptance of homosexuality. Finally, General Conference was urged to extend the study on sexuality an additional four years.

Conference at its 1992 session, acting on a resolution from the Board of Church and Society, encouraged every congregation in the conference to engage in study ban, about a dozen Affirmation members gathered outside the Civic Center in Baltimore and passed out brochures to General Conference delegates and visitors inviting their congregations to become Reconciling Congregations, in essence to dissent from the unwelcoming policies approved by the UMC. There were nine Reconciling Congregations by the end of 1984.

By 1986, the "reconciling issue" was becoming a national debate within the US portion of the UMC. At its session, the Northern Illinois Annual Conference became the first to officially declare itself a Reconciling Conference. In 1987, three more annual conferences—California-Nevada, New York, and Troy—voted to become Reconciling Conferences in their early summer sessions. By the end of 1987 there were 30 Reconciling Congregations nationwide, and by the end of 1997 there were 137 Reconciling Congregations and 19 Reconciling Campus Ministries.

General Conference 2000 in Cleveland saw an even greater outcry from within the UMC to "extend the table" to our gay, lesbian, bisexual, and transgender sisters and brothers. The reconciling movement asked the church to recognize that "Wide is God's Welcome" and that the UMC's exclusive positions were not. After the votes were taken to maintain the denomination's exclusionary position, a peaceful protest began on the floor that threatened to temporarily halt the conference proceedings. When protestors, including delegates and bishops, were threatened with arrest if they did not stop, a number of the protesters decided to accept being peacefully arrested as a part of their witness to the general church. Among those arrested was Troy Annual Conference's own Bishop Susan Morrison.

and discussion regarding a decision to become a Reconciling Congregation. As the report of the board puts it, "... thereby celebrating the diversity that God created, which is our richness as children of God."

It needs to be noted repeatedly that conference did not come easily to these positions. The tension was extreme and so was the degree of civility and mutual respect. In 1993, there was a particularly difficult vote that asked

The Rev. Steven Clunn

General Conference to, among other things, remove language prohibiting the ordination of homosexual persons. After the vote, the Rev. Steven Clunn and the Rev. James Proctor, strong advocates for the non-traditional and traditional positions respectively, stood together to offer prayers for healing the anguish of conference.

Another resolution condemned applying a different code of military ethics to persons on the basis of their sexual orientation. In other, largely symbolic,

The Rev. James Proctor

action the conference resolved that "covenant services" were not marriage services and thus could be celebrated by conference clergy. Bishop William Grove, presiding at the session, explained that this resolution needed to be referred to the Judicial Council for a declaratory decision, and it was so referred.

At the 1994 conference a whole morning was given to the topic of human sexuality. The Rev. Arthur Hagy sounded the note of radical hospitality as he introduced the teaching session by reminding those gathered that the discussion was about "us" as a family and not about "them" as outsiders. Dr. Catherine Clark Kroeger, a professor at Gordon-Conwell Theological

My Journey as a Homophile

Rev. Bill Barney

In 1972, when the General Conference declared that "the practice of homosexuality is incompatible with Christian teaching," it seemed all right to me. I was in my second year of ministry and as far as I knew I was opposed to "the practice of homosexuality." Then in 1973, as the new Conference Youth Coordinator, I became an adult member of the United Methodist Council on Youth Ministry in the general church, representing the Northeast Jurisdiction. Little did I know how it would change my life.

At a meeting in Denver, the Council hosted Bill Johnson, the first self-identified homosexual pastor ordained in the United Church of Christ. I found out that the youth leadership of our church was very upset by the action of General Conference and set out to change it. My uncomfortable encounter with the pain-filled story of Bill Johnson's battle with injustice brought about in me a conversion to activism—as I said then, "from homophobe to homophile" (one who expresses loving acceptance of homosexual persons). From there, I went on to chair the first churchwide forum on "Sexual Orientation," which led to the UMC mandating the first churchwide study of homosexuality. In 1975, our own TAC youth led our Annual Conference to be the first to support the call for this study by an overwhelming vote, submitting its petition to General Conference.

I have remained a radical homophile since that time and have participated in every initiative by Troy Conference and joined a minority of delegates at General Conference to overturn the 1972 language. The work of the "reconciling movement" in Troy Conference has been, for me, among the proudest and most spiritual moments

Seminary, presented what we are calling the "traditional" view. Her position was that God's moral absolutes are found in the scriptures. At the same time, she was quick to note that "the faith journeys of homosexual persons have much to teach us." Dr. Victor Paul Furnish, a professor from Perkins School of Theology, outlined why he did not share the church's traditional view on homosexuality. One key point in his argument was that our understanding of the Gospel needs to be reconceived and reformulated to take into account the things we learn along the way. The morning closed with a Service of Silence, Surrender and Healing.

This event was typical of the way conference tried to work through all its issues—a full and frank presentation of agreement and disagreement, followed by a genuine attempt to affirm ongoing Christian unity amid ongoing divergence of thought.

Later in that same session, Rutland UMC was acknowledged as the conference's first Reconciling Congregation. The report of the Cabinet given by the Rev. William Lasher noted wryly, "We are one of four Reconciling Conferences in the UMC. However, we recognize that not all of us celebrate that status as good news." The stress in Troy Conference could be found across the whole denomination. Two documents, "A Time of Hope—A Time of Threat," and "An Invitation to the Church," reprinted in the 1994 Journal, outline some of the tensions. Even so, Troy Annual Conference remained committed to fruitful dialogue in a "context of trust and respect" with "an openness to one another and a confidence of the Holy Spirit within our midst."

The 1995 session dealt with a petition, "Blessing Loving Relationships," in a non-legislative manner because Bishop Grove noted the thrust of the legislation was in violation of the *Discipline* and he could not allow it to be passed. At the close of discussion the bishop led the conference in prayer. Later in the day, conference affirmed a petition, "Supporting the Covenant of Marriage," which stressed the of my ministry. As I became convicted that gay, lesbian, bisexual and transgender (GLBT) persons deserve complete access to all levels of life in church and society, the issues have become ramped up and divisive. I remain proud that TAC has never wavered for over 30 years in its support for homosexual rights and participation in the church.

I am aware that this has been a painful journey for those who felt they were opposing a challenge to traditional "Christian teaching," always finding themselves in a voting minority. Those of us who were in the TAC majority and, by the way, in a General Conference minority (we felt the ultimate legislative pain), have always supported an open and fair discussion of the issues by persons of all persuasions on these issues. I do not remember a person on either side ever being attacked personally in all of this time—as spirited as the debate may have been, almost annually. I do believe that eventually the youth of our church will be the ones to lead us out of the prohibitive position of the church against GLBT persons. The Troy Annual Conference will be remembered as a leader in the church among annual conferences on this issue, and I will acknowledge with a thankful heart that I was probably the one who first stirred up the "hornets' nest". Long live the spirit of Troy Annual Conference!

A Stranger in a Strange Land:
Life as an Evangelical in Troy Annual Conference

Rev. James Proctor

Home. This ordinary but astounding word was spoken into my soul in the most unlikely of places—a meeting of Troy Annual Conference. During a communion service in the gym at Green Mountain College in the late 1980s I wondered, "What in the world am I doing here?" Then traditional language about marriage used in *The United Methodist Book of Worship* and the Social Principles found in the *Book of Discipline.*

The report from the delegates to the 1996 General Conference noted that a statement acknowledging a division of opinion on the matter of homosexuality and reconciling congregations was rejected on the floor. Essentially, the general church did not want to go on record as admitting there was disagreement within the denomination regarding the official statements of the *Book of Discipline.* Yet clearly, in Troy Conference as well as other places, such disagreement was very real. One sign of that reality was the passage of a resolution recognizing, affirming, and congratulating the United Methodist churches of Rutland, Saratoga Springs, First UMC in Schenectady, and Plattsburgh for declaring themselves Reconciling Congregations.

In 1997, three petitions to General Conference regarding homosexuality came to conference for action. Each one began, "In observance of over 20 years of opposition by Troy Annual Conference to the official position of the UMC, and in celebration of our 10th anniversary of becoming a Reconciling Conference ..." One sign of the division within conference was that in each case there was a move to table, and none was approved. The first petition laid out the ongoing tension: many believe that living out one's homosexual orientation is incompatible with Christian teaching, while many others believe it is compatible when done in the context of human covenantal faithfulness. The second called for deletion of the disciplinary paragraph barring "self-avowed, practicing homosexuals" from ordination or appointment. Both petitions passed by show of hands.

The third petition called for deletion of the disciplinary language that bans the celebration of homosexual unions by United Methodist pastors and within United Methodist churches. This last petition was passed by paper ballot with 263 in favor, 189 opposed, and 4 abstentions. Those

God spoke into my soul and told me that Troy Conference was indeed my ministry home.

What makes this unusual is that I am not exactly a good fit with Troy Conference. Using the old "left/right" spectrum to describe theological leanings, I am considerably to the right of most of the people I meet in Troy Conference. It makes conference life a bit uncomfortable at times. It is often contentious, frustrating, discouraging and disappointing.

This is home? By God's grace, yes. I have grown and received nourishment from my time in Troy Conference. I can only pray that my presence has given the same opportunities to others.

Life for an evangelical is difficult when conference takes actions that seem quite far from the Christian faith as I understand it. Year after year I am identified with a body that doesn't seem to resemble me in significant ways. Just one example—I recall the time the presiding bishop declared a sense of joy and freedom when she came to the conclusion that it was not the job of the church to worry about getting folks saved. Many in attendance cheered and applauded. Into my mind came a favorite quote from our Methodist founder, John Wesley: "We have nothing to do but save souls." Are we in the same household? Is it possible to feel like an outsider in your own home? Most certainly. What would it be like if your whole family were red-headed, freckled sports nuts, and you were a black-haired, olive-skinned, computer geek? You might feel a little out of place. And certainly sometimes as resolutions were debated and decided, it felt like that.

This sense of alienation was what prompted formation of the Fellowship Inspiring Scriptural Holiness (FISH), an evangelical fellowship within Troy Conference in the late 1990s. As one of the founders of this group, I recall many conversations where deep and numbers help to show the depth of division that existed within the membership of conference. All three actions came back to conference the next year in the form of a petition to rescind the previous year's decisions. After discussion and prayer the vote to rescind did not prevail.

In 1998, the Judicial Council ruled that Annual Conferences could no longer identify themselves as "Reconciling." But in 1999, a petition was presented affirming that Troy Annual Conference would "continue its historic and vital affirmation of local congregations, pastors and laity who choose to participate in the Reconciling Congregation Program." A move to table the petition failed and the resolution was approved. Also, Slingerlands UMC was added to the list of Reconciling Congregations within conference, bringing the total to five.

At the 2000 session of conference, the issues of division were raised in a new way with a petition to establish a non-geographical "Wesley District" that would allow like-minded clergy and congregations to be an identified, functioning sub-unit of annual conference. After a lengthy and often highly technical debate, the petition was amended to call for the development "of a process of dialog and Christian conferencing ... to explore areas of difference and unity."

The task force created for this work reported back in 2001 that they had undertaken a process of conversation within the group and hoped to bring something suitable for the whole conference the following year. However, radical hospitality was evident in an approved resolution that encouraged all congregations to participate in welcoming training, under the general church media theme, "Open Hearts. Open Minds. Open Doors."

The report from what was now called the Theological Diversity Team in 2002 indicated some progress toward their assigned task. They identified some seventeen key issues that underlay the tensions felt in conference. They difficult thoughts and feelings poured out as we tried to sort out our place in this sometimes homey, sometimes alien, environment. This tension motivated our controversial and troubling proposal, brought forth at the 2000 Annual Conference, to create a "Wesley District," a non-geographical, evangelical district within the conference. Regardless of what folks thought concerning the wisdom, practicality, need, or appropriateness for such a district, it served to alert the conference to the inner struggle of the evangelicals in our midst. This proposal reflected our conflicted longings to stay connected with, and also to separate from, Troy Annual Conference.

So why did God tell me this place that was pulling me apart was to be my home? Because there is much more to the story than debates and resolutions. The heart and soul of Troy Conference for me is found in the relationships with the people. In the break times, in the hallways and dining rooms, in the common and unscheduled moments of the day, opportunities abound for God's people to draw closer together, to share faith, to teach and learn from each other. More than once at troubling moments at conference, people would make a point of coming to me to check how it was with my soul. I had opportunity to be gently reminded that a significant portion of the actions of the conference were things I endorse and agree with. How I value that perspective! A number of people went out of their way to spend extended time with me, listening deeply to my thoughts on controversial matters. How I value that listening! Others took the time to speak their hearts to me, knowing I would likely not agree with them, but still valuing the chance to air their thoughts, trusting me to think deeply with them and not simply reject them. How I value that trust! Many in the conference inquired concerning my family after my wife and I adopted three children from Ethiopia. The children generally are not comfortable with continued to aim toward fulfilling their purpose: "to create and model a climate in which theological differences can be acknowledged and explored in our search for unity in Christ."

In 2003, the team offered one resolution in support of an attitude of theological diversity and two resolutions in support of a process of theological diversity. The common goal of these resolutions was to promote the respectful hearing of all voices even when the divisions of opinion were painfully deep. One resolution, seeking a way to move to a consensus model, was referred back to the team with the request that they develop suitable training and clarify how a consensus process would work. The other two, one urging a respectful hearing of divergent views, and the other allowing for a dissenting opinion to be included in the official record, were approved after extensive debate.

This attention to a mutually respectful process was important because that same conference passed seven petitions touching difficult and contentious issues. Conference approved trying to find a way to extend its own health care coverage to "domestic partners" (regardless of married status or homosexual unions, though the petition mentioned neither). Also conference petitioned General Conference to change the Social Principles by deleting the thought that sexual relations are only affirmed in the marriage bond and by expanding the language on support for human rights and liberties to specifically include gay, lesbian, bisexual, and transgender persons. Additional action regarding ordination requirements asked to substitute "responsibility in all relationships" for the phrase "celibacy in singleness" and to remove language stating that the practice of homosexuality is incompatible with Christian teaching. Further legislation asked that annual conference be allowed to decide whether or not to authorize homosexual unions and to remove restrictions on the use of church money for the support of any gay caucus or support of the acceptance crowds or strangers, so I have never felt it wise to "put them on display" at conference. Despite the disappointment this causes for folks who desire to meet them, people still ask about them regularly, pray for them and us, and have even made donations to support this part of the family they have never met. How I value that understanding and support!

Two events in particular stand out that testify to our desire as brothers and sisters to walk through tough issues together. The first was "a dialogue on reconciliation," an overnight retreat in 1991 where a dozen clergy with widely disparate views on homosexuality gathered. Organized primarily by Arthur Hagy and myself, with Carrol Newquist as moderator, we spent the first day sharing faith stories with each other, cooking supper together, and generally getting to know each other apart from areas of contention. Based on this foundation of fellowship, we spent time on the second day seeking to hear each other's perspectives on homosexuality in a small group setting. The time ended with communion.

The second event occurred at Annual Conference in 1994. The organizers of the conference session agreed to dedicate an entire morning of our time together to discuss the issue of homosexuality in some depth. What was especially unique and helpful about this session was the agreement that there would be no resolutions on the issue presented for vote at Annual Conference that year. This allowed us to ponder, pray, speak and listen without the pressure of being concerned with who would "win."

These events help us to see one another, not as enemies, but as sojourners on the road of faith together. Obviously we have not come to a place of agreement on contentious issues. However, I believe the open and charitable attitude we are developing with one another is rare, and is to be greatly valued.

There have been a few times when individuals have

of homosexuality.

These petitions were passed after extensive debate and over considerable opposition. The agreement passed earlier in the session to publish dissenting opinions was put to immediate use, with 48 persons going on record as opposed to the domestic partners legislation and 78 opposing the petitions that would weaken the traditional stance that sexual relationships are only affirmed within the bonds of marriage. In the light of emphasizing radical hospitality, it needs to be noted that opposition did not extend to the broader statement that those deserving equal rights should specifically include gay, lesbian, bisexual, and transgender persons.

In a related matter, the Small Membership Church Award went to Old Stone UMC in Isle LaMotte, VT. Speaking for the congregation, a layperson from the church said, "About the only thing we did was open our doors a bit wider. We looked out into our community and saw some gay and lesbian people and we invited them in." In her additional remarks she spoke more about inclusion and extending invitations to diverse people whom they found were "strangely familiar." Old Stone UMC was not officially a Reconciling Congregation, but it extended radical hospitality all the same.

At the conference session of 2004 the Theological Diversity team asked to be decommissioned. Conference disagreed and instead called for the Cabinet to meet with the team to explore how the congregations of the conference could be helped to deal with issues of theological diversity. Also, once again conference passed a resolution (207 for, 155 opposed, and 14 abstaining) seeking health care coverage for domestic partners. On a point of order questioning the constitutionality of the issue Bishop Morrison, presiding officer, agreed to prepare a ruling for the Judicial Council to consider. In addition, a small group of those opposed to the resolution took the time to prepare been extremely uncharitable in response to my actions or statements. These times stand out very clearly because they are so out of step with the response of the vast majority of people in the conference. There have been times I have been so frustrated that walking out seemed to be the only way to keep peace of mind. But the call of God to make this my "home" has enabled me to stick it out, find the blessing in the midst of the turmoil, and, hopefully, be found faithful. I have sought to speak and live the truth as I understand it, and to love others regardless of their perspective. In the process I have found meaningful fellowship in this family.

Being an evangelical in Troy Annual Conference has been quite difficult. Being a brother in the Troy Conference family has warmed my soul. Thank you, brothers and sisters, for walking this road with me.

Rev. John Marshall remembers

I was ordained a deacon in 1987. That was the first year I attended all of Annual Conference. It was also the year the Methodist Federation for Social Action brought forward, and conference adopted, Petition 9, Reconciling Conference and Congregation. That was a difficult thing for me because I was new in the conference and because I felt myself in support of the Discipline as it was and the rulings of the Judicial Council.

I found that action, and related ones that conference took through the years, to be troublesome. I didn't think the labels were helpful. It was particularly hard when "Reconciling Conference" was written on the cover of the Journal. In a small conference like this one there was no evangelical caucus and sometimes that led to a sense of isolation. Some of my colleagues who thought the way I did were afraid to speak up and voice their disagreement. Some of those votes were taken at the time when the district superintendents sat together up a dissenting opinion, noting that the approved action went beyond the traditional views of marriage in relation to both heterosexual and homosexual couples.

Again at the 2006 session, numerous petitions dealt with issues surrounding the church's best response to homosexuality. Several petitions were affirmed by conference, and a minority report outlining more traditional views was offered the day after the initial votes were taken. Several other related petitions were tabled and then referred to the Theological Diversity Critical Issues team for study and future discussion.

The 2007 session, on Friday morning, used the Circle Process to help members speak their minds and hear what others had to say. On a common motion made by representatives of both the traditional and non-traditional views, the five resolutions on human sexuality tabled in 2006 were taken off the table and made the topic of conversation within the circle of those sitting at each table. The question to be addressed was, "What is your understanding of God's will in regard to homosexuality, what is the church's faithful response, and why do you believe this?" In the afternoon the rules were suspended, and a vote was taken on the resolutions individually. The resolutions, urging General Conference to ease financial restrictions in supporting gay rights, allow ordination of homosexuals and celebration of homosexual unions, and support a non-traditional stance on human sexuality were all approved. In an additional action, conference reacted to a pastor in another conference who refused church membership to a homosexual. Troy Conference affirmed instead a willingness to "welcome persons of any age, gender, race, ethnic background, sexual orientation, economic condition and physical or mental ability as full participants in our community of faith."

The Theological Diversity Ministry Team offered a report in 2008 rating the Circle Process of the prior year as an overall success because discussion was freed from front. So when we took standing votes some didn't want the DS to see how they voted. I wish we had thought to call for a written ballot as that might have changed the outcome.

At the same time, I thought the bishops were fair in the way they handled the debate. The elimination of applause and the stress on civility was important. I found Bishop Morrison especially determined to be fair. After the debates she checked to be sure that she had been even-handed. And after conference, there was always a time of reflection—a time to be sure that my stands did not show aspects of homophobia.

I didn't feel that taking the positions I did took bravery. I knew I could hold a minority view and still belong. The appointment process seemed to treat me fairly. After the debates, I could count on the Saturday night program (or Friday night sometimes) and the or-dination service to bring us together. Though, it didn't feel good that at the 2009 ordination wearing my robe and stole became a political statement. Still, I never felt that the stands we took defined who we were as a conference. We as a group had a diversity of opinions and, even in later years, had the option of presenting a minority resolution even when the body voted to take a particular stand.

I'm anticipating that in a larger conference there will be more voices, and that we might be more diverse and more moderate.

Christ Church, Troy Becomes a Reconciling Congregation

Bob Blackmon, Chair
Social Awareness and Action Team

For several years we had been aware of the reconciling movement from conversations with people within The

the constraints of parliamentary action. By the same token, with discussion centered on the handful of people at the same table it was impossible for everyone to hear all the points of view as would have been the case with a discussion on the floor. The team acknowledged that more work was needed at all levels to help make positive conversation a priority over divisive arguments. In an additional comment revolving around the topic of radical hospitality, the team noted that youth in particular found even the Circle Process a barrier to discussion with some of their adult counterparts. Still, solutions were closer once the problems were more clearly identified.

At the last full session of annual conference in 2009, a substantial number made a symbolic statement regarding their desire to change the denomination's current stand on homosexuals in ministry. At the suggestion of the Rev. Bill Barney, the "No-Robes Project" invited all interested clergy to process into the ordination service without a clergy robe in support of those who were denied participation "because of sexual orientation or gender identity." A related witness came in the form of rainbow stoles worn either with or without a robe to show support for the desired change in policy. Many of the clergy at the ordination service took this stance for wider inclusion.

The very difficult conversations on homosexuality through the years were important dimensions of radical hospitality in two ways. First, within the conference those conversations made clear the central importance of being willing to listen to divergent opinions and to keep those differences from becoming barriers to Christian fellowship. Secondly, as the church looked to the world, the conversations helped the conference make a vigorous affirmation of the worth and value of all people. Regardless of the ways specific points of view differed, the common commitment was to welcome each person as a child of God.

United Methodist Church. The decision to become a Reconciling Congregation was a logical decision for us because Christ Church is diverse and active in societal issues. It is a welcoming congregation, totally comfortable having gay and lesbian people as part of our community of faith.

After some conversations with Pastor Nina and some discussions within the Social Awareness and Action Team (SAAT), we quickly found we fully supported our becoming a Reconciling Congregation. We then took a series of steps to engage the whole congregation with the issue.

We held several well-attended Coffee Talks on the topic immediately following Sunday morning worship. We invited a pastor and a lay person from a nearby UMC that had just completed the process of becoming a Reconciling Congregation. Approximately 40 people attended that evening workshop, and the discussion was wonderful. Everyone went away feeling the event had been very helpful.

In case there were parishioners who might have doubts about supporting the movement but were not willing to express their concerns in a public forum, we provided the opportunity for private meetings with the pastor. Only a few people took advantage of that option, and we found that people who were rumored to not support the movement were actually comfortable with it.

The worship experience was part of our process. Several times during the 18 months of our effort the pastor spoke of inclusiveness, openness, and love, sometimes directly mentioning the reconciling movement. It is important to point out that our tradition is to be very specific in inviting ALL, no exceptions, to the communion table. Obviously, that invitation was extended several times during our process.

As part of our Summer Festival of the Arts, members of the congregation gathered one evening to watch and discuss the film Milk. On the following Sunday, a member of SAAT delivered a three-minute "Reflection" as part of the service, recalling <u>Milk</u> and pointing out that basic human rights are still denied members of the GLBT community. Another member of the team followed with a brief statement tying this issue to the struggle for African-American civil rights.

We used other methods to raise awareness as well. We secured pink lapel buttons with the words "All Means ALL" printed on them for team members and others in the congregation to wear to worship and church events. We had an article in the church newsletter describing our process. We offered a suggestion box as an opportunity for commenting on the reconciling process. A few people left notes in the box. All were positive.

In the last summer of 2009, the nine-member SAAT created a draft statement expressing our position. On November 19, the draft statement went to a well-attended meeting of the Church Council. There was a fair amount of discussion, all positive. The Council approved the final statement, recommended to the Church Conference that the statement be approved and that Christ Church become a Reconciling Congregation. Church Conference met on November 22. Following some positive discussion, the motion to become a Reconciling Congregation was passed unanimously with no nays or abstentions.

It is important to note that people of all ages supported this movement with enthusiasm. There were many pink buttons at both Church Council and Church Conference. Some were worn by people in their 80s. Without question there was broad-based support for our becoming a Reconciling Congregation. We are aware that some other congregations have taken years to come to this conclusion. Our process took only about 18 months, but the speed with which that happened in no way minimized the opportunity for full and complete consideration of the issue. Rather it reflects our church's strong commitment to diversity and inclusiveness.

Christ Church UMC Statement

God intends the church to be a community that embodies love, grace, and justice for all people. As a Reconciling Congregation, we therefore affirm the sacred worth of and welcome persons of any sexual orientation, gender, gender identity, age, marital status, race, ethnic background, economic condition, and physical or mental ability as full participants in our community of faith. God's love includes everyone, as does Christ Church United Methodist.

Reconciling Congregation: A label we shall proudly wear!

Rev. Nina Nichols, pastor

I was a student intern at Holy Covenant UMC in Chicago while in seminary at the University of Chicago Divinity School. Holy Covenant was a Reconciling Congregation, and the experience of serving there made a deep impression on me. I volunteered at General Conference 1996 with the "Open the Doors" Campaign and again in 2000 in Cleveland with the "Extend the Table" Campaign. I was on the strategy team for the Rev. Greg Dell during his trial when he was suspended from appointed ministry for doing a same sex blessing for two men in his congregation, Broadway UMC in Chicago. In 2008, I was in Fort Worth for General Conference working on the amendment to Article 4 of the constitution to clarify our welcome to all persons. I love The United Methodist Church, but our hard heartedness regarding welcome and inclusion regardless of sexual orientation saddens me. I think, therefore, that getting to be on the journey with Christ Church from consideration of making this statement to adopting it unanimously by Church Conference action will always be one of the most joyous highlights of my ministry.

Thoughts on the Future

Rev. Steven Clunn

As the Troy Annual Conference begins to structurally wind down, many of us look forward to a new Upstate New York Annual Conference, a larger New England Annual Conference, and a continued witness of God's great love through the efforts of reconciling congregations, clergy and laity. We give thanks for the role that TAC has played in its twenty-two year history of official witness for a more inclusive church! We prayerfully support our newly fashioned annual conferences and the reconciling congregations from the former TAC, who have and will continue to make a part of their faithful witness to God's love in the name of Jesus, a witness that is both inclusive and reconciling.

Written and Offered With Great Love!

Women in Leadership

A Flame of Fire dedicates a whole chapter to the role of Troy Conference women and the uphill struggle required to get general acceptance of their call and recognition of their leadership abilities. While that struggle is far from over, it seems valuable to outline just how those efforts played out in Troy Conference in recent years. Progress and transformation taken for granted can obscure how much has actually changed.

For instance, while through the years many women were ordained as "Local" deacons and elders, Doris Hartman, a missionary to Japan, was in 1963 the first woman received into Troy Conference in full connection. Barbara Bingham Gardner became the second woman in full connection in 1964 and was the first to serve Troy Conference churches.

The Rev. Barbara Bingham Gardner

When the Rev. Gardner retired in 1983, fourteen other women shared her status, and five more were under appointment in probationary status. Those numbers represented about ten percent of the clergy in full connection and twenty-five percent of the probationary members. That same year the Commission on the Status and Role of Women celebrated ten years of existence. The Commission went on to note concerns about non-inclusive language and hard-to-pin-down inequities in the appointment process. "The hard facts of statistics," they said, "do show that there is financial discrimination against women clergy."

To help put things in perspective, it was not until 1980 that the first woman, Marjorie Swank Matthews, was elected a bishop of The United Methodist Church. It was also noteworthy when she became the first woman bishop to preside over General Conference in 1984.

Showing how much, or how little, progress was made, in 1984 the Conference Commission on the Status and Role of Women offered three resolutions, all of which were approved, encouraging the study and use of inclusive language. The next year conference recommended to all local churches the study and implementation of the document, "Words that Hurt and Words that Heal."

In 1989, the Board of Church and Society put forward, and conference affirmed, a resolution stressing the need for day care for children. Local churches were urged to find ways their members and facilities could be involved in ministries of this sort. That same year, the Rev. Marcheta P. Townsend was appointed Superintendent of the Green Mountain District, the first woman in Troy Conference to hold that position of leadership.

Conference celebrated the 100th anniversary of the birth of theologian Georgia Harkness in 1991. Worship, drama, and music, supplemented by two lectures from Professor Mary Elizabeth Moore from Clermont School of Theology, helped interpret Doctor Harkness, a Troy Conference native, as a thinker, teacher, and model for Christian living.

In 1993, Bishop William Grove preached an ordination sermon in which he celebrated the central role of women in church leadership. His message took embodied form as of the six persons ordained and consecrated that day, five were women.

The first woman bishop to lead Troy Conference was Susan Murch Morrison, who served here from 1996 to 2006. Her tenure was marked by general acceptance of her leadership, though some people were uncomfortable with her advocacy for a more accepting view of homosexuality.

Two events in 1998 particularly serve to dramatize issues surrounding women in leadership positions. A first concern was the non-payment of the salaries of women clergy in the Mozambique Conference. In a poor country with very limited exposure to women clergy, these persons were financially shortchanged to an even greater degree than their male colleagues. The women clergy of Troy Conference made a commitment to contribute to these salaries. The Rev. Kelly Warner invited others to assist in this effort, and the Journal reports that assent was by "thunderous applause matching the thunder and lighting engulfing the campus" at the time as a result of a spring storm. The second event, while less dramatic, was equally noteworthy: Barbara Zittel became the first layperson to chair the Commission on the Status and Role of Women.

While the vision of the Commission of the Status

The Rev. Ruth Gray Barr

Ruth G. Barr was born in Greensboro, VT and graduated first from Hardwick Academy and then from Johnson Normal School. Later training included a year at Moody Bible School in Northfield, MA. In 1896, she graduated from New England Deaconess and Training School, Boston, Mass.

She did deaconess work first in the Boston area and then for five years at Methodist churches in Springfield, MA. In 1906 she returned to Greensboro Bend, where she acted as superintendent of schools as well as church organist and Sunday school superintendent. She was active in local, district and statewide religious organizations such as the Woman's Christian Temperance Union and the Woman's Foreign Missionary Society.

She did extensive pulpit supply work and in 1917 acted as pastor's assistant at Grace Methodist Episcopal Church in Saint Johnsbury. In 1925 she was ordained a deacon by the Vermont Conference of the Methodist Episcopal Church. She is listed in conference journals as serving in the pulpit rotation of the Greensboro Bend church. Her studies for elder's orders were complete, and she was to have been ordained at the 1929 session of annual conference.

Ruth died at the home of her sister on July 8, 1928. An article about her in the July 19, 1928, Hardwick Gazette said, "She has left behind a 'trail of light' leading upwards to God and the world is better because she lived in it." Her funeral was held in the Greensboro Bend Methodist Episcopal Church. Officiating were District Superintendent C. C. Chayer and the Rev. J. J. Snellgrove.

(Thanks to the Rev. Patricia Thompson for her research on Ruth Gray Barr, who is believed to be the first woman ordained in the Vermont and Troy Conferences.)

and Role of Women is far from complete, some markers show the progress that has been made. In 2006, Troy Conference was operating under the leadership of Susan W. Hassinger, its second woman bishop; the Rev. Janice Palm was superintendent of the Embury district; and the conference statistician, the conference secretary, the chair of the Board of Ordained Ministry, the president of the Conference Council on Youth Ministries, the Conference Lay Leader, and the four District Lay Leaders were all women. In 2007, conference elected delegates and alternates to General and Jurisdictional Conference. Of the twelve, the first layperson elected was a young adult woman, and the final delegation included two women of color, one Native American woman pastor, two additional clergy women, and two additional lay women. This was not by design or for lack of numerous other qualified persons; rather the elections represented recognition of and appreciation for the leadership these persons had given through the years.

The drive for radical hospitality and the tensions induced by efforts to extend hospitality are clearly part of the history of Troy Annual Conference. A learning process was necessary, and sometimes progress was slower than it should have been. Nevertheless, many bright spots mark the record, the boundaries have been stretched, and the goal of a truly inclusive church is closer now than it has ever been.

Commissioning of
Meredith Vanderminden, 1999

Mary Barry Webb

Mary Barry was born in Cambridgeport, VT in 1851. She was precocious. Legend says she first gained her license to teach at age 15. After attending Mount Holyoke College, she returned to teaching and eventually became assistant principal of Bellows Falls High School. In 1894 she married the Rev. Alfred Webb, a Methodist pastor serving Montpelier. She was very active in the Ladies' Aid Society and became president of the Vermont Conference Women's Home Missionary Society. In 1904, the first year that women were eligible for election, the Vermont Conference chose Mary Webb as a lay delegate to the General Conference of the Methodist Episcopal Church held in Los Angeles.

Chapter 3

Passionate Worship

Praise the Lord with the lyre; make melody to him with the harp of ten strings. Sing to him a new song; play skillfully on the strings, with loud shouts. Psalm 33:2-3

Passionate worship is really in the blood of United Methodists. We take a certain pride in recalling that John Wesley was criticized for being "enthusiastic." Passionate worship—dynamic preaching, powerful singing, heartfelt prayer—was the core of the camp meeting experience and what folks expected when the circuit rider came to town. You can trace the ministry of a few pastors by the new organs they encouraged their congregations to obtain. So it is no surprise that passionate worship is a meaningful part of the heritage of Troy Conference.

Worship at Annual Conference

The worship at annual conference sessions was always intended to be something special. Lay and clergy alike had opportunities to experience the traditions of the church expressed in new ways.

Anniversary Celebration In 1983, Troy Annual Conference celebrated its one hundred-fiftieth anniversary. The session opened on Thursday, June 2, at Christ Church, Troy, the site of the first session of Troy Conference in 1832. Led by a band, participants paraded through the streets of Troy to the opening communion service at Russell Sage College. On Sunday morning, 3,000 United Methodists gathered for worship at the Colonie Coliseum. Bishop Nichols preached in the round from a rotating stage. The massed choir, nearly 300 voices strong, came from over twenty-five conference churches.

Musicians Through the years Troy Conference has been blessed with pastors who were talented organists as well. Among those who at various times stimulated conference with their music were the Revs. Thomas Blowers, Jim Borden, Paul

Bishop Roy C. Nichols

Crowder, Mark Demers, David Giles, Tim Klasnick, Howard Stimmel, and David Vallelunga. Their diverse musical interests enhanced the experience as we worshiped and sang together.

Other musicians also brought unique talents to help clergy and laity alike recognize additional potential for worship services. The Rev. Robert Long often used his trumpet to accent special music. In 1989, the Council on Finance and Administration presented a resolution, which conference accepted, offering a one-time forgiveness of past apportionment indebtedness to all churches that had fallen behind. This "Year of Jubilee," once made official, was celebrated with the Rev. Long blowing the shofar. It made a stirring sound as it echoed through the Russell Sage Auditorium where conference was in session.

The Conference of 1999 featured a jazz band at the opening communion service. A later session that year was set aside for the music of the Africa University Choir, which was touring the Northeast Jurisdiction at the time. Sessions were held at Green Mountain College in Poultney, VT. Things were tense when it was discovered that their bus had brought them to Putney, VT instead. Those two locations are on opposite sides of the state with over eighty miles and nearly two hours of driving time between them. However, the choir arrived just in time and "uplifted us all with their gift of music."

One year the Covenant Players, much better known for their dramatic presentations, came to annual conference with a musical group. After hearing their upbeat version of "A Mighty Fortress Is Our God," it was hard to listen to Martin Luther's hymn the same way again.

Another musical group that enlivened worship at annual conference was the praise band, "One Achord," from Round Lake UMC. They have appeared at many other local churches, played at a coffee house sponsored by a Christian bookstore, and led outdoor services during an antiques festival. This group, accomplished in several styles of contemporary Christian music and often playing their own compositions, was chosen to receive the 1997 Denman Evangelism Award.

Drummers also brought a unique dimension to conference worship. In 2002, in celebration of the Vermont Korean-American Church, Korean drummers in traditional dress rocked the Sheraton Convention Center in Burlington. At the 2005 session, a team of women drummers, a lay and clergy group, enlivened worship with a rhythmic, percussive sound.

Barb Lemmel and Dana Carroll on the drums

A whole series of song leaders brought their personal passion to conference worship. The best known of these was probably Francois Clemons, familiar to many as Officer Clemons on "Mister Rogers Neighborhood." His strong, mellow voice inspired our conference sessions in 2003. But there were others as well. In 2004, the Rev. Michael Padula, then a probationary member of conference, led the music from the keyboard of his Hammond organ with rotating speaker. For 2008, our song leader was the Rev. Grace Cajiuat, a native of the Philippines, who had recently completed her Masters in Divinity and held three advanced degrees in music.

"Trees," danced by Wendy Guay 1992

Other Modalities in Worship There were many additional efforts to make worship especially uplifting at annual conference. Art, for instance, came in many forms. the Rev. J. Coolidge Hand, particularly when he served at Poultney from 1971 to 1974 and conference was held at Green Mountain College in that community, produced graphic arts items that stirred the imagination. In 1994, the Rev. Thomas Shanklin, conference secretary, brought a large cross into the conference hall. Between sessions he often redecorated the cross so the impact was always fresh. The worship center featured nails on which to place prayer concerns. As conference concluded, the cross was decorated with butterflies and flowers.

Bishop Susan M. Morrison

Sacred dance frequently was part of worship at conference. With space to move and a more flexible time frame than many local churches could offer, individuals and groups interpreted scripture and spiritual concerns in a variety of ways.

Bishop Susan M. Morrison always marked the sacrament of communion

Rev. Michelle Bogue-Trost reflects

Creating an annual conference session is rather like co-ordinating air traffic control for butterflies. Although planning begins almost immediately following the close of one conference, all the planning in the world can't prepare the planners for the next session. A dozen people scheme to organize, make plans, pull things together, and get it all to work, yet annual conference takes on a life of its own when exposed to time, air, and the community of faith.

What will be the theme? It must be timely, engaging, easily represented by an image or logo, and able to be expressed creatively through worship. What will worship look like--ancient, traditional, contemporary, postmodern?

Some will be happy with what we plan, and some will vehemently dislike it. There is the possibility that we will make everyone happy, and an equal possibility that we will make no one happy with the work we have done. Great philosophical wrestlings ensue; will we do conference like it's been done before, or will we dare to do a brand new thing?

Logistics can drown a soul. Venues, meals, special guests, registrations, reservations, materials for meaningful worship, people resources, time constraints, too many minutes at a microphone—get too deep into these, and one can lose sight of Wesley's "holy conferencing" idea. No matter what is planned, something always happens to thwart the best intentions for time and resources, and someone at some point along the way will object to what has been planned. Having a head for details and a hide like a rhino help, for it is difficult to hear criticism of that which one has worked so hard to accomplish in seeking to serve the conference.

Working with bishops is grand fun; it keeps the improvisational muscles flexed. One learns that time is

and service of ordination with her particular style. Breaking the bread was always a dramatic act for her, with the
loaf held high overhead. In some rituals she moved up and
down the aisles, generously flicking holy water with a green
branch and urging all who felt the drops to remember their
baptism and be thankful. She also brought to conference
the custom of washing the feet of ordinands before inviting
them forward again for the laying on of hands. In a tribute
to this moving dramatization of servitude, during her last
session with Troy Conference Bishop Morrison had her own
feet washed by conference lay leader Ilah Sisson Walser.

Technology Modern technology came to the support of
passionate worship during the close of the twentieth century. For many people, it was at annual conference that they
first sang hymns by read-
ing from video screens
rather than paper copies.
Video clips appeared as a
supportive aid to preach-
ing. Video cameras put
the preachers and choir
on the big screen and
gave everyone a front row
seat. The video screens
sometimes became "can-
vases" for meditative art.
One speaker suggested
video screens were the
equivalent of stained glass
for the modern world. For
those who could not read,
the stained glass told a

Technology table (2003): Bill Stewart,
foreground; Bill Pattison; Susan Fenimore (hidden); James Fenimore (hidden) and Ralph Marino.

memorable story. For us today, the images also tell a story,
but a dynamic one that can be easily changed to suit the
mood, purpose, and flow of our worship on a given day.
For many, technology's potential to enhance passionate

fluid, schedules are bendable, and anything can happen at any given moment. Yet it is in this setting that one sees the gifts of our bishops: grace, patience, stamina, and their great and abiding love for the Church they serve.

Somehow, it all comes together. Annual conference happens: the planned and the unplanned, the fights and the forgiveness, the expected and the unexpected, the moments of grace and the moments when we all gasp. The gathered faithful of Troy Conference meet and have fellowship and are at a family reunion once again. Friendships are renewed, fresh relationships are celebrated, our work in the world is affirmed and our people recharged.

It is a beautiful thing.

worship became clear at conference sessions, paving the way for more and more local churches to bring the ancient good news to life through the use of modern technology.

At annual conference, clergy and laity found ideas, themes and practices to take home. They had help in making sure that the regular practice of worship did not become the routine practice of worship. Conference played an important role in keeping alive the excitement and enthusiasm that have been part of passionate Methodist worship from the beginning.

Lay Speaking

Another way Troy Annual Conference sought to make worship dynamic and fresh was by giving strong support to the ministry of lay speaking. Lay speaking, of course, has a long and honorable tradition in United Methodist life. In this case, however, leaders made an intentional effort to keep lay speaking as an important ministry. They enthusiastically supported the ministry with significant human resources.

The Journal for 1984 has several pages listing the lay speakers connected with conference churches. It also reports the passage of a resolution creating the "Conference Coordinating Committee on Lay Work." The next year, William Woodman, committee chair and conference lay Leader, reported that the new committee had begun its work and that lay speaking was an important part of the focus.

In 1986, Woodman reported that work spearheaded by Ruth Harlow brought training in lay speaking to 250 laity in conference churches. The journal now also lists separately "Local Lay Speakers" who have taken the basic course that makes them eligible to speak in their own congregations, and "Certified Lay Speakers" who have taken an advanced course so they may fill pulpits in other churches.

The Coordinating Committee reported in 1987 that 92 people were trained in basic courses and 90 in various advanced courses. In addition, the committee held a conferencewide Lay Speaking Convocation in the spring of that year.

Woodman began to write his 1988 report as conference lay leader but died before he could complete the task. Ruth Harlow, his predecessor as conference lay leader and vice-chairperson with him of the Coordinating Committee on Lay Work, completed the reports on his behalf. Lay speaker training was offered twice on each district, with the strong support of district directors of lay speaking. Iris and Joe Civalier, both certified lay speakers on the Adirondack District, held a conferencewide course at Skye Farm titled "Leading in Small Groups." The committee also held a spring convocation for lay speakers and pastors, with a leader from the General Board of Discipleship. Over 60 persons attended.

Shirley Byers, the newly elected conference lay leader and chairperson of the Coordinating Committee on Lay Work, issued the committee report for the Journal of 1989. She noted that Don Waterfield and Iris Civalier offered

Lay Speaking Ministry

Darlene Suto, Embury District Director
of Lay Speaking Ministries

I cannot remember any one particular event, word, or person that moved me along in my faith journey. It was, I believe, a series of happenings. It was a consistent path and a sense of the church as being always present in my youth, and through the years that has brought me to where I am today.

I have been involved in lay speaking for some time now, and it has been a fulfilling experience for me. One of my strengths has always been in public speaking and dramatization (I was a theater major and involved in theater for a number of years), and that has served me well in the lay speaking ministries. It is a gift that I have, and it has been utilized in many churches throughout the Embury District.

Lay speaking ministries has brought a fulfillment to my life. There have been a number of people over the years that have encouraged me—pastors, family and friends who took the time to say, "Thank you for sharing your message with us." I enjoyed teaching basic and advanced classes and the people I met while doing this. There are many good Christian people I have found throughout Troy Conference who have abundant spiritual gifts to be shared in a variety of ways.

It is indeed bittersweet to see the Embury District and Troy Conference coming to a close, but in this time and in this place as a lay speaker, I am lifted up by these words, "To every thing there is a season and a time to every purpose under heaven." Amen.

a basic and an advanced course on every district, as well as a conferencewide weekend advanced course. Byers also urged churches, pastors and district superintendents to make more use of the skills, gifts, and graces that lay speakers were trained to deliver.

In 1990, the Journal shows 12 basic and 14 advanced lay speaking courses offered and two additional weekend courses. the Rev. James M. Perry, conference council director, noted in his 1993 report that lay speakers were a vital resource for the church. "Their training is not only in speaking but in caring, visiting, and teaching." All of these are aspects of a passionate approach to worship and to the Christian life. How passionate? Byers, the conference lay leader, reported that fifty basic and advanced lay speaking courses were held around the conference. The end result was a corps of 450 local church lay speakers and 275 certified lay speakers.

Reporting for the Cabinet, the Rev. William A. Lasher indicated that more use should be made of lay speakers as more of them were being trained each year. The Adirondack District Council on Ministries credited Grace Morehouse, district director of lay speaking, with holding fifteen basic and advanced courses with a total of more than one hundred persons attending.

In 2002, Julius A. Archibald, chair of the Board of Lay Ministry and conference lay leader, noted some progress on the goal of having all local church lay leaders be certified lay speakers. The Journal shows that about two-thirds of the approximately 300 churches have at least one lay speaker, with 395 certified lay speakers in 143 local churches. Sixty-one churches, about 20%, have a lay leader with advanced lay speaker training.

The decade-long emphasis on lay speaking produced a major response across the

Iris Civalier and Julius A. Archibald

conference. Simply by taking one or more of the courses, many lay people showed how eager they were to participate in a passionate, personal, heartfelt worship experience.

Thus, while local church worship is local, Troy Conference made support and enhancement of those local efforts a significant part of its ongoing activities. Passionate worship was a familiar aspect of conference activity and intentionally supported in many ways.

Chapter 4

Intentional Faith Development

[W]e have not ceased praying...that you may lead lives worthy of the Lord, fully pleasing to him, as you bear fruit in every good work and as you grow in the knowledge of God. Colossians 1:9

The concept of intentional faith development affirms that spiritual maturity is a goal best reached by deliberate, sustained effort. Like the idea of going on to perfection, the emphasis is on the journey as much as the destination. We need not only a good goal but also a good way to get there. Through the years, Troy Annual Conference has undertaken initiatives in support of church unity, strategic planning, and spiritual growth, with the intention of seeing faith clearly and visibly developed. Some initiatives brought us farther along our journey than others.

Ecumenical Action:
Consultation On Church Union (COCU)
and Christians United In Mission (CUM)

Interest in, and support of, the Consultation on Church Union (COCU) was natural for United Methodists since John Wesley himself displayed deep interest in the underlying oneness of faithful people. His sermon, "A Catholic Spirit," stresses how there can be unity in the midst of diversity. Thus, it is not surprising that Methodists and a number of others in the Wesleyan tradition were early supporters of the vision of a reunited church when COCU began to flourish in the early 1960s. The large number of federated churches in the conference also spurred interest in the topic of faithful, Christian unity.

Christians United in Mission (CUM) began in 1971 as a practical way for Christians of the New York Capital District to engage in cooperative efforts across a broad range of topics and geographical areas. Troy Conference was one of the founding communions. Ten years later, that agency was supporting a variety of ecumenical social service and advocacy ministries, and Troy Conference was still an active supporter of those efforts.

General Conference in 1980 called for the creation of a commission on Christian Unity and Interreligious Concerns in each annual conference. In Troy Conference the commission was formed in 1981, and its first report appeared in the Journal for 1982. By then the commission was already involved with the Roman Catholic Diocese of Albany, the New York State Council of Churches, and the Vermont Ecumenical Council. In line with that emphasis on unity and cooperation, one of the offerings at Summer Learning Fellowship was "Pilgrimage in Faith—Oneness in Christ."

In 1984, the commission noted it was exploring the possibilities for dialogue among Christians, Jews, and Muslims. The following year the commission undertook a survey on the "ecumenical climate at the local level." The response rate was a modest 25%.

In a practical demonstration of unity, Bishop C. Dale White invited the Rev. James Miller from the Albany Presbytery to assist in the ordination of twelve deacons at the 1987 conference. That same year, Troy Conference also passed a resolution inviting General Conference to claim "The COCU Consensus," as urged by the sixteenth plenary session for Consultation on Church Union in 1984.

The ordination service in 1988 included the participation of the Rev. Joseph Kerr, presiding elder of the Western New York Conference AME Zion Church. In a further practical affirmation of interdenominational cooperation, Covenant Hills the new Troy Conference camping site in Vermont, came into being with the support of human, financial, and material resources provided by the Vermont

Conference of the United Church of Christ. This cooperative relationship continues and makes Covenant Hills a tangible symbol of Christian faith in action untroubled by denominational bounds.

In 1990, the work through CUM moved forward on a variety of fronts. One especially vital effort was the founding of the Regional Food Bank, essentially a warehouse serving a twenty-county area and distributing vast quantities of supplies to local food pantries and soup kitchens.

The 1991 Journal notes practical cooperative efforts made through CUM, as well as expressions of hope for organic unity through COCU. Beyond the food bank, CUM sponsored the creation of the Support Ministry for Persons with AIDS, coordinated a "Help for the Homeless" Campaign, and held a conference on "Navigating Older Adulthood." Conference also urged the 1992 General Conference to enter into covenant communion with the Churches of Christ Uniting (COCU).

The Conference Commission on Christian Unity noted six areas of interest in their 1993 report: helping local churches understand COCU, urging federated churches to assess their effectiveness, developing an interfaith relationship with Islam, raising interest in contemporary interreligious issues, increasing the level of United Methodist self-understanding, and facilitating healthy relationships in the case of interfaith marriages.

In 1995, among other actions, CUM reported having sponsored the largest CROP Walk in New York State, an effort involving over 1,000 Capital Region walkers that raised over $125,000. At the same time, with the guidance of the Commission on Christian Unity and Interreligious Concerns, Troy Conference once more urged General Conference to move forward and approve "The COCU Consensus."

Somewhere along the way, the high point of enthusiasm for church unity was reached and passed. While the Conference Commission on Christian Unity faithfully continued its work, local churches became less and less supportive. The theory remained attractive, but the actual consensus to proceed with structural changes in the United Methodist denomination and other judicatories was elusive.

Even so, the call to unity was still important. For instance, the 2003 service of ordination under the leadership of Bishop Susan M. Morrison included the participation of the Rev. Arnold Thomas, conference minister from the Vermont Conference of the United Church of Christ. Also, in 2007 Bishop Thomas Ely of the Vermont Diocese of the Episcopal Church concelebrated communion at the memorial service with Bishop Susan W. Hassinger. This Episcopalian presence was a first for Troy Conference.

Meanwhile, the interest in cooperative efforts remains strong. Beginning in 1998, Christians United in Mission became the Capital Region Ecumenical Organization (CREO) to emphasize that other ecumenical organizations, as well as judicatories, were represented in its membership. Troy Conference participation in the ongoing efforts of CREO remains as a substantial testimony to the desire to work together and be intentional in faith development and faithful action.

Drawn by the Millennium

Another intentional effort by Troy Conference used interest in the new millennium to bring focus to the work of the church. Some were not sure that their clocks were going to work correctly after 2000, and some made the point that the millennium didn't really begin until 2001. Nevertheless, since the 20th century was about to become a thing of the past, this was an opportunity to be sure that the church did not become a thing of the past as well. While it wasn't obvious at the time, conference was beginning an experiment in the power of intentionality.

The Enlarged Cabinet presented conference in 1988 with a major petition, "Task Force 2000: Where in the world are we going?" The purpose of the task force, which conference endorsed, was to study the past, examine projections for the future, and provide strategies to meet the inevitable change. Bonnie Totten and the Rev. William Lasher served as co-chairs. The interim report in 1989 noted that local churches were invited to be part of the process of discernment and looking ahead.

In 1990, the task force requested, and was granted, an additional year to prepare the final report and recommendations. The difficulty of their task may be illustrated with a quotation regarding anticipated trends from one of the task force's major resources (*Megatrends 2000: Ten New Directions for the 1990s* by John Naisbitt and Patricia Aburdene): "At the dawn of the third millennium there are unmistakable signs of a worldwide multi-denominational religious revival." As of this writing the trend remains spotty at best. Future generations will be in a much better position to judge how well placed this hope turns out to be.

The final, full report, prepared under the leadership of the Rev. Lasher, took up eighteen pages in the Journal, with an additional five pages of notes. Clustered around six themes (Local Church Spiritual Growth, Focusing Effort for Outreach Ministry, Setting Priorities, Deployment of Clergy, Stabilizing Conference Finances, and Establishing a Committee on Future-Driven Strategic Planning), the task force offered twenty-eight recommendations. The central recommendation appeared in the form of a resolution, which was affirmed, and established "VISION 2000."

VISION 2000 was a call to all congregations to engage in the kind of prayerful examination of the future that characterized Task Force 2000. The concept was for each congregation to find its own way forward to stronger and more effective ministry. VISION 2000 was launched with a one-day special session of conference on November 2, 1991 devoted to programmatic concerns. The Cabinet report in 1992 showed 36% of the churches were engaged in the work of VISION 2000.

The Strategic Planning Committee, the formation of which was recommended by Task Force 2000, then began its work. At the 1993 session, six resolutions from the committee came before conference and received approval. Matters as diverse as parish alignment, clergy deployment, program development, resources for local congregations, financial stewardship, and coordination of conference efforts all prompted suggestions for the future.

During 1994, another related approach to the many concerns began to attract the attention of conference. Quest for Quality, a broad conception of how the church might find its new direction, was introduced to the denomination by Dr. Ezra Earl Jones, general secretary of the General Board of Discipleship. Initially, a small group of lay and clergy attended two training seminars. Then in 1995, more church leaders were exposed to the concept at the Albany Area Pastor's School and at a series of District Days undertaken by Bishop William B. Grove. Quest for Quality, described as a "vehicle for the introduction of the principles of continuous quality improvement in the church," came to be known as QUEST across the conference. The push of QUEST urged immediate changes in the work of district superintendents, the council director, and the Council on Ministries, with the expectation that further changes would follow across the whole of conference structure and operation. Further, local congregations were expected to use the QUEST concepts to examine their own operating systems.

The Rev. James Perry, conference council director,

moved and the 1996 session of conference approved, that the Quest for Leadership Team study the structure of Troy Conference with the intention of bringing recommendations to conference the following year. These recommendations would have brought about the first major reorganization of conference structure since 1973.

However, the report was delayed. The Rev. Perry responded to an opportunity for ministry in the Minnesota Conference, and the Rev. Garry Campbell was named interim council director. Bishop Susan Morrison, new resident bishop of the Albany Area, formed a Vision Team to further the intentions of annual conference. The Vision Team presented a report-in-progress to the 1998 session. Under the leadership of Nancy T. Foltz, a consultant to non-profit organizations, work on transforming Troy Annual Conference had begun.

At a special session of annual conference held in September 1998, the extensive work of the Vision Team came up for consideration, revision, and approval. Discussions moved from the conference mission, to core values, to critical issues, and finally to the formation of a Transition Team. The amended report as a whole was adopted and approved. The 1999 session of conference reviewed the work undertaken and approved the recommendations of the Transition Team on a standing vote of 340 for and 20 opposed. Then conference approved the formation of an Implementation Team to bring a final report to the 2000 session of annual conference.

The 2000 report of the Implementation Team was, in a sense, the final report of the Vision and Transition Teams. When conference voted approval it affirmed statements of mission and vision and acknowledged a set of critical issues that were to be intentionally addressed in structure and in effort.

One new direction chosen to help insure that the new operating agencies were staffed with enthusiastic persons was called "self-nomination." Rather than relying on the Nominating Committee to seek out people to fill slots, the hope was that people would be drawn to the work that suited them best. They could apply for positions, "self-nominate," and then be elected by annual conference. This process began right away, and some were elected to positions in the new structure before the close of the 2000 session of conference. With this running start, the work of the new councils and teams began immediately.

Over time, the results of this major experiment became clear. Among all aspects of the endeavor were at least two very positive outcomes and one disappointing failure.

The Futures Council, which provided steering and evaluation functions for the conference, in 2002 called for the creation of a half-time Faith Development Coordinator. Rev. DeeAnn Lowman had served in a position with some similar responsibilities from 1997 to 2000 in her role as Director of Camping and Spiritual Formation. However, when she took a new appointment, the spiritual formation position was left unfilled. Now the Rev. Meredith Vanderminden was chosen to oversee this aspect of conference life. She began her work in 2003. One of her major efforts was the creation of a two-year Spiritual Director Training course that filled to its maximum capacity of thirty-five within two weeks after registration opened. This training met a substantial felt need for many. Planning for the second course began long before the first was over, and again registrations quickly filled the available openings. In 2008 Evie Doyon, a lay person, became the Faith Development Coordinator, and the various spiritual concern initiatives continued to flourish.

Another highly successful innovation in the new structure was the Administrative Services Council. One key task handled by this body was the distribution of funds for emerging missional priorities. Normally conference operated on a planning cycle that involved a minimum delay of six months between approval and the availability of funds. The budget voted in June was for the fiscal year beginning the

Mission Statement

The mission of Troy Annual Conference is to provide, equip, and resource lay and clergy leaders for the purpose of helping churches make, nurture, and send forth disciples of Jesus Christ and to connect congregations with ministries around the world."

Vision Statement

Do not be conformed to this world, but be transformed by the renewing of your minds, so that you may discern what is the will of God—what is good and acceptable and perfect." Romans 12.2

Critical Issues

- Spiritual formation
- Leadership ministries
- Mission and faith
- Relationship between congregations and conference
- Ethnic, cultural and racial diversity
- Theological diversity

from Implementation Team report, June 2000

Growing the Spiritual Life

Rev. Meredith Vanderminden
Conference Faith Development Coordinator (2003–2007)

From early in my ministry, I was aware that there exists in individuals and churches a deep longing for something more meaningful than what we usually provide, especially as we moved further into a time of decline, challenge and change. We ask people to pray, but we often don't teach them how.

When the Faith Development Coordinator position was created, and I accepted the position, the conference was beginning to form an alphabet of ideas around next January, and even then additions to the budget were through the existing groups and agencies of the conference. In the new system, the Administrative Services Council was given charge of a pool of money for undesignated critical issues. When local churches, districts, or conference agencies developed plans related to the critical issues, they could apply for these funds, with the expectation of a decision and support forthcoming within a few weeks. In 2001, the council approved over $41,000 in support of ministries focused on responding to critical issues. That amount was typical of the annual expenditures in the coming years for dozens of programs, projects, and missional efforts.

On the other hand, the attempt to generate greater enthusiasm for certain vital ministries through the self-nomination process was a less successful dimension of the new structure. Self-nomination worked well as a process. The conference councils (Covenant; Futures; Administrative Services; and Ethnic, Racial and Cultural Diversity) and the critical issue teams on Spiritual Formation and Theological Diversity all attracted enough interest and leadership to function effectively.

But in 2003, just three years after the new structure went into operation, the critical issue teams of Leadership Ministries; Faith, Mission and Evangelism; and Congregation and Conference Partnership; along with the Board of Discipleship and commissions on the Small Membership Church and On the Status and Role of Women were all placed on a "year of Sabbath rest." This indicated that no new persons would be elected to the bodies. Their work was put on hold for a time of rest, prayer, and discernment. This was a setback for the conference because the critical issues were defined as being vital for an effective, healthy future. Since certain of these issues failed to attract enough self-nominations to create strong creative organizations, the work assigned to them went undone.

After a year of reflection, conference decided to discontinue the Leadership Ministries and the Congregation spiritual formation. When my leadership in these ministries came to a close, I believe the alphabet had grown to a whole language instead.

All the programs we developed focused on meeting those needs, which slowly became clearer. The aim was a deepening of our relationship with God, God's people, and God's creation. I grew spiritually myself, and I stood witness as clergy and lay people grew in their faith. I saw lives transformed by the work of God. I know mine was transformed during that time.

Clergy Soul Care urged clergy to enrich their own prayer lives. The Way of Forgiveness taught people how to deepen and better their relationships with each other through prayer. These two programs were developed here in Troy Conference, with no previous models to go on. We did use Companions in Christ's forgiveness study as a resource for the forgiveness series, but much of the work that we did came straight from the people of Troy Conference and their gifts. Karyl Hopp was one of those gifts and resources.

Spiritual Director Training taught people how to care for the souls of individuals and congregations. That training was originally modeled on the training offered in the Louisiana Conference with Rev. Wendy Miller. But it quickly became a unique program here as it grew to encompass the unique needs and talents of our folks. Components were added—for instance a focus on worship as spiritual formation, led by Nancy Dibelius—that were not part of the other programs Wendy organized.

Also original was the consulting I did with individual churches. My presentations and suggestions were custom-designed to fill the spiritual needs of each unique congregation. In all these programs, we wanted participants to experience a profound sense of God's care for them and presence with them, to learn how to create and provide sustaining soul care for themselves, and to and Conference Partnership Teams. The work of the Faith, Mission and Evangelism Team was disbursed among the Spiritual Formation Team, the Board of Global Ministries, and a newly created Evangelism Team. The 2004 Journal lists just two persons as members of the Evangelism Ministry Team.

From then on, the Evangelism Team has neither a report nor resolutions listed in the Journal. This effort to intentionally respond to a clearly identified critical issue—while extending over more than twenty years—eventually ended without an effective response. The projections of decline offered in the 1980s essentially match the reality faced in the new millennium. Overall, the efforts to respond produced much good, but the answer to the question of how to be effective in evangelism eluded the searchers.

Troy Conference Theological Academy

Troy and its predecessor conferences had been supportive of theological training since the very earliest days. For instance, back in 1944 conference approved a resolution to General Conference calling for the creation of an earned advanced academic degree for pastors. "Doctor of Applied Christianity" was suggested as a degree title to emphasize the point they were making. Other examples can be found in Chapter X, "Some Were Educators," in *A Flame of Fire*. Similar motives were at work in 1975 when the Troy Conference Theological Academy was organized as a deliberate effort to encourage intellectual and spiritual growth. The Rev. James M. Lavery became its fourth director in 1982. In the spring of that year he offered the course "Don't Bet on the Lions," which reviewed the context of the Christian faith in the first century. A sub-group with a slightly different focus, called the Lay Institute Committee, was also active and began to expand course offerings.

In 1985, some of the concerns of the Lay Institute were transferred to the newly established Conference Committee on Lay Work, while the academy focused exclusively be able to care compassionately for the souls of those they ministered to in many different contexts. I think we were able to do this.

Overall, the reaction to my ministry was extremely positive. There was a deep spiritual need out there, and people in Troy Conference felt it. We sadly turned a few people away because of lack of space when many of these programs started, but the conference continued to put resources in place to meet the spiritual need. The Covenant Council was one of our biggest supporters year after year. The spiritual hunger is great, and the Spiritual Director Training continues to this day to meet that need. That is something I am very pleased to see.

My appointment as Faith Development Coordinator was a wonderful experience! While Troy has a variety of strengths to bring to the new conference, I'm happy and excited to be able to say that one of the gifts we offer is our strong understanding of the need for both discipleship and spiritual formation.

on theological concerns. That year the academy offered four courses and, with the Continuing Education Committee, coordinated the Pastors' School. Through a resolution, the academy leadership was structured to provide members on each district, and funding was channeled through the benevolence budget and the Conference Council on Ministries. They also began to emphasize courses offered at the district, rather than the conference, level.

Regrettably, in 1987 the district level courses, despite their wide variety of topics, were all forced to cancel due to lack of registration. After regrouping, the academy offered courses in 1989 and 1990 that met with much greater success. In 1992, the academy presented educational opportunities on feminist spirituality, the Bible in life, conflict management, reconciling congregations, and Vision 2000.

The academy continued to struggle to find its footing.

Some effective and well-attended courses were presented in 1994. Academy leadership explored the potential for computer-assisted learning. A basic Bible study course and one on feminist spirituality attracted substantial interest, but the vision of regular offerings on each district remained only a vision. In 1996 and 1997, there was no report from the academy in the Journal, and in 1998 the academy disappears from the organizational chart.

Actually, in 1997 the Conference Council on Ministries called for, and conference agreed to fund, a five-day Academy for Spiritual Formation. The academy was held at Green Mountain College in 1998, with strong participation by persons in the area. Once again, in 2002 conference approved a resolution commissioning a "Wesley Learning Academy" to create, sponsor, and support continuing education opportunities. The Wesley Learning Academy received some modest funding from the Critical Issues Fund in 2003 and regular funding through the conference benevolence budget in 2004 and 2005. But in 2006, that funding line went to zero. Thus, the vision that inspired the Learning Academy was unable to find continuing expression in reality.

Three major factors were involved in this tapering off of intentional educational offerings. First, Troy Conference is relatively small, so while each offering attracted some people, respondents were typically too few and lived too far apart to make the courses generally feasible. Second, numerous other educational opportunities, in and out of the church, were abundant at the same time. Summer Learning Fellowship, sponsored through the years by United Methodist Women, constantly drew a substantial number of those who were eager for richer offerings. The lay speaker movement was gaining strength, and many laity found their needs met through those course offerings. And, third, many other things were going on in Troy Conference at the same time. Discussions of the future and the long-anticipated realignment of conference boundaries took energy and leadership that otherwise might well have supported these important educational efforts. At the very least, the intentional search for ways to provide relevant education opportunities for clergy and laity kept the importance of the task clear in the mind of conference.

Walk to Emmaus

Women's Walk #88, Rutland UMC, 2004

Perhaps no effort of Troy Conference better exemplifies the concept of intentional faith development than the Walk to Emmaus. From the time the concept was first embraced to the present, lay and clergy of all theological perspectives have taken the Walk and found it immediately rewarding as well as deeply satisfying in the long term.

In 1983, the Board of Discipleship Division of Laity noted an exploration of interest in the Emmaus Program offered by the Upper Room. The steering committee came together, and the first Emmaus Walk was scheduled for October 1984. Sometimes described as "a basic course in Christianity," the program was designed to show a "concern for the spiritual renewal of each person." The Walk grew out of a Roman Catholic renewal program, Cursillo, begun in Spain in the late 1940s. The event is outlined as a three-day weekend of clergy and laity talks, worship, and community building, followed by ongoing support from a caring community.

The first Walks in Troy Conference, with separate weekends for men and women, occurred somewhat later than scheduled at Brattleboro UMC in April and May 1985. Brattleboro was selected "because the event requires the support and participation of a large number of persons who have previously participated in a similar retreat." There were many such persons in the Brattleboro area. At the following session of conference, Bishop White received a collage of pictures taken during the events.

Very soon, the Board of Discipleship reported that 80 clergy and laity had attended the Walk to Emmaus. New events were scheduled at Hudson Falls UMC, and a midwinter reunion was held at Rutland UMC. By 1988, conference had held 14 Walks for adults. Chrysalis, the parallel event for youth aged fifteen to twenty-one, was held for the first time in the conference at Hudson Falls UMC later that year. Fifteen "butterflies" participated. Events for adults drew 100 new pilgrims to Jonesville UMC and Albany Street UMC in Schenectady.

Support for new pilgrims by those who have already taken the Walk is a significant part of the program. In 1990, Debbie Richardson from Troy Conference went to South Africa to participate in the first Walk held there. In 1992, the Rev. Philip O'Hara was the spiritual director, and his wife, Dr. Sabine O'Hara, was on the speaking and music teams of the first Walk to Emmaus held in Germany.

The report to the 1994 Conference noted five Emmaus weekends were held, two for men and three for women, with a waiting list for additional women's weekends. Approximately 1,100 in Troy Conference had taken the Walk since the first local opportunity in 1985.

By 1996, there were over 1300 Emmaus pilgrims in Troy Conference. There were 263 similar communities around the world, including Hong Kong, Singapore and

Walk to Emmaus

Rev. Thomas Shanklin

My experience with Emmaus goes back to 1976, when I was a student pastor at Port Morris, NJ. There were two lovely members of that church who had gone to Cursillo in New Jersey and were taken with it. Back then, Cursillo was quite ecumenical, although it was sponsored by the Catholic Church. I was taking a course on Cults and Sects at Drew and I did an in-depth study on the Cursillo movement.

Even though I had done a semester's study and read the manual, I still did not "GET" what the whole thing was about. When I became pastor of Brattleboro in 1979, a lady from St. Michael's Episcopal Church asked, "Would you like to go to Vermont Episcopal Cursillo?" Without hesitation I said, "Yes."

It was held at a big Catholic convent in Rutland. There were all sorts of men on the weekend, very ecumenical. And it was there that I was blown away by the possibility of love. On Sunday morning of that weekend, someone stuck a Bible in my hand and said, "Here's today's scripture. Would you read John 15." As I read, the circle of men disappeared and I was standing there alone with what I was reading. Suddenly I got it: God loves me. I am Chosen. God speaks in a still small voice.

Eventually, we got word that the Upper Room was coordinating a Methodist Cursillo. The Upper Room rewrote the materials, changed the scheduling a bit, changed some of the talks and titles of them, and called it the Upper Room Walk to Emmaus.

In the early 1980s, the Board of Discipleship began to explore the Walk to Emmaus. The Rev. Denise Dillon came to me and asked if I would lead a steering committee. I refused. About a year after my refusal, I got a big GOD NUDGE and agreed to chair a steering

Estonia. The Walk to Emmaus became a program with a strong component of lay leadership, even though clergy are part of each event. The Walks and Chrysalis proceeded without direct conference oversight and are independent of conference funding.

In January of 2006, Troy Conference celebrated its twenty-year anniversary of participation in the Walk to Emmaus. Nearly 2,700 youth and adults had participated by that time. One indication of the meaning of the Walk to Emmaus is found in the laity memoirs of 2007. The celebration of one man's life notes the profound impact the Walk to Emmaus had on him, even after many years of interest in, and support of, the church. Another memoir reports that among the high points of one woman's ministry was her role in assisting in the formation of the Walk to Emmaus as a member of Brattleboro UMC.

The Walk to Emmaus, after 102 sessions and an additional 37 Chrysalis Flights, continues to be a prime example of intentional faith development. It is intentional for those who take the Walk and become new members of the community, as well as for those who continue to be involved in sharing their faith, supporting each new Walk when it is held, and maintaining regular opportunities for additional fellowship, spiritual encouragement, and singing.

In its 2009 report, the Emmaus Board of Directors looked ahead to the conference mergers of 2010. They indicated enthusiasm for working with the Emmaus communities in the New England and other New York conferences. They also plan to maintain the fellowship already established among the "pilgrims" and "butterflies" across Troy Conference. There is every reason to anticipate that these intentional faith development activities will continue for years to come.

committee to begin the program. Loren Mills, Don Lewis, and I flew to Nashville to attend an Upper Room Walk to Emmaus. We were hosted by committee members there and participated in a weekend as candidates.

Upon our return, I formed a steering committee. After about a year of work, we held our first two weekends at Brattleboro UMC—first a men's weekend, then a women's. I visited a number of churches prior to those weekends working to recruit candidates. It was touch and go. I think we only had about 12 male candidates. Half of our teams were probably Episcopalian or Catholic. I was the head spiritual director of the first teams. On at least one of the weekends, we held the community gathering worship at the Catholic Church in Brattleboro where, with the priest's approval, I served communion at their altar.

Those first weekends at Brattleboro were amazing. The small church was transformed into a dormitory, worship space, and prayer space. The participants were trucked down to Brattleboro Union High School daily for showers. The presence of such prayer-spirit-learning activity in the local church transformed many.

My Walk to Emmaus

George Holzhauer

My involvement with the Walk to Emmaus began when I attended a similar ecumenical event called Tres Dias. For that experience they didn't even tell you where you were going. It was all on faith. I discovered myself in the midst of a very warm caring community. The experience drew me first to Bible reading, then to Bible study, and more recently to a strong interest in facilitating adult Bible study.

After the Tres Dias experience I was invited to give one of the talks at Brattleboro on Troy Conference

Walk to Emmaus #3. I was hesitant but found it a rewarding experience. With the sharing, skits, singing, and small-group experience, you go from not knowing anybody to being part of an amazing community. That event led me to other involvement. I was lay director for Walk #5 in Hudson Falls. I also came to participate extensively in Lay Witness missions. I've been on missions all across Vermont and New York, as well as some in Maine, New Hampshire, Connecticut, Massachusetts and New Jersey.

Some people I recall who were extensively involved in getting the Troy Conference program going were Loren Mills, Don Lewis, Susan Hager-Smith, Tom Shanklin, and Erik Smith. Betty Burbank did a great deal of work getting the necessary rights to use much of the music that is central to the Walk experience. To thank the Corinth congregation for sharing their space with us, we sang in their service on Sunday morning. "Our God is an Awesome God" had them on their feet and singing in the aisles. Large churches like Rutland and Burlington supported the Walk, as did much smaller congregations like Porter's Corners.

Some have gone from the Walk to providing leadership for the prison version of Emmaus, called "Kairos." The Rev. Don Aiken, at the time chaplain at Dannemora, was a key person in getting that aspect of the program organized. The Kairos ministry in turn continues to support the Walk. Many of the "Agape" letters to pilgrims are sent from prisoners. One other thing the Troy Conference Walk did was sponsor the start-up of the Emmaus movement in Maine. I also know that a number of lay people in Troy Conference have chosen to change careers and become clergy due to their Emmaus experience.

My involvement with the Walk through the years has been a very special and meaningful experience.

Chapter 5

Risk-Taking Mission and Service

He has told you, O Mortal, what is good; and what does the Lord require of you but to do justice, and to love kindness, and to walk humbly with your God?
Micah 6:8

In some ways mission work is always a risk. By its very nature, mission is going from the known into the unknown, typically from the more comfortable to the less comfortable, from the place where one is to the place where one believes that God intends. Mission is outreach. It is offering the Good News in tangible form, expecting,—but never sure—that the offering will be received and appreciated.

Tracing the history of mission work in the Troy Conference presents an interesting challenge, because of course at the start Troy Conference was itself a mission field. The circuit riders headed out, not to established churches, but on routes where they were expected to establish churches.

Yet early on, the people of Troy Conference picked up a concern for those in other places and in need of support. For instance, George Brown, an African-American preacher of Troy Conference, went to Liberia in 1836 because he felt a call to the mission field. Through the years, various people from this area headed to the western frontier of the United States, leaving a legacy of local churches across the country. Even international mission work continued in a variety of ways.

In more recent years Troy Conference, along with supporting the denomination's mission work, responded to some particular needs in four rather different ways: an attempted church start just north of Albany, investment in a number of urban missions, expansion of the Saratoga

Retirement Center, and strong involvement with the Volunteer in Mission program.

Congregation at Exit 8

In the early 1960s, Troy Conference was successful in starting two new churches—one in South Burlington, VT, the other in Queensbury at Exit 19 of the Adirondack Northway. In 1987, as part of an ambitious plan developed by the Committee on Parish and Community Development, the conference made a major effort to establish another new congregation. The location chosen was southern Saratoga County, near Exit 8 of the Northway, an area identified as the fastest growing in New York State. Eight United Methodist churches existed nearby, but the expectation was that this new ministry would have no adverse effect on them.

The committee had already selected the Wilton area of Saratoga County; the Groton circuit in Vermont; the Schoharie County cluster; the Rutland County, VT UMCs; and the two United Methodist churches in Rensselaer for strong new outreach and cooperative initiatives. Each of these efforts were to be made and coordinated through existing congregations. Some of these congregations were very small, but they all were active. The Exit 8 ministry was the only project seeking to create a new congregation. It was a risk-taking mission.

The estimated necessary financial support for all projects over the next five years was $1,224,000. This amount included the costs of land acquisition, salaries, and some program expenses. The funds were to come from annual conference reserves, conference loans, anticipated support from a planned 1,000 member "Builder's Club," and grants from the General Church.

In its report to the 1988 Annual Conference, the Committee on Parish and Community Development noted an early complication for the Exit 8 ministry: "Land in the area is scarce and expensive." The $60,000 budgeted was not really enough to purchase adequate, desirable land in

North Adams Supports School in Korea

A nearly forgotten aspect of Troy Conference mission work was a generous, risk-taking effort in Korea. Methodist work in Korea began in 1903. In 1923, First Church of North Adams, MA, then a part of Troy Conference, donated $10,000 for the construction of the Samil School for Boys in Suwon. In the following years, owing, among other things, to what the Board of Foreign Missions called a growing "communistic spirit," conditions became less favorable to the effort. An additional gift

of $250 from North Adams in 1926 boosted the school, which now had six teachers and 265 students. In 1957, despite the great stress of the Korean War, the school had over 700 boys in attendance and a sister school for the education of girls. Due probably to the loss of the North Adams church and all its records by fire in 1927, the connection between the conference and the school dropped from sight, except for the marble slab proclaiming "North Adams Church Memorial" over the front door of the school and a small photo of the school hanging in the rebuilt North Adams church. A native of North Adams stationed in Korea in 1953 helped renew memories of the bonds between the two when he happened to be in Suwon. Also of interest, the walled city of Suwon is just 25 miles south of Seoul; Rev. Yoo-Yun Cho-Chang, a native of Seoul, was appointed pastor of the First United Methodist Church of North Adams from 1995 to 1998.

an area of high growth that was already under heavy commercial and residential development.

Again the next year the report was negative: "Our 'Exit 8' project has been a frustrating one for us, with possibilities for the purchase of land appearing and disappearing like mirages." While site location people had been active, nothing of the budgeted amount for the project had been expended.

Finally in 1990, the Rev. Carrol Newquist, superintendent of the Bennington-Troy District, reporting for the Enlarged Cabinet, celebrated the launching of the new congregation. A commissioning service held at Pawling Avenue UMC recognized the appointment of the Rev. Christopher Dillon as the founding pastor of "Clifton Park, Exit 8 Ministries." The Rev. Robert Long, reporting for the conference trustees, noted the anticipated purchase of land and a parsonage for the ministry. Enthusiasm continued to grow across the conference. Churches were invited to donate a few hymnals and Bibles apiece in order to support the beginning congregation and to share in a physical presence in the midst of the new gathering. A suitable nine-and-a-half-acre site was located for the church, with a price tag of $122,000. The trustees outlined a combination of grants and loans to cover part of the purchase price but noted an additional unbudgeted $60,000 would be required. The trustees received the direction to put a $40,000 down payment on a suitable parsonage and assume the mortgage.

The Rev. Dillon oversaw the work of contacting potential members for the congregation. Fifty-five volunteers from twenty neighboring United Methodist churches made 4,500 phone calls to households in the target area. Of those responding, 400 requested a follow-up mailing. The conversations and mailings created a central core of persons interested in becoming members of the new United Methodist church.

The church held its first service on December 2, 1990, at a temporary location some five miles away from

Exit 8 Ministry remembered

Rev. Christopher Dillon

A key part of the vision for the Exit 8 Ministry came from Rev. David Giles and his gracious wife, Rev. Joyce Giles. That vision energized the enthusiasm, courage, and sacrifice of Troy Conference.

Words are inadequate to express my appreciation to the multitudes deserving thanks for their exercise of faith, creativity, and generosity commissioning Exit 8 Ministries to make disciples of Jesus Christ for the transformation of the world. The new church development training offered by the UMC was world class.

Troy Conference support was substantial, providing funding and years of planning. Fifty-five volunteers from twenty congregations spent hours making thousands of phone calls to identify those interested in becoming part of a new faith community. One hundred-twenty congregations took part in a shower of hymnals to provide that resource for the Clifton Park Family of Christ.

The congregation that emerged was full of the hospitality borne of God's love. Dozens of people gave their hearts to Christ. HIV positive people found dignity and respect. Ecumenical ties were strengthened. Thirty thousand dollars was raised by visible faith witness for local and global hunger relief. Advocacy for low-income senior citizen housing bore fruit. A determined group of children from a housing project led an innovative urban camp meeting that raised support for their Volunteer in Mission trip to Puerto Rico, plus a love gift of $2,000 for their sister church there.

When it became clear that the experiment was not financially viable, the congregation refused to disband. And then, with impeccable timing, the members of Waterford UMC invited them to share space and eventually to become one. To God be the glory!

the identified center of the population area. Exit 8 Ministries became a worshiping congregation officially known as Clifton Park, Family of Christ. Slightly more than one hundred people attended the first service. About one quarter of them represented other United Methodist congregations in the area. Three dozen of those attending that Sunday became the Family of Christ faith community.

Despite an enthusiastic pastor and a broad program that included intentional outreach and active interest in social concerns as well as a Sunday worship experience, the new congregation faced severe financial difficulties. The Cabinet found it necessary to add an out-appointment, some 45 minutes away from Clifton Park, in order to help cover the pastor's compensation. The congregation and the conference gave sacrificially, but the church did not grow fast enough to sustain itself before outside funding was exhausted.

The Journal for 1993 includes a resolution noting that the Family of Christ had to be relocated to share space with Waterford UMC. The Rev. Dillon became pastor of both congregations. The conference trustees were authorized to sell the recently acquired parsonage of the Exit 8 ministry. In fact, the Exit 8 parsonage was, as noted in the 1994 Journal, sold to the Korean United Methodist Congregation of Albany so, in a sense, it remained in the family.

The 1995 Journal gives the final summary report of Exit 8 Ministries. The Family of Christ merged formally with Waterford UMC in January 1995 and remained under the leadership of the Reverend Dillon. The files on the whole project from 1986 to 1995 were placed in the conference archives under the heading "Exit 8 Ministries." A related disappointment was that membership in the Builder's Club was reported to be only 140, some 860 short of the original goal. Ironically, Bishop Ruediger Minor of the Eurasian Area of The United Methodist Church, conference lecturer in 1995, noted that between 1992 and 1994 the number of United Methodist churches in Russia had risen from twelve to twenty. Yet, risk-taking mission had not produced the hoped-for result of a new congregation in Troy Conference.

Urban Ministries

Urban ministries in Troy Conference took place in a variety of settings. Many churches were located in urban areas and took advantage of that setting to move into, sponsor, and enhance mission to the community beyond the local congregation.

AUMS An early example of clear interest in supporting urban ministries took substantial form with the creation of the Albany Methodist Society in 1961. The society, the first of its kind in Troy Conference, is now called the Albany United Methodist Society and is typically known as AUMS from its pronounceable initials. *A Flame of Fire* outlines the establishment of the society and how it came to maturity as a force in New York's capital city.

From then until now, the society has continued to function and serve as a way for churches outside the city to participate in downtown mission. Financial support of course has always been welcome. But, for instance, the Summer Educational Enrichment Program takes a different tack. Local churches in other cities or even rural areas may serve as hosts for busloads of children for a day. Thus, the inner city and suburban cultures can experience each other. Through this program and others, many have received the opportunity to interact, to learn about similarities and differences, and to appreciate diversity.

The core of sponsoring congregations continued to grow through the years. In 1995, twenty-one churches were participating, including the Korean Church of Albany, a number of nearby suburban congregations, and South Cambridge UMC, a small-membership church over an hour away from downtown Albany.

The details of programs sponsored by AUMS naturally varied over time. However, the report to conference in 2009 can serve to express the range and depth of the inner city ministry through the years. One key ministry is the food pantry, which operates under the leadership of a staff person and with the support of numerous volunteers. Funding for the pantry comes partly from New York State, as well as from the member churches, and a line item in the conference benevolence budget. The Boy Scouts and the US Postal Service are credited with coordinating special food drives. The pantry offers regular food supplies as well as special baskets at Thanksgiving and Easter. The pantry also distributes toys for children at Christmas. In addition to providing food, the staff also serves as a resource to keep clients informed of opportunities and programs available to them.

A program for seniors, "Kindred Spirits," meets three times a week, providing fellowship along with low impact exercises, nutrition training, and other information. This group is in ministry itself in the form of a choir, which provides entertainment at nursing homes, schools, and churches.

The After School program provides safe sanctuary for children, hot snacks, homework assistance, a computer lab, a reading program, and gym time. Three AmeriCorps members run the program, with assistance from students at the College of Saint Rose and the University at Albany.

Other ways of ministering to the community include the AUMSAmeriCorps, which links seventeen AmeriCorps trainees to the community, and the Clothing Room which, as the name suggests, offers clients access to good clothing through the year.

AUMS celebrated its fiftieth anniversary in April 2009 under the leadership of Peter Fish, the tenth person to serve as executive director of the organization. Those first tentative efforts to faithfully support the wider community in the name, and with the backing of, Troy Conference have matured into a strong and diverse ministry. Today the society continues to bear witness to a desire to care and to be in mission.

In addition to inner city work in Albany, Troy Conference supported urban ministries in several other communities.

Burlington Ecumenical Action Ministry The Burlington Ecumenical Action Ministry (BEAM), an interfaith cooperative venture, was founded in 1968. BEAM was established to "provide the space for individuals and organizations to experience wholeness and to understand that collaborative efforts contribute to the welfare of the community." United Methodists were part of the core group and continue to be involved.

One of the unique and non-traditional ministries of BEAM is the Vermont Developmental Credit Union established in 1989 to bring "fair and affordable financial services" to families "not well served by traditional banking institutions." The credit union has made thousands of loans with a cumulative lending total of over $100 million. People served came from more than 200 towns throughout Vermont.

Schenectady Inner City Ministry Schenectady's Inner City Ministry (SICM), founded in 1967, always did have a strong United Methodist presence. Numerous local churches from many denominations were members, and Troy Conference for many years provided direct financial support.

A typical program was the emergency food distribution center. For many years the center was located in the First UMC of Schenectady. In 1981 the center made 13,088 distributions; in 2008 it made 37,200 distributions. These were emergency distributions, as individual access to the resources is limited to just four times a year. Once a month the center also offers a mass distribution of food from supplies obtained through the Northeastern New York Regional Food Bank.

Other SICM programs in 1981 were Youth Services, which often provided support for battered children; a cooperative nursery school; a Security Deposit Loan Fund to help low income people obtain housing; and an Enriched

Housing Program for older persons. In 2009, additional programs included tax preparation, flu shots, voter registration, and testing for lead. The Damian Center has a major emphasis on assistance to victims of AIDS. SICM presents a range of summer programs for youth, including a service that in 2008 provided over 27,000 lunches. Adults have access to a fitness, nutrition, and exercise program. SICM's approach to reducing childhood obesity appears under the title "Safe Parks and Edible Playgrounds." "Safe Parks" seeks to advance community policies and environmental changes to provide access to safe places for children to play. "Edible Playgrounds" are gardens for and by children.

Troy Area United Ministries Troy Area United Ministries (TAUM) was formed in 1986 by the union of the United Urban Ministry (founded in 1969), in which Troy Conference participated, and the Troy Area Council of Churches, to which several United Methodist churches belonged. In 1987, TAUM facilitated a number of significant programs, including campus ministries at Rensselaer Polytechnic Institute and Russell Sage College, hospital and nursing home chaplaincies, week-end meal delivery to an overnight shelter for the homeless, and a Walk for Hunger. The organization also focused on such things as emergency food supplies, the Capital District Community Loan Fund, and the Community Dispute Settlement Program to support the justice system with trained mediators.

TAUM mission interests in 2009 included campus ministries, "Computers for Kids," support of a CROP Walk, a furniture program helping hundreds of families to secure good used furniture free of charge (as well as providing employment for persons at risk of homelessness), the Damien Center relating to over 150 persons with HIV/AIDS, a scholarship program in honor of the Rev. Dr. Martin Luther King, Jr., and the "Adopt a Family" program at holiday times.

Urban and urban-based ministries continue to be a major emphasis for the churches and people of the Troy

Conference area.

The Saratoga Retirement Center And The Troy Conference Geriatric Foundation The Saratoga Retirement Center was one of the most exciting mission efforts of Troy Conference from the time it was initiated in the early 1960s. The Schwartzes' book, *A Flame of Fire*, documents the various steps taken in preparation for the first residents to move into Embury Apartments in Saratoga Springs, in October 1972. The associated Wesley Nursing Home began taking patients in April 1973. Keeseville Country Gardens, another Troy Conference related residential center, opened in 1980.

These successful adventures in risk-taking mission served to encourage Troy Conference to continue looking ahead for additional opportunities to serve. The 1982 report of the Troy Conference Geriatric Foundation noted significant progress on plans for a major expansion at the Saratoga site and expressed hopes for a new facility in the vicinity of Saint Johnsbury, VT.

The foundation report in 1984 outlined how the vision for an expanded facility in Saratoga had been transformed into reality: "This tangible witness to the caring mission of Troy Conference was the cooperative effort of federal assurance of a loan, a finance company who issued bonds of $11.5 million dollars, an architect who was willing to chance its final construction, a contractor who extended a firm bid before final construction costs were known, an executive director and staff at Wesley Nursing Home, and the directors who supervised

Saratoga Retirement Center

and who ultimately take final responsibility for the project." That sentence spells out a message of excitement, of people wanting to proceed under the enticement of a powerful dream.

President of the Board Rev. Leon M. Adkins Jr., welcomed Bishop Roy C. Nichols to the official expansion groundbreaking ceremony on May 27, 1984. The consecration ceremony was held on May 15, 1985 with Bishop C. Dale White presiding. At that time, Iris Civalier was president of the foundation, and the Rev. Ralph J. Barron Jr. still served as director. In fact, the board of directors celebrated the thirteenth anniversary of Embury Apartments by naming this major new addition in honor of the Rev. Barron.

Two items of special interest occurred in 1987. First, the board chose to have the Health Care Center participate in a peer-reviewed, educational assessment program developed by the United Methodist Association of Health and Welfare Ministries for the purpose of promoting, pursuing and recognizing excellence in Christian ministry and mission. Second, the foundation received authorization to proceed with an application to construct a center for independent living in Green Island, New York.

In 1988, the Foundation reported that Embury Apartments had received a New York State Achievement Award. The presentation noted, "Embury Apartments is a showcase development for senior citizens." Embury also received an excellent rating in the educational assessment undertaken the previous year.

The Geriatric Foundation report to conference in 1989 noted several key events. The Rev. Ralph Barron retired as executive director after having given key leadership since the original planning of Embury Apartments. The board gave him credit for bringing about the intergenerational nursery school operating in the Activity Room of the Health Care Center. The board chose G. Neil Roberts, first as acting administrator to succeed the Rev. Barron, and then as the new executive director. One disappointing piece of news was that the Green Island project was put on hold because the necessary approvals could not be secured. At the same time, conference authorized proceeding with plans for a nursing home and adult home in the Clifton Park area that Executive Director Roberts had begun to explore with members of the Health Continuum Development Group.

The 1990 report of the foundation shows progress toward goals. They had received preliminary approval for the Clifton Park-based Georgia Harkness Health Care Center and Epworth Manor Apartments. For the second year in a row, the New York State Department of Health survey found no deficiencies at the Saratoga Springs facility. The credit for this good report went to the full range of employees, from department heads to part-time workers. Their constant attention to quality care produced this exceptional result.

The 1991 report of the foundation notes some frustration over the inability to move the Clifton Park project forward to completion. The hoped-for Vermont project was also at a standstill. Yet, the state approval process and a funding package for a light care unit attached to Wesley were both in place. This addition would allow a full range of care, from fully independent living to skilled nursing care, all on the same Saratoga Springs campus.

By 1992, it had become clear that with the nation in an economic recession, the Clifton Park projects were not going to become a reality. Before the year was over the proposed Green Island project was rejected by the federal government. At the same time, the complex in Saratoga Springs was doing well and moving forward. In addition, Keeseville Country Gardens was held up as a model for expansion of the work at additional sites being explored in both Vermont and New York.

News in the 1993 report of Executive

Keeseville Country Gardens

Director Roberts included the announcement that the foundation had awarded four scholarships to assist people pursuing health related careers, affiliated with The Weathervane Project in Lincoln, VT, and begun developing assisted living programs in Saratoga Springs.

The Geriatric Foundation report in the 1995 Journal made an interesting comparison, noted an upgrade, and raised a concern. The comparison was that when the Embury complex was built in 1972 the average age of a resident was 70 years, while in 1984 the average resident was 83. Keeseville saw an important upgrade: the addition of an elevator which much improved handicapped access to the building. The concern was that changes in the rates of reimbursement were not keeping up with the cost of operating the facility. The conference commitment to providing housing, support, and services to the aging was under great stress.

Work in 1995 saw major improvements to the already excellent Saratoga Springs facility. The latest addition to the Wesley Health Care Center was completed and opened. With an additional 80 beds, adult day care, and a primary care clinic available, along with an in-ground therapeutic pool and a heated walkway connecting the Wesley and Embury sites, programs were now blended together more efficiently than ever.

The 1997 report of the executive director noted that things were generally going well in Saratoga but warned that the Keeseville site was suffering from the opening of a similar facility nearby. This led to the unusual problem of vacant apartments. There was also the threat of yet another housing project in the vicinity, which would stress the market even more.

January 1998 brought a staggering ice storm to the Adirondack North Country. Keeseville Country Gardens, while unharmed, was without power, and the residents had to be evacuated to the local firehouse for a day and a half. Response to this ice storm provided many in the conference with their first opportunity to be a Volunteer in Mission. Director Roberts, reporting to conference in 1998, noted that the Gardens received a community vehicle from the Geriatric Foundation. This allowed much greater flexibility in transporting residents and was part of the plan to help people "age in place."

At the 1998 session of conference, after supper on Friday evening, May 28, Director Roberts explained and led conference through a complex series of resolutions relating to the foundation. When the foundation was initially chartered it was set up to be a housing corporation. Through the years that description had become less and less applicable to the actual work of the board, which now focused on expanding the level and variety of care at the existing facilities. The easiest way to meet the new situation was through some complex legal maneuvering. Step by step, conference voted the necessary changes. A newly formed corporation, United Methodist Health and Housing, Incorporated was named to replace the Troy Conference Geriatric Foundation as the parent organization for Wesley, the Saratoga Retirement Center, and Keeseville Country Gardens. The Geriatric Foundation was renamed EK (for Embury & Keeseville) Housing and placed as a (completely inactive) corporation in the United Methodist Health and Housing structure. Ronald Brown, president of the (former) Geriatric Foundation, was named interim president of Health and Housing. Then finally, Ronald Brown and the complete slate of previous directors of the Geriatric Foundation were properly elected to the Board of Health and Housing, now operating as a management company. (The by-laws of United Methodist Health and Housing appear in the 2000 Journal.) As one last touch, the name "Troy Conference Geriatric Foundation" was resurrected to serve as the title of the fund-raising arm of United Methodist Health and Housing. Annual Conference breathed a sigh of relief once that work was done.

The 1999 report of United Methodist Health and

Housing noted another deficiency-free survey from the Department of Health; the construction underway for another 60 units of housing, to be named Woodlawn Commons, at the Saratoga site; and optimistic talk of sponsoring a new facility in Vermont.

In 2001, the board reported an ongoing, and so far successful, struggle to maintain adequate staffing. Burlington and Middlebury were mentioned as possible sites for new facilities in Vermont.

The report to conference in 2002 indicates retrenchment in several areas. Ownership and operation of Keeseville Country Gardens was turned over to National Church Residences. The operational size of Wesley was reduced "to better match the available labor market." It was a continual challenge to "balance the budget and maintain the mission of excellence." And the adult daycare program was reduced "to match society's willingness to pay."

On December 31, 2002, Chief Executive Officer Neil Roberts retired. J. Brian Nealon, after eighteen years of service to the organization in other roles, took his place as CEO. It was a difficult time for United Methodist Health and Housing. In order to protect the assets of Troy Conference in a time of economic difficulty, conference severed the long-standing relationship with the ministry at Wesley and the related facilities. CEO Nealon reported that due to significant under-reimbursement for Medicaid residents, the corporation sustained a loss of $2,500,000. This was part of a widespread problem at the time. In 2003, eight upstate nursing homes had to close due to financial difficulties. The Wesley commitment to provide quality care remained, but attracting staff was a major problem due to the shortfall in revenues. At the same time, four fourteen-story elevators were replaced in the now thirty-year-old Embury complex. The Wesley Foundation, now the fundraising arm for UMHH, had very difficult work laid out before it.

In the 2006 report to conference from CEO Nealon, some very positive news appeared. Despite the pressure of

Refurbishing Embury Towers

J. Brian Nealon, Wesley Community CEO

Both Embury towers were fully occupied the day we received notice of our award, August 8, 2007. Over the next twelve months we defined the scope of the project, selected an architect, put the job out to bid, and chose a general contractor. We stopped admitting people into Embury. By attrition we had nearly forty apartments vacant by August 2008.

The construction process involves renovations being done on at least three contiguous floors at a time. So that means, at a minimum, twenty-four apartments need to be vacant at once.

The way it has worked for the vast majority of tenants living on floors that have been renovated is that we have hired additional staff to pack up the residents and move them from the apartment that is about to be demolished to an apartment on a different floor, then unpack them. About eight weeks later the process gets reversed, and the resident is back "home," but in a renovated apartment that is safer and more convenient for a senior, as well as being much better insulated.

We kicked off on September 2, 2008, and expect to be finished around April of 2010. I can't give enough credit to the Embury staff for their thoughtfulness, diplomacy, and dedication to the process. I also am very grateful to the Embury tenants for their cooperation and support.

reduced funding, aging buildings and changing demographics, the Wesley Health Care Center had "a positive operating margin." An application went in to New York State seeking low income housing credits for the rehabilitation of every kitchen and bathroom in the 208 apartments in Embury. (The credits, worth $13,000,000, were granted in 2007 with the work scheduled for completion in 2010.) The executive director of the Wesley Foundation also reported good news in the form of a $150,000 grant for an emergency generator at Woodlawn Commons and over $90,000 donated for the purchase of a 10-passenger bus.

The risk-taking mission in support of care for the aging and elderly begun by Troy Conference in the late 1960s produced a significant outcome. While in 2010 UMHH is no longer an organization directly responsible to Troy Annual Conference, it retains a commitment to the principles and goals that were fundamental in establishing it over 35 years ago.

Volunteers in Mission

The roots of what we mean by Volunteers in Mission run deep. Exodus 23:5 puts it, "When you see the donkey of one who hates you lying under its burden and you would hold back from setting it free, you must help to set it free." The "must help" may have been partly for the donkey's sake, but even more we understand it to be a covenant requirement.

Certainly the covenant requirement to lend a hand in time of need must have been fulfilled again and again on an informal basis by Troy Conference folk through the years. In his report to conference in 1983, the Rev. William Cotant, Director of Camping/Local Church Youth Enabler, lists among his many efforts, "putting together a massive work bee at Missisquoi for the centennial celebration." The report of the Conference Board of Global Ministries notes with disappointment that a hoped-for work camp to Henderson Settlement, Kentucky did not happen, "but we are still working on one for the summer of 1984." Unfortunately that didn't happen either, but the 1985 Journal reports that "opportunities for short term Volunteers in Mission will be one of the new emphases" for the coming year.

In 1986 the program really came to life. The Rev. Harold Robinson and Shirley Byers attended a training conference for short term Volunteers in Mission. A work team from

Burlington went to Americus, GA; a Delmar group headed off to Saint Croix, VI; while a third group traveled to a VIM project in Salem, ME. The United Methodist Men held a work weekend at Skye Farm as well.

The Rev. Leon Adkins, Albany district superintendent, led a team of thirteen people to Puerto Rico in January of 1987. It is possible that the time of year for that trip was not accidentally chosen. From then on, the District Council on Ministries continued to provide support and encouragement to the VIM program.

Through the remainder of 1987, VIM teams went to nearby sites such as Albany United Methodist Society, the Ganienkah Community, and Skye Farm and to more distant locations such as Mexico and Nicaragua. Along with conference-sponsored visits to at least seven other locations, one team traveled to Brazil in 1988 and worked at two sites some 1,500 miles apart.

By 1990, VIM demonstrated a wide appeal across the conference. Youth from some modestly sized churches such as Keeseville, Harkness, Westport and Port Henry went to work with the poor and homeless in New York City. A team from Waitsfield, VT, traveled to Montserrat Island in the Caribbean to assist in the recovery from Hurricane Hugo, which had struck the island in September 1989. Still other teams traveled to Saint Croix, Puerto Rico, and South Carolina.

In 1991, fifteen volunteers from the Adirondack District took a VIM trip to the Oklahoma Indian Mission, investing some 900 hours in renovating and refurbishing a church and parsonage.

Here is a sample of one important way the people and churches of Troy Conference became involved with the VIM movements. In the summer of 1993, a nineteen-member VIM team went to Mozambique. Delmar UMC placed two twenty-foot shipping containers in their parking lot. These gradually filled with donations of building materials. The team also brought along nineteen large suitcases of medicines. In addition, they raised a quantity of cash to allow them to purchase more building supplies once they arrived on site. The collection of materials, medicines, and money allowed strong support of the ministry even by those who never left the country. On their return to the U.S., members of the mission team made themselves available and shared their stories with all interested audiences. That pattern of telling the story not only helped more people support each individual ministry but also encouraged an ever increasing number of people of all ages to take on a VIM project of their own.

And what kind of work did they do? They repaired a buried water line, reconstructed a windmill and a pump, dug ditches for foundations, excavated a 10 foot (3 meter) deep cesspool, repaired a war-damaged clinic, laid bricks, mucked out flooded cellars, replaced and taped flood-damaged wall board, and purchased supplies and appliances to help families enjoy living in their homes again. Some of these VIM team members had special technical skills, some of them learned on the job, and some just did the grunt work necessary to bring the job closer to completion.

In 1995, VIM coordinators explained the overall operation of the program this way: "The General Board seeks places for work opportunities throughout the world; the VIM committee brings opportunities to the attention of the conference churches; local churches or clusters of churches initiate projects; and individuals give their time and pay their own expenses to work so that the love of God and Christ can be expressed." On September 23, 1995, conference held its first VIM rally at Christ UMC in Glens Falls to "celebrate all past, present and future Volunteers in Mission." The purpose of the rally was to honor those who had made VIM commitments and "to inspire others to become involved in future missions."

In 1996, new projects included renovation of a hospital in Budapest, restoration of homes and youth work in Bosnia, and the sending of at least five other VIM teams

Art Hagy remembers

I was in Mississippi in 1994 for district superintendent training. While there I heard Bishop Ann Sherer speak about the devastation from the flood in Missouri during the previous summer. When I returned to New York, I asked Ed Osterhout to put a team together to go out and assist with the rebuilding.

A major rally in Glens Falls a year or so later got more people focused on the possibilities. We made contact with the Salem ME United Methodist Economic Ministry and encouraged people to go there. Other trips followed to Georgia and North Carolina.

The 1998 ice storm in the North Country showed how willing people are to respond and help others. Harold Shippey asked several of us to organize teams to meet at Skye Farm and then head into the area for a half-week, starting on Easter. I agreed to try to put a team of six together but ended up having to turn people down after twelve of us signed up. There was just no more room for us in the church that was to be our headquarters.

As we move to become part of the Upper New York Area, we are the ones with the depth of experience and ongoing enthusiasm for VIM.

Carol Osterhout remembers

Our first mission trip was to Missouri in April 1994. Art Hagy, our DS, received a call asking for help after the summer 1993 flooding of the Mississippi River. He in turn asked my husband Ed to put together a team. Ed gathered six of us—Dick and Judy Palmer, Bill Pattison, Kirk Daniels and the two of us—rented the Skye Farm van, took out the back seat, and off we went on our spring school break. We were new at this and made no hotel reservations. We stayed outside Cleveland on the way out. At breakfast the next morning we had a very from local churches. Natural disasters in both Vermont and New York offered fresh opportunities for VIM experiences without requiring a passport. Many felt called to respond to the needs within the conference.

It was in 1996 that conference resolved to explore ways to bring a VIM team from Mozambique to itinerate around Troy Conference. Brenda Arley introduced the Mozambique VIM team to conference on May 28, 1998. Bishop João Somane Machado from Mozambique presented conference with a wooden sculpture showing dozens of interconnected individuals carved from a single piece of wood. He commented at the time, "When we are connected, we can never be separated."

Also in 1998, Henry Coghill received the Harry Denman evangelism award for his work as disaster coordinator. In accepting the award he noted that he was often told, "You (Troy Conference and UMCOR) are the first relief agency that brought what we really needed." The VIM response was part of turning that desire to be helpful into a reality.

As the years passed and the VIM program grew, conference decided to make the VIM coordinator a part-time member of the conference staff. Troy was the second conference in the Northeastern Jurisdiction to turn this coordination into a paid position. In 2003, Peter and Janet Huston accepted that 500-hour-per-year position and began to oversee a complex VIM program. VIM teams not only went on scheduled trips, typically at least a half-dozen per year, but also responded to emergencies that required immediate action and other projects that a

Jack and Sue Hill, TC VIMs, with a client in South Carolina, 2003

carful of volunteers could handle in a day. Communication

friendly waitress who even came outside to say goodbye to us when we left. That warm response was one of many we've had over the years.

We stayed at Mount Oliver UMC in Taylor, MO, and worked at West Quincy. The six of us lined up cots in the church basement, put our belongings on church tables, and showered at the parsonage next door. The people of the church fed us meals.

Early the next morning Judy and I went for our walk. We met a woman who hugged us as soon as she found out why we were there. She told us her flood story and walked with us each morning. Later in the week we met her in the hardware store. That hardware store, by the way, cut the bill in half when the owner discovered we were working for flood victims.

Our job was to help Dave, a single father with two children who had lost his business in the flood when the water rose to the middle of the second story of his business building. During the week we removed old sheetrock, carpet, insulation, and plumbing. We put in new electrical outlets, set up two greenhouses, and hooked up the electric, gas, water, cable, and sewer connections to his mobile home.

When the men were digging in the rain to find the septic tank, they remarked about the thick Missouri mud. A local man helping them said, "That's not Missouri mud. That's Iowa mud!"

On Monday night, Dave arrived at the church door in full uniform with his limousine. He took us all—his two children, the pastor, and his mother—sightseeing in Hannibal. He had been running a limo service to earn some money while his business was closed.

On Saturday, Dave opened his greenhouse business for the first time since the flood, and his family moved back into their mobile home.

Kirk was encouraged to go on our trip by his

became a very significant part of the coordinators' job. Subspecialties under the VIM umbrella include "Primetimers," which combines service and educational travel for people over 50, and NOMADS, which coordinates service by persons with RVs.

The VIM experience became a more and more significant part of the Troy Conference self-image. In 2003, the Board of Ordained Ministry proposed, and the clergy executive session approved, that Volunteer in Mission service be a prerequisite for ordination as deacon or elder in the conference.

Also in 2003, the conference celebrated a VIM trip to Cuba made during the previous fall by the Area Cabinet under the leadership of Bishop Susan Morrison. In the summer of 2003, several teams went to the Salem ME UM Economic Ministry while others went to North Carolina, West Virginia, Green Mountain College, and Springfield, VT. One week Skye Farm campers worked on homes in the North Country.

Another sign of the significance of the VIM program is found in the memoir for Bruce Conklin, which appears in the 2004 Journal. The memoir emphasizes how this active layman found great satisfaction in his VIM experiences. Bruce was a highly successful builder in the Saratoga Springs area. He had a long and productive connection with Habitat for Humanity, not only raising money but being involved with the hands-on construction as well. He led a number of major work projects at Skye Farm and Covenant Hills. He also led international mission projects, including building a Methodist church in Hermosillo, Mexico. Beyond that, he led seven VIM trips to Brazil, where he was involved in the construction of parsonages, churches, and buildings at a youth camp. On his premature death from cancer, Bishop Adriel de Souza Maia of Brazil said the notice of his death "leaves us sad, considering the importance of this brother in the life and ministry of the missionary region of the northeast." A service of celebration of Bruce's life was held at the Nova Descoberta Methodist church in 2004 when the VIM team pastor. He had never experienced the kind of fellowship we always have on mission trips and was thrilled by it. Pastor Bill led a Bible study each evening. Sometimes we'd all be falling asleep, but Kirk insisted that we not skip the Bible study because he had never done that before, either.

Sarajevo Mission

Dick Palmer, VIM volunteer

In 1996, I went to Sarajevo as part of a team of about 16 members responding to a need identified by Dirk Van Gorp from Troy Conference, who was serving as an UMCOR coordinator. Our primary task was reintegrating boys and girls, Muslim and Croatian, in the 13- to 15- year-old age bracket into society following the war. The issue was building trust and generally we did this by playing games with them. We used activities like "Set," card games, basketball, kickball and four-square, where problems caused by the language barrier were minimal. The parking lot initially was covered with broken glass so we did some outside clean up. In the youth center we did some general sprucing up, replaced carpets and did needed repair work in the gym.

We always felt safe there, although our feeling of security was helped by the regular patrols of the French soldiers in battle gear. Walking down the street one day, someone on our team wondered aloud, "Do you think they know we're Americans?" I replied, "We're fat, they're thin. They know we're Americans all right!"

Another part of our work involved helping the school, which had been closed by the fighting, get ready to reopen. One morning we arrived to find the principal and staff had a "Thank you" reception ready for us. So even though it was well before noon, we shared Turkish coffee and brandy with them.

was in Recife. His ashes were scattered in several places, including, fittingly enough, VIM sites in Mexico, Brazil, Skye Farm, and Covenant Hills.

The growth of the VIM program in Troy Conference is suggested by the report in 2005. Teams worked on at least four local projects, numerous national projects (several trips to Salem, ME and three other states), and two international projects. The conference treasurer processed $165,000 given for VIM travel, expenses and ministries. Also in 2005, conference purchased a tool trailer. Proudly labeled "Mission in Motion," the trailer supports the collection and distribution of flood buckets as well as local and national VIM projects.

Just to underline that VIM experiences have long been part of Troy Conference life, the 2005 memoir of Lavena Brown Falls, who died at the age of 106, notes that she and her husband volunteered for a year at the construction of the Jesse Lee Home for Children in Anchorage, AK. Lavena was born in 1897. The Jesse Lee Home was built in 1965 to replace the home destroyed in the earthquake of 1964. Lavena Falls was a VIM for a year at the age of 66.

The laity memoir of Henry 'Jim' Requate in the 2006 Journal also notes the major role VIM had in allowing him to express his faith. Among other involvement, he was a key person on three trips to Brazil. Jim, we are told, "lived the Volunteer In Mission motto: Christian love in action."

John Underhill, TC VIM, talks with clients in Mississippi, 2006

The 2007 memoir of Marilyn Brownell gives a prominent place to her VIM service. She made three trips to Brazil. Her ministry was summarized this way: "Marilyn offered the cup of cold, safe water to the Brazilian

Remembering Mel McGaughey

Carol Osterhout, VIM Volunteer

The VIM Primetimers took a trip to the Hinton Rural Life Center in the Blue Ridge Mountains of Western North Carolina in late October 2003. One of the team was Rev. Mel McGaughey, 89 years old, ordained a deacon in 1940 and, with his wife, a missionary to Tonga early in his retirement. He loved mission work and enjoyed it greatly even though he found it physically challenging. He was not one to sit around wasting time with idleness. We were finishing up the punch list for a new home being built for a single mother. On the way into the house, Mel slipped and fell into the sludge from the well drilling. He was completely covered, including his face and glasses, with sticky, slimy mud. He looked terrible and at first we were really concerned about him. We sat him on the steps and began to clean him up as best we could. He took it all in stride and said with a laugh, "I've been bragging about going on a mission when I'm nearly 90. I guess pride really does go before a fall."

VIM Frustration

The Rev. Ralph Marino, VIM Volunteer

Probably one of the most frustrating aspects of a VIM project comes when you can't quite finish the job and have to leave it for someone else.

We were working on a trailer bathroom renovation. Each step of the work seemed to lead to yet another problem that needed attention before we could start to put things back together. Finally, on Friday afternoon, our last day, all the loose ends were tied off neatly. We set the bathtub in place for a trial fit, and it looked good. Then as we juggled the tub one last time, we happened to get a look at its underside. At that point we

Volunteer in Mission team, both to the Brazilians and to the members from Troy Conference. We thank God for the gift of her life among us."

In 2007, the role of VIM Coordinators passed from Peter and Janet Huston to Jay and Cathie Dunkleberger. Jay and Cathie inherited a very active program, with six teams having gone to help the Gulf Coast respond to Hurricane Katrina, flood relief work needed in the Mohawk River valley, multiple teams going to Maine, another off to the Blackfoot Indian reservation in Montana, two international teams, and numerous training sessions to attend and schedule, as well as the conference-wide VIM rally.

The Dunklebergers' first report in the 2008 Journal lists seventeen teams acting locally, nationally, and internationally, putting in over 8600 hours of service. After attending a number of training sessions and rallies from Arkansas to Pennsylvania themselves, they were anticipating a full schedule of training to be offered across Troy Conference in support of nine mission venues already on the calendar.

Obviously, Volunteer in Mission projects can take many forms. This makes providing a summary of work and its impact very difficult. Still, common features include, on the one hand, an investment of time, money, energy, and comfort on the part of the missioners and, on the other hand, the intention to be a blessing in the lives of those served.

Bishop Morrison with Mozambican VIMs, 2003

"Blessed to be a blessing." In one way or another, that has been an essential part of the Wesleyan tradition, across the world and in Troy Conference, from its beginnings and through even our own contemporary times.

discovered the fiberglass shell had delaminated from the internal frame. There was no installing that tub.

The tub was a special order, and nothing like it was to be found within a two-hour drive of the project site. We had no choice but to lug the thing outside and order another. We told the disappointed homeowner she was going to have to bathe the children in the sink for another few days and packed up our gear in the pouring rain.

Our satisfaction came in the middle of the next week when we got word from the team that followed us. The new tub was in and fully functional.

Liz Hill remembers

I went on my first mission trip—to the Salem, ME, United Methodist Economic Ministry—with Rev. Art Hagy when I was twelve. I was bummed not to meet the homeowner at the site where I was working but I did get to meet the community at the Wednesday night picnic. I learned some plumbing and carpentry but I learned much more than that. I learned how much more I have than so many others.

Dealing with natural disasters is even worse. On a VIM trip to Mississippi I remember a homeowner coming back to her house two years after she had to leave it because of Hurricane Katrina. She wanted to gather some things left on the floor, and we had to tell her that she couldn't because everything was contaminated with mold. I'll never forget the look on her face.

I learned many lessons on the trips. I got skills to do repairs and can use those skills in other places. I impressed my brother recently when I soldered copper pipes for a plumbing job. You learn patience, for instance, when doing finish work. And when you get a teacher who doesn't explain things well, you learn to pay close attention. As a young person, you get to work with people with great experience and that encourages you to higher standards. And the chance to be in other parts of the country is interesting, too. In one store, I wanted a soda and the clerk kept insisting I wanted "pop."

Sometimes because of my size and age, and because I'm a girl, people try to tell me how to use my tools. They have trouble grasping that women can do things.

The work can be hard, but it's also fun to joke and wisecrack with co-workers on the team. I'd like to see more teens be part of VIM teams.

A Flood Victim Says Thank You

Joe Ford

*Adapted from remarks presented to the
2009 session of annual conference*

On August 11, 2008, my home in Rensselaer, NY was devastated by a flood. Inside my home, to a height of almost 3 feet, everything was covered in a layer of water, mud, and contamination from the backed-up sewers. The water rose so quickly that I only had time to hand my dog and two cats to someone in a boat outside my home, and I entered the boat through my front porch window with just what I had on and a plastic bag of my medications.

In the four days afterward, I called my insurance company and found out I was not covered at all for my loss. I called FEMA, only to learn that the federal government was not going to do anything to help me or anyone else in my city. And, finally, I called various state agencies, only to be told there would be no help from them as well. It seemed to me that no one cared what had happened to me. It was then I realized that I had lost my home and most everything that I owned. I suppose it was only natural that I fell into a state of depression, but it was so deep a depression that I even thought of ending my life.

On the fourth day after the flood, when I had lost all hope, I received two telephone calls: one from Jay Dunkleberger and the other from John Hill. They told me they were from the United Methodist Church's "Volunteers in Mission," and they were going to come to my home and help me. It was those two phone calls and the arrival of volunteers the next day that gave me hope to go on, because I knew that somebody really did care about me, someone they didn't even know.

The volunteers that came to my home came from all walks of life and all professions. The most senior of them were in their eighties while the youngest were young men and women in their teenage years. There were 76 volunteers from ten United Methodist churches and two volunteers from Faith Lutheran Church in North Troy.

Over the more than four months that the volunteers were at my house, I saw them working so hard to make my home a beautiful one. I saw them drying out the mud and water and removing it shovel by shovel in temperatures that ranged between 90 and 100 degrees. I saw Jack Hill with a protection suit, boots, gloves, and a mask, going into my house repeatedly, disinfecting the contaminated walls and floors in that same unbearable temperature. I saw people doing the arduous work of ripping up wooden floors and several layers of linoleum with crowbars, stripping the walls down to the supporting beams, and then digging out the remainder of the mud from crevices, handful by handful, all the time in that same unbearable heat.

During this time and the succeeding months spent on rebuilding the walls and floors, recreating new wider door frames to make my home handicapped accessible, laying down new floors, creating new walls, covering them with new paint and wallpaper, and replacing my furniture and appliances, I often had to go outside my home because I was so moved by what all the volunteers were doing for me that I knew I was on the verge of tears and didn't want to upset them.

On December 20, 2008, I was able to return to my home, and it is beautiful—more beautiful than it was before the flood. It is not only visually beautiful but spiritually too, because it was built with love. Even to this day, as I walk from room to room, I still see and feel the presence of the volunteers there. Each wall, each floor, each room, the wallpaper, paint, reconstructed doorways, furniture, and appliances bring back the memory of the smiling faces saying "hello" to me and asking me how I was doing, all the time caring more about me than they did for themselves.

Although I thought of my fellow Jews throughout the world as "my family," I came to realize that I had a much larger family because all of you have become a part of my family, too. I made the decision to visit each of the churches the volunteers had come from. Over the past several months, I have visited each of the eleven churches. I told them I knew they had helped me through their donations, their sales, and the gifts of furniture and appliances. I also told them I knew I was not the only person they had helped; there were many others here in America and in other countries they had helped too. I told them that if those people could travel the many miles to thank them, they would, but because they were unable to, I thanked them for those people, too. When people ask me about all of you, I tell them you are my angels, because to me that is what you really are.

When I visited your churches, I had the same warm feeling that I have when I am in my synagogue. In our daily prayers we say the Hebrew words, "L'dor V'dor," which means "from generation to generation." I have felt the warmth and seen the beauty of the generations in your churches through an acolyte lighting the candles, pastors setting aside special time in the service to talk with young children, and the beautiful voices of your choirs.

Although the flood had been very devastating for me if it hadn't happened, I would not have met all you wonderful people whom I have come to know and love. To me, your coming was and always will be a miracle. I know that for whatever time I have yet to live, each and everyone of you will be a part of my very being, and I hope that, if there is some good in me, I will always be a part of you.

I am receiving newsletters now from some of the churches, and I sometimes wonder what my mailman thinks of my identity. He has seen me with my kippah on, and for years has delivered mail from my synagogue and other Jewish organizations. Now that I am receiving Christian newsletters too, he's been looking at me as though he is a bit puzzled. If he ever asks me about the mail I receive, I will tell him that all of the Jewish and Christian mail is from my family.

The Hebrew words todah rabah mean "thank you very much." Todah rabah for being my angels, my friends, and my family.

May our Heavenly Father bless all of you and your families, now and always.

Chapter 6

Extravagant Generosity

And God is able to provide you with every blessing in abundance, so that by always having enough of everything, you may share abundantly in every good work.

2 Corinthians 9:8

Extravagant generosity always needs to be measured by the dimensions of the attitude rather than the size of the gift. The value Jesus placed on the widow's mite—she put in more than all the others—is proof enough of that. Such generosity, spending on others rather than on ourselves, is frequently a challenge. The people of Troy Conference often rose to meet that challenge.

World Service

There was a time when conference typically struggled to meet connectional responsibilities in full. Many local churches could not pay their apportionments, so conference regularly found itself not meeting World Service at 100%.

In 1980, annual conference initiated a plan to accomplish two financial goals simultaneously. The Crusade for Ministry and Mission sought to raise $3.2 million—$2 million for pensions and a half million for missions. An additional $.7 million was for administrative expenses and contingencies.

The amount for pensions was to provide mandated reserves for the support of present and future retirees. At the time, the unfunded pension liabilities were nearly six million dollars. This amount was not due all at once, but it did increase each time the pension rate was raised and each time a pastor retired with years of service under that plan.

The amount for missions was intended to pre-fund the benevolence side of the conference budget, which included both actions intended by conference agencies and the World Service apportionment from the denomination. Under the old system, all conference benevolences were funded largely as receipts arrived from the churches. Typically, income lagged far behind budgeted expectations. Some churches waited until the end of the year before they forwarded anything to the conference treasurer. This in turn meant that operating budgets had to be watched carefully and planned programs might or might not be funded in timely fashion. But with pre-funding, conference would have the financial resources for the year ahead on hand January 1. Income from the churches through the year would then go to replenish the reserves rather than to meet current needs.

The Crusade for Ministry and Mission was a massive effort. The first team leaders were Harold Wusterbarth and the Rev. Garry Campbell. They became co-chairs of the Crusade Continuation Committee, while in 1981 the Rev. Kenneth Beatty was elected director of the follow-up program and Ruth Harlow was chosen as associate director. The Rev. Oren J. Lane used his photographic skills and worked with the Interpretation Committee to prepare a slide show illustrating the theme and purpose of the crusade.

The churches responded fairly well. The report in 1984 showed 42% of the hoped-for money had been received. Conference voted to extend the campaign an additional year and a half, to December 31, 1985, to give churches more time to meet their fair-share askings. The final report in the 1986 Journal shows all expenses paid, a benevolence fund of $500,000 on hand, and $1,020,000 put toward reducing past-service pension liability. This last allocation had the effect of reducing administrative apportionments for the years ahead. The total collected, $1,681,546 by April 30, 1986, was the largest amount conference had raised for any purpose at that time. The Rev. William Lasher, council director noted in his report that, due to the Crusade, World Service was paid at 100% in 1985 for the fourth year in a row.

In the initial years following the crusade, invested funds produced enough interest to keep the program working as originally intended. But by the late 1980s a problem began to appear. Income from the churches dropped along with interest rates on conference investments. Nevertheless, annual conference determined to continue to support World Service at 100%. In 1990 the trustees voted to "insure" the benevolence program for 1991 and 1992 through the use of undesignated funds under their control. At the same time, annual conference charged the Council on Ministries and the Council on Finance and Administration with the task of preparing a comprehensive stewardship effort to bring the giving back to a higher level.

With that decision to move forward, conference was able to maintain support for World Service at 100% despite the often significantly-lower level of giving from the churches in a given year. For instance, the conference treasurer reported that in 2008, World Service was paid at 100% despite the fact that only 87.4% of the total came from the churches.

Additional factors need to be included when considering the frequent struggle to reach and continue the 100% support of World Service. First, through the sustained efforts of United Methodist Women, the churches regularly gave annual amounts of well over $100,000 in support of missional needs. Further, the churches continued to respond with extravagant generosity to a variety of serious emergencies around the world. The chart that follows lists some of the efforts conference made to meet the needs of others.

This record shows the churches, both large and small, reaching out to people in need around the world. World Service was paid at 100%, and $2,800,000 more was raised in addition to the ongoing efforts of the UMW and continuing support of other advance specials.

Special Mission Giving by Troy Conference Churches		
Year	Emergency	Amount
1987	Bishop's Appeal UMCOR World Hunger	$37,000 $13,000
1988	Bangladesh, Armenia	$97,000
1989	Hurricane/San Francisco earthquake	144,000
1991	Bangladesh/Persian Gulf	$124,000
1992	Florida hurricane/Somalia	$172,000
1993	Midwest flooding	$51,000
1994	General miscellaneous	$99,000
1995	Oklahoma City/Bosnia/ Vermont flood	$91,000
1996	Brazil/Bosnia	$98,000
1997	Brazil/Bosnia/floods	$97,000
1998	NY ice storm/hurricane	$260,000
1999	Turkey earthquake/Kosovo/hurricane	$270,000
2000	Mozambique floods	$52,000
2001	El Salvador/India/Love in the Midst of Tragedy (9/11 response)	$180,000
2002	General Advance Specials	$144,000
2003	Mozambique land mine removal	$39,000
2004	Flood buckets/Heifer International/tsunami/hurricanes/land mine removal	$113,000
2005	Hurricanes/tsunami/Heifer Project	$566,000
2006	Flooding/Heifer Project/Pakistan earthquake	$61,000
2007	Heifer Project/Mozambique/UMCOR	$49,000
2008	Disaster relief	$70,000

Mission Work

The 1991 Journal shows the Covenant Agreement created between the Methodist Church of the Northeastern Region of Brazil and Troy Conference. A key sentence is, "As the world becomes a global village, we are aware of our interdependence and God's call to faithfulness to his gospel." That awareness was deeply rooted in Troy Conference from its earliest days and has continued to encourage extravagant generosity through the years.

One type of extravagant gift is human resources. The people of Troy Conference sent out missionaries to extend the reach of compassion and make awareness of interdependence a reality.

The memoir for Leona Aldrich Reid in the 1990 Journal records how, as the wife of pastor Frank Reid, she supported mission work in a variety of ways. Perhaps the most telling observation is that on the day of her husband's retirement from active ministry in 1967, her daughter, Sonia Reid Strawn, was commissioned as a missionary to Korea. Sonia and her husband Dwight continued to serve there for many years.

The parsonage family of Bristol and Muriel Chatterton also raised their daughters with a drive for mission work. Sue went to Korea while Lois served in the United States.

In June of 1996, conference lecturer Ruediger Minor, bishop of The United Methodist Church in Russia, offered a prayer of blessing on the Rev. and Mrs. Jim Proctor as they went off for a year of mission work in Kazakhstan.

Also in 1996, conference heard reports from local residents Dirk and Carol Van Gorp regarding their work with UMCOR in Bosnia. The Rev. Lee and Bonnie Adkins also had recently returned from that country.

Also in 1996, Bishop Paulo Ayres Mattos of the Northeastern Region of Brazil attended the Troy Conference session to sign the Covenant Agreement. The following year, the Rev. Lawrence Curtis, district superintendent, along with Madeleine Robinson and Shirley Byers, representing the conference Board of Global Ministries, traveled to Brazil to sign the covenant there on behalf of Bishop Susan M. Morrison, newly assigned to the Albany Area.

In 1993 and again in 1995 persons from Troy Conference traveled to Mozambique on mission trips. They returned with stories of the faith, spirituality, and gifts of the Mozambican United Methodists. These experiences led the Board of Global Ministries in 1996 to propose, and conference to accept, the idea of a team from Mozambique coming to Troy Conference to share their gifts, demonstrating a genuine partnership in mission. Two-thirds of the conference Sunday offering in 1997 went to funding the Volunteer in Mission Team coming from Mozambique to the United States. The team of twelve was present at the 1998 session of annual conference and after that itinerated to many of our local churches.

This exchange experience meant so much to all involved that a second VIM team came to Troy Annual Conference from Mozambique in 2003. Again the funding for the trip came from local churches eager to share and be generous. The dynamic enthusiasm was captured in a remark by Bishop Morrison: "Troy Annual Conference and Mozambique area are one church."

Mozambique VIM team visits Troy Conference, 2003

The sense of unity was underlined in another way in 2003. Warfare in Mozambique had left many parts of the nation littered with landmines. To purchase a mechanical mine sweeper, the Rev. George and Margaret Klohck offered to match donations from Troy Conference dollar for dollar in the hope of raising $45,000. A year later, the Klocks reported that the total raised was $54,000. Land was already

A Woman Missionary in Korea

Sue Chatterton Pak

After two years of college, going in the direction of social work, I felt I had to make a decision to work more directly with God through the church. I chose to transfer to Scarritt College where I could be trained as a Christian worker. Through this experience I received marvelous training in a variety of fields that prepared me for being a missionary.

One of my classes was led by David White, who had been a missionary to Cuba. He inspired me greatly. I had several Korean friends and enjoyed their company. I felt that I wanted to go to the mission field but knew that language was vital for communication. Korean was a challenge with no familiar roots to build on. So when the form asked where I felt led to go I listed it this way: South America because I felt the language would come easier, Korea because of my acquaintance with Koreans, and anywhere God needed me to go.

God sent me to Korea. Of course, this was extremely wise as I do not do well with heat and humidity and probably would have been miserable in that setting. I guess God figured He could help me with the language! And he did, because after three years of study I was dreaming in Korean! Here I would like to say that when I look at my "call," I would say "yes," God guided me to Korea. But if I am honest, I am an adventuresome soul and a lot of the reason I went there was to have a unique experience. However, the Korean Christians and other missionaries on the field influenced me greatly and deepened my walk with the Lord so that I would say I became a missionary on the field due to the devoted Christians I encountered in my life experiences.

As a single woman from the United States from 1966-69, I found the experience to be exciting and a time being cleared with the machine funded by the extravagant generosity of Troy Annual Conference.

Central Conference Pension Initiative

Along-standing tradition at conference was the presentation of a check from Cokesbury representing profit sharing from The United Methodist Publishing House. According to the *Discipline*, Article VI of the Restrictive Rules, such profits are only to be used for the support of people in the ministerial pension system. These checks were always received with enthusiasm and applause. Beginning in 2004, Troy Conference voted to channel that annual check not to its own pension fund but instead to the Central Conference Pension Fund. The Central Conferences at the time included mostly African and Eastern European Methodists. Clergy in those conferences typically had very small salaries, which not infrequently they failed to receive. On retirement, they lost even that inadequate amount of financial support. The Central Conference Pension Initiative was intended to provide a realistic level of annual support to retired pastors, dependents and survivors in those settings.

In 2008, the Conference Board of Pensions recommended and conference agreed to put an additional $15,000 from the Retired Pastor's Emergency Aid Fund into the Pension Initiative. This action was taken in honor of Bishop Machado of Mozambique.

In 2009, due to economic conditions, there were no profits for Cokesbury to share. In place of that, conference voted to take an extra offering in the middle of the Celebration of Ministry Service. Between what was received at that time and what came in later, the contribution to the Central Conference Pension Initiative totaled more than the typical check from the Publishing House would have been. Again in 2010, there was no profit sharing check from Cokesbury. The Board of Pensions voted to recommend that conference again put $15,000 to the initiative, this time from the retired Pastors Pension and Health Insurance Reserve Fund.

of learning from the Korean Christians. Koreans were used to American women missionaries so the adjustment was fairly easy. We had an advantage in that we could be free to be who we were and share the Gospel. Korea had women Bible teachers even at this time in their history, so they paved the way. I can say that leading Lenten services as a youth probably gave me confidence to lead worship and stand up in front of others. I taught English conversation at the college level at Mokwon Methodist University for ten years and then worked at Taejon Christian International School in various capacities for another twenty years.

The cultural difference hit home when I returned to Korea in 1979, married to a Korean and with three young children. We had done things together as a couple in the U.S., but in Korea men do their thing and women do theirs, especially in our generation. The first year back was a huge adjustment. I was rarely invited to functions my husband attended and David was gone much of the time, leaving me with most of the responsibility for the children. I hit rock bottom and went into a depression. I did not know many foreigners at this time and we were living on campus and there was no help for counseling. You have to understand that David had little choice as the society demanded his time and energy, and the "group" is of prime importance in Asian society. If you do not participate in the social gatherings you hurt the "keepun" or the feelings of the others, so even though my husband wanted to be home more, he had to accommodate the group. Seeing my depression, David encouraged me to read the Psalms for comfort. I followed his suggestion and began reading the Psalms. I can say that God became my counselor at that point. Slowly and gradually God pulled me out of my depression.

Another hard thing as the wife of a Korean man is that women do not have much opportunity to speak in

This was extravagant generosity in action.

Health Insurance

Provision for health insurance for pastors and their families was a long-standing concern in Troy Conference, and responding to the challenge took considerable time and energy. Insurance is an issue with many technicalities and in some ways the attention it required was a diversion from the real work of conference. On the other hand, it was an aspect of modern life that required careful thought and deliberate action. Despite the costs, many efforts were made to minimize the impact of increased premiums on clergy. The story of those actions tells something about the expectations, mindfulness, and generosity of Troy Conference.

The 1981 Journal has several references to health insurance. At that time the concerns were more technical than financial. The Commission on Equitable Salaries made it clear that churches were expected to cover hospitalization premiums for Blue Cross-Blue Shield Standard Plan B or equivalent. The Committee on Insurance Plans noted that annual conference covered the cost of a Major Medical Plan for expenses beyond those of Plan B. The cost of this coverage for 456 pastors and dependents in 1980 was $16,702. A conference Medicare subsidy for retired ministers and surviving spouses was $36 per individual or family, available "if requested." The cost of adding Major Medical coverage to the basic health insurance plan was $3.98 per month for an individual and $9.66 per month for a family. (Just to put those numbers in perspective, the 2010 health insurance premium mandated to be paid by the local church for each full-time clergy is $1,268 per month.)

In the coming years, health insurance coverage came to have an increasingly strong impact on the budgets of local churches. Despite rising costs, conference generously continued to view health insurance as a fundamental part mixed groups of men and women. Also, sometimes language prevented me from talking more in public. This caused me to lose myself for a while as I considered myself an extrovert. But I could exercise my personality more fully when working with children, youth, and college age people, so I wasn't completely tied down.

I cannot emphasize enough that working with Korean Christians and fellow missionaries deepened my faith and broadened my walk. I was blessed far more than I think I gave to others. Being a missionary is not an exceptional thing, really; it is just that we are privileged to work more intensely with outstanding Christians and probably pray far more than the average person. We work on God's strength and not our own. When He is in command and control, things we think are impossible happen and He is honored.

of ministerial compensation.

There was a period of calm before the storm, but in 1983 the situation began to get complicated. "In June, when the Blue Cross-Blue Shield Insurance Contract was renewed, in addition to the increased premium cost each subscriber experienced, the Major Medical Cost, borne by the conference, more than doubled." The anticipated $24,000 bill became $37,000 (the quarterly increase came mid-year) and the projection for 1984 was for $50,000. Through a competitive bidding process the Committee on Insurance Plans was able to negotiate a new plan that reduced rates and increased coverage for 1984.

This negotiation worked for one year. However, the 1985 Journal reported that at the last minute the New York State Insurance Commission nullified an extension of that contract because claims in 1984 drastically exceeded the premiums. Facing an additional $60,000 premium, the conference Committee on Insurance Plans switched carriers and was able to provide insurance at an only slightly higher rate.

By this time Major Medical coverage disappeared as a separate policy and had been folded into the regular plan. Conference noted in a resolution that it had "affirmed and fulfilled an intent to underwrite a portion of the ... Health Insurance Premium," that is, Major Medical, amounting to about 20% of the total cost. So, the resolution continued to commit conference to a 20% subsidy of the insurance plan costs borne by the local churches.

The rates remained stable for one year. In 1987, the quarterly costs rose to accommodate increased coverage and to keep step with inflation. The individual quarterly premium went up 55% to $180. The family premium increased by 51% to $468, and the Medicare premium soared 76% to $156. These greater costs were understood as employee (clergy) benefits.

The 1989 report of the Committee on Insurance Plans notes first that premiums had increased another 12%, and that this was a much smaller increase than could be obtained from other carriers. The guideline the committee followed was "the avoidance of reducing coverage or in any other way shifting health care costs back to the recipients." Further, due to the way insurance was now provided, retirees had become responsible for a substantially greater premium. Conference voted a subsidy to cover 20% of the retiree's costs even though this meant practical elimination of the reduction in premiums paid by local churches for active pastors.

More bad news came in 1990. Costs for claims exceeded premiums by over $280,000 for the prior three years, so premiums had to increase by 35%. The family rate was up to $1,047 per quarter. It is perhaps not coincidental that conference passed a resolution calling for a greater federal effort to provide universal health care.

In 1991, conference grappled with a variety of health insurance-related issues. It was voted to bill on the basis of a "Uniform Insurance Premium" so that churches with a single pastor, a pastor with a family, or a pastor with insurance coverage obtained in another way, such as through a spouse, would all pay the same rate. (Later this action was rescinded before it went into effect at a special session of annual conference held on December 7. The decision made then, accepted by a vote of 205 to 97, restored part of the differential between premiums for single and married clergy and also called for an additional apportioned amount from each church.) The conference subsidy was exclusively devoted to reducing the premiums of retirees and their spouses. An attempt to make clergy responsible for part of their own insurance costs was not approved.

The 1992 Journal indicates that the Committee on Health Insurance Plans reviewed over twenty bids before deciding to remain with the then-current carrier. Once again conference passed a resolution calling for national health care. One additional resolution indicated a desire to hold premiums at the current level. Anticipated future actions that might be effective were spelled out in detail. The first step would be to increase deductibles. The second would be to eliminate dental, vision, and hearing coverage. Only then, if necessary, would subscribers have to help pay the premiums.

In 1994, the Committee noted with approval that by joining HealthFlex, a denomination-wide program run through the General Board of Pensions and Health Benefits, conference was able to maintain benefits with only a modest increase in rates. The committee also suggested that participant contributions would become necessary when annual charges for family coverage reached $7,500.

The rising expense of health insurance created a certain amount of tension. In 1995, a petition was presented voicing frustration with "mandated" costs and asking that "the Health Insurance Committee be reconstituted so that no more than three of the nine be clergy or clergy family members." The petition was referred to the Committee on Health Insurance Plans. The following year, conference voted to make that suggested change in the makeup of the committee.

However, also in 1996, the issue of pastors sharing the cost of health insurance created extended debate, so much so that the final decisions were made at a rare late-night session convened at 9:05 p.m. following the informal Saturday night program. After extensive discussion, conference again decided not to have pastors share the cost of health insurance premiums. This was at least partly because the conference minimum salary was among the lowest in the denomination. The tax-free health insurance benefit was a step toward more equitable compensation. An additional resolution from the Committee on Health Insurance Plans placed a strong emphasis on wellness promotion; that is, taking a proactive stance toward health issues that would help reduce the use made of health insurance, improving the "experience" of plan members, and thus ultimately reducing health insurance costs.

For a few years the situation remained fairly stable with rates rising very slowly. In 2002, however, the rate for a family plan jumped 20% to $9180. That same year, a highly technical resolution addressed the issue of eligibility criteria for the retiree health insurance benefit. The plan at the time simply called for conference to pay 20% of the retiree premiums. The new plan, covering those who joined the system after July 2002, established a vesting schedule with six years of full-time service required to gain any portion of the benefit credit and thirty years of full-time service needed to reach 100% of the conference subsidy.

In 2003, premiums again rose substantially to $11,000 for family coverage. The Conference Board of Pensions provided $46,000 in supplemental payments to retirees to ease the transition to the newer, higher rates for their coverage.

Conference 2004 addressed several different aspects of health insurance. One decision required that all full-time pastors be covered by the conference program. This meant that churches with pastors who had coverage outside the

Ralph Craw's Legacy

Rev. Bill Lasher

Ralph Craw was a very committed church member. He was a schoolteacher, never married, taking care of his parents at their farm until they died. He continued to care for neighbors and friends his whole life. He was a great cook—known especially for his pies.

The church was his family, and he was active for many years at Wilton UMC and later at Saratoga Springs UMC. Bruce Conklin and Will Chamberlin were his "boys" and they looked after Ralph as he grew older. He was extremely frugal yet very generous. He took tithing to his church seriously, but more than that he considered all that he had to belong to God.

Ralph read and studied his Bible daily. He prayed for his church and especially for his pastor every day and was always affirming and supportive of pastors. He was a regular worshiper. He loved the church, especially when it was reaching out to help persons in need.

In the early 1990s, he became concerned about the "unfunded liability" of the Troy Conference part of the pre-82 UMC pension plan—a plan that provides retirement benefits for pastors and spouses who had service years prior to 1982. He invited me, the conference pension officer, to meet with him and his lawyer to draft his will so that his entire estate would go to Troy Conference and be used to help fund the pre-82 pension plan. Several years later, when it was announced that the Troy Conference pre-82 plan was fully funded, Ralph came to me (at this time, I was one of his pastors) to discuss other possibilities. Ralph wanted to make sure his gift would be used where most needed, so he changed his will so the proceeds would be used instead to help fund retiree health insurance.

Ralph died in 2006, but because of the downturn in

United Methodist system still were required to pay the premiums. This inability to opt out brought about a slight reduction in overall premiums. Retirees again received a modest supplement to cover the cost of their premiums. The Committee on Health Insurance Plans also was directed to seek ways to provide health care coverage for domestic partners, such persons not being eligible for coverage at that time. That petition passed by a vote of 207 to 155 and generated a dissenting opinion signed by seven members of conference.

As already noted, one concern through the years was a focus on wellness and the use of screening tests to assess risks ahead of time. The 2006 report of the committee noted that those participating in an on-line health risk assessment would receive $100. In addition, premiums would be reduced if a large enough number of participants undertook the assessment. In a positive reflection of that concern, Bishop Susan Morrison noted that a major consideration in her decision to retire in the midst of the quadrennium was her desire to model wellness. She felt her continuation in service would have a negative impact on her future and chose to make a healthier choice.

Once again, in 2007 conference approved a resolution in support of universal health care. In addition, reflecting a generous bequest made by Ralph Craw, a long-time active lay person, conference voted to increase the subsidy of retiree health insurance premiums from 20% to 30%.

A growing concern through the years was the provision of health insurance for part-time pastors. A serious complication of using the United Methodist HealthFlex system for this coverage was the necessity of inclusion. That is, for some three-quarter time pastors to be covered, all three-quarter time pastors would have to be covered. This approach was deemed far too expensive for the typically-small local churches using part-time pastors. Even so, the Committee on Health Insurance Plans was directed to seek a solution to the problem. This generous impulse was the housing market, the sale of the property was delayed. Will Chamberlin, a lay member of the Saratoga Springs UMC and a long time friend, is the trustee of the Ralph Craw Trust Agreement. He gave much time and effort to completing the eventual sale of the property. In 2009, the trustees of the Troy Annual Conference received a check for $1.3 million dollars from his estate.

Ralph would be pleased to know that his desire to support pastors in their retirement is being implemented. In anticipation of this gift, the conference voted in 2007 that the 20% subsidy for retiree health insurance cost be raised to 30% beginning in 2008. In the allocation of assets to take effect in July 2010 as we change conference boundaries, 30% of the Ralph Craw gift will be transferred to the New England Annual Conference and 70% to the new Upper New York Conference to be used for the purpose he intended. The legacy of Ralph Craw continues to provide support for many pastors of The United Methodist Church. Praise God for this saint who lived among us.

thwarted by the anticipated changes in conference configuration. As the committee worked through 2008 and early 2009, there was no decision as to when boundaries would change or how the Troy Conference system would fit with the systems of the other conferences involved in the mergers. The committee could only informally suggest the hope that some local sources of insurance could be found to meet the need.

As discussions regarding the new conference alignment proceeded during 2009, the issues of health insurance were a major priority in the soon-to-be-established Upper New York Area. The resulting recommendation to the new conference is not easily summarized. However, one key component of the plan is that mandatory enrollment of full-time clergy in HealthFlex will be continued, and participants will be assessed a contribution equal to 15% of the premium. The health insurance experiment in extravagant generosity had come to an end.

Through the years conference has had an attitude of generosity. Money for local church operations, missions, clergy housing, and salaries has been tight. Even so, congregations repeatedly have gone the second mile to respond to the needs of others. Open-handed giving has frequently marked the actions of Troy Conference people.

Chapter 7

Troy Conference Camps

Come, let us go up to the mountain of the Lord, to the house of the God of Jacob; that he may teach us his ways and that we may walk in his paths.

Micah 4: 2

The Early Days

Between the example of Jesus giving His Sermon on the Mount and John Wesley offering a strong affirmation of "field preaching," it comes as no surprise that Methodists were and are partial to the religious experience in the great out-of-doors. From nearly the earliest days of Methodist work in Troy Conference, the camp meeting, in its various forms, was the means of sharing the Gospel and building commitment to the work of Christ.

The Rev. Charles and Ouida Schwartz, in *A Flame of Fire*, explored the roots of camping in Troy Conference. This chapter owes a debt to their research and writing.

Presbyterian revival meetings held in Kentucky and Tennessee seem to have stimulated similar efforts by the Methodists. In 1810, Bishop Francis Asbury set a goal of six hundred camp meetings a year. More than likely one reason for his enthusiasm was the first camp meeting held within the bounds of Troy Conference in 1805. Bishop Asbury and Bishop Richard Whatcoat, along with ministers from Canada, Vermont, New York, New Jersey, Massachusetts, and Connecticut, held a four-day gathering at Stillwater, NY, on the banks of the Hudson. This event made a great impact on the people and served to encourage additional gatherings across the territory. Communities such as Petersburgh, Mooers, and Riverside Campground in Riparius, New York, along with Barre, Taftsville, Morrisville, Northfield, Lyndonville, and

Sheldon, VT, are recorded as having hosted camp meetings.

In the early days, a camp meeting site would be just an open place close to a source of water and firewood, where visitors could erect tents. These gatherings could easily draw hundreds or even thousands of people from distances of a hundred miles or more. Clearly, such a crowd could quickly overwhelm limited local resources. Families typically would bring a quantity of food from home for their stay, while keeping the need for on-site cooking to a minimum. Individual campfires kept water hot for tea or coffee all day and weekends. Such hospitality made it easier for those who were far from home.

Often a large tent was located at the center of things for the mass meetings. At some meetings, several such tents were erected so more than one preacher could speak at the same time. The days were full. The horn signaling morning prayers would blow at 6 a.m. Preaching occurred at 10 a.m., 2 p.m., 7 p.m., and again at midnight. Sermons often were followed by an exhortation that might be as long as the message itself. The Love Feast was celebrated, and many additional prayer meetings were part of the daily schedule. In addition, those who gathered found many opportunities for praise and personal testimony.

While religious fervor might have run high at these meetings, conversions were actually relatively rare. Some estimates put them in the neighborhood of only 1%. And even then, backsliding after a powerful experience was common. Since meetings were generally open to all comers, rowdies and troublemakers frequently were part of the crowd as well. Indeed, there were those who claimed more souls were conceived than saved at these sessions.

And yet for the majority, despite the complications and negatives, something highly spiritual was going on. Author A. P. Mead, writing in 1859, expressed a Methodist view: "The campground is a hallowed place. Every tree seems clothed with richer verdure, and becomes sacred. We worship in the shady grove with peculiar emotions. The places where camp meetings are held are consecrated. We feel that we are treading on holy ground."

Claremont Junction

Some insight into how campgrounds emerged and operated comes from records of Chapel Grove in Claremont, NH. Three area railroads were asked to allow free passage for all freights necessary to build up and sustain a camp meeting at Claremont Junction. Preachers and their wives were to travel free to and from all meetings. The further request was that those attending be charged half-fare plus ten cents. The ten cents was to cover the expenses of the association. All these terms were generally agreeable to the railroads. The association bought property and divided it into parcels 24 feet wide and 28 feet deep—essentially a size that would accommodate a tent. According to a newspaper of the time, site preparations were done by asking "those interested in...giving a day's work...[to] come with horses, carts, hoes, shovels, picks, bars, scrapers, chains and axes."

When in 1941 the Vermont Conference merged with Troy Conference, the Claremont Junction Campground Association was reported to be a self-perpetuating organization, incorporated under the laws of New Hampshire. Church related activity continued on that site for many years, but in 1967 the situation changed. Citing the area around the campground as being predominantly commercial and not conducive for use as a summer camp for youth, annual conference gave permission to sell the campground.

Lyndonville

In the 1800s Lyndonville was a major railway hub. Through the joint efforts of the Saint Johnsbury District and the Connecticut and Passumpsic Rivers Railroad, a "Monstrous Camp Meeting" was held there in 1867. Trains brought in at least twenty cars full of attendees. A bystander counted some 400 wagon teams of participants going by a corner in three hours. Railroad Grove, as it was called then, hosted an estimated seven thousand participants. Some brought their tents, while others stayed in the lodgings available in the area at a cost of $1 a day, or $4 for the whole event.

The Lyndonville Epworth League ran a fruit stand on the grounds featuring mostly grapes. The meetings of course were planned for the purpose of spiritual uplift, but additional attractions certainly included socializing, along with some horse-trading by the men and the swapping of recipes and patterns by the women. As a practical matter, bonfires were kept burning to keep mosquitoes away.

Annual camp meetings of this sort, typically lasting ten days, continued on the site until 1915. After that, the property was given to the Village Improvement Society of Lyndonville for use as a community playground.

The sense of community interpreted through the religious experience surely was a significant part of what lead to the next development: permanent sites with buildings specifically designed to serve the camping experience. Once a religious association owned rather than borrowed or rented the property, other use could be made of it. A covered tabernacle replaced the preaching tent, and cottages for the better off replaced family wagons and temporary canvas hung from ridgepoles.

Round Lake

Perhaps the prime example of this kind of intentional upgrade was undertaken by the Round Lake Camp Meeting Association. The association was formed by a group of laymen from Troy, one of whom was Joseph Hillman, who had returned inspired from a camp meeting he had attended at Oak Bluffs on Martha's Vineyard, MA. In 1867, the association purchased forty acres of land in Round Lake with ready access to the Rensselaer and Saratoga Railroad. The first camp meeting at the site, beginning September 1, 1868, attracted eight thousand people during

Lyndonville Camp Meeting Reenactment

In 1984 Methodism celebrated 200 years of work in the United States. An afternoon of annual conference was given over to a camp meeting experience. The event began with a "Nooning," an outdoor meal together. Each district offered a pageant relating to a different 50-year segment of history while, in the spirit of the camp meeting, "brush arbor" preachers vigorously proclaimed themes from John Wesley's sermons.

In September of that same year, the Methodist churches of Lyndonville and vicinity held a one-day re-enactment of a camp meeting, though at the fairgrounds rather than what was now Powers Park. The Rev. Dr. Stanley Moore, then superintendent of the Burlington District, preached in the morning, and the Rev. Charles Warner from Hudson Falls, NY led an evangelistic service in the afternoon.

its ten-day duration.

The National Camp Meeting Association for the Promotion of Holiness held a session on the grounds in 1869. One hundred fifty clergy were present and the Sunday attendance was twenty thousand, even though no trains ran to the grounds on the Sabbath. Those in attendance came from all across the country.

Round Lake Auditorium

Round Lake also hosted the "Great Fraternal Camp Meeting" in 1874, when bishops, clergy and five thousand laity from ten different branches of Methodism came together. The event took place over two weeks, and more than fifty sermons were preached. President Ulysses S. Grant visited the grounds one day.

In 1885, the association built the Round Lake Auditorium with seating for about 1,000 persons. The auditorium now houses the oldest, largest three-keyboard organ in the United States that is still operating. This Ferris wooden tracker was built in 1847 for Calvary Episcopal Church in New York City and installed in the auditorium in 1888. The bell tower was rebuilt in 1986 as one of the final phases of refurbishing the entire structure. The auditorium hosted a "Great Day of Methodist Singing" in October 1981, with music workshops, children's choirs, anthems from participating churches, and a great massed choir for the concluding evening worship service.

The program booklet for the 1922 season touts an institute featuring addresses by four bishops, as well as numerous other educational offerings. Specific opportunities were the School of Missions, the Troy Conference Summer School of Theology, and a School of Religious Education, each offered on a different week. Recreational features offered by the association included picnics on Lookout Mountain in Lake George, music by the women of the Aida Brass Quartette of New York City, and a variety of sports, including basketball, baseball, tennis, croquet, and golf. Nearby places of interest included the Saratoga Battlefield; the Witenagemot Oak Tree planted in Schaghticoke in 1676 as a sign of peace; the "Cryptozoon Ledge" in Saratoga Springs, where marine fossils could be seen in limestone; and the remains of an extinct volcano just north of Schuylerville.

In 1928 the village, on the main line of the Delaware and Hudson Railroad, offered eleven trains each way daily except Sunday. The colony included 270 cottages, two hotels, and "other facilities contributing to the comfort and convenience of the large summer colony." Using typewriter and mimeograph, the Epworth League published a daily newsletter, "The Institooter," printed in Troy and delivered to Round Lake each day. The two pages had a mix of news, poetic thoughts, inspiration, puzzles, and a quantity of humor. For example: "Miss Turner said at the close of the first session yesterday, 'Some time ago my doctor told me to exercise early every morning with dumb-bells. Will the class please join me tomorrow before breakfast?'"

At the time of its founding, the Round Lake Campground was not expected to become a permanent community, but as the area developed so did the need for a resident caretaker. Other families also established homes on or near the grounds. Through the years, some tent platforms were upgraded to cottages. Then, as time, opportunity, and changing needs allowed, some landowners were able to acquire still more space to build. A Sunday School began in 1875, and in 1894 the first sections of the present Methodist church were erected. Tradition says a wedding in the church took place even before the pews were installed. Round Lake Village is now on the National Historic Register because of the many Victorian period houses erected on the grounds.

Enthusiasm for these gatherings ran high. In 1874, conference passed a resolution advising each presiding elder to hold at least one camp meeting at a place big enough to accommodate the churches of his circuit.

Riverside Campground

Another New York site where camp meetings matured into permanent campgrounds was Riverside at Riparious in the Adirondacks. The following story of Riverside Campground from 1873 to 1939 comes largely from materials prepared by the Rev. Thomas M. Bishop, who was born in Troy, NY in 1871, became a member of Troy Conference in 1900, and served for 41 years. His memoir in the 1943 Journal says, "Brother Bishop had the honor and privilege of being one of the founders in 1912 of the Riverside Institute for young people's summer gatherings, and across the years he was one of the enthusiastic officers and eager teachers." Thanks to him we have an inside look at the early history of Riverside campground. His manuscript is dated March 17, 1939.

The Camp Meeting Ground

About sixty-five years ago, around 1873, when old-fashioned camp meetings for religious services and revival purposes were popular gatherings in the woods and beside the rivers and lakes, a camp meeting was held in Warren County near Pottersville. The Methodists living at Johnsburg wanted to have meetings at a location nearer their village. One Monday morning, so tradition says, the Rev. Aaron Hall, then pastor at Johnsburg, having been told of a favorable site near the Riverside Bridge, started out on an exploration. He traveled eastward to the Hudson River, waded across it, and tramped south along the bank. Soon he came to a level piece of ground, well wooded, not far from the eastern approach to the bridge. Convinced that he had found the location he sought, he inquired as to its ownership and arranged for its use for a camp meeting.

Reporting to his church at Johnsburg and receiving the approval of its members, Mr. Hall and they decided to clear the ground and hold services there that very summer. Led by their pastor, a group of men with oxen and axes, accompanied by their wives with cooking utensils, journeyed to the chosen place.

It is said that Pastor Hall was the first to sink his axe into a tree, starting to cut it and its comrades down. Many hands made light work, and soon the "circle" was cleared, and planks were laid across the stumps for seats. A platform for the speakers and the organ was built and roofed over at the south end of the circle.

Old-fashioned jacks, so called, were built to give illumination and to attract the mosquitoes away from the worshipers. The jacks were made of wooden boards, put together like an old mortar box about four or five feet square and one foot deep, placed up on four stout posts four feet high. These boxes were filled with cobblestones from the river and sand from the road. Underneath them was piled the reserve supply of firewood. When the time for the evening service approached, the caretaker would start the fires, making the rounds all through the hours of the service, replenishing them from the material beneath the jack, and putting out the flames when the box itself began to burn, as it often did toward the end of the evening. How the children liked to help him keep the jack fires burning.

The families who came to stay through the camp meeting brought tents for shelter, straw for bedding, and supplies for man and beast. A barn was built for the horses, a dining hall for the transients, and a cottage for the preachers. The preachers' horses were fed and cared for free of charge, with hay provided by the association. The preacher himself had to supply the oats.

The control of the grounds and the running of the boarding hall were in the charge of the camp meeting association, which was soon formed by the leaders of the enterprise. Plots of ground were assigned to the members, leased to them for ninety-nine years.

Around the circle were built thirty or more little camps, or cottages as we now call them. They were simple structures of wood, really shelters only, usually with two rooms downstairs, one big room upstairs divided by curtains, and a big porch toward the river. These camps were just places to eat and sleep. Usually they were thirteen feet wide, twenty feet long, and a story and a half high, all set up a foot or so from the ground on stones or posts. They were so close together that one could hardly pass between them. You can get some idea of how closely the cottages were built to each other from a serious fire that occurred in 1924. Thirteen cottages were destroyed. In the rebuilding, just six took their place. While the earlier arrangement didn't allow for much privacy, the many children on the grounds found it ideal for games of hide-and-seek. Later some larger and more substantial cottages were built.

In the summer of 1908, workers went into the nearby woods to cut the timbers for the tabernacle. Clergy and laity worked together on the construction. Eventually the structure was named in memory of the Rev. Aaron Hall, who is considered the founder of the grounds.

For forty years, Methodist camp meetings were held at Riverside in the Adirondacks. Usually the presiding elder of the Saratoga District had charge of the religious services, filling the days with meetings and securing the speakers and leaders. From the platform, searching and stirring gospel sermons, some of them long and loud, were given by prominent preachers of Methodist and other denominations. Bishops and secretaries and others in high places, and also ministers in humbler positions but equally powerful in proclamation and prayer, instructed the people and sounded the call to follow the Christ. Riverside for years was a place of much emotion in religious experience and expression. "Amens" and "Hallelujahs" were shouted often. It was also a place of serious thought about religion, deep conviction of sin, sincere repentance, saving faith, and definite consecration to the Christian life.

The women organized a missionary society. Special meetings were held for the young people. Crowds attended the Sunday services. It was a great meeting place for relatives and friends. It was a notable place for the beginning and continuance of many a courtship that led to the establishing of Christian homes.

When the founding fathers ceased from their labors at Riverside, some of their sons continued carrying the burden of Riverside control. Among others A. Edson Hall, Embury Moston, Thomas R. Kneil, Charles Lavery, and Mrs. Haviland, Aaron Hall's daughter, gave their personal attention and volunteer services through many years. Later, these and a few others formed the Riverside Grove Association, which succeeded the Riverside Camp Meeting Association in the holding of the property.

With the passing years, interest in and attendance upon these camp meetings declined, and steps were taken to increase the interest of the younger generation in Riverside. These efforts at last led to the offer of the use of the grounds and buildings, with a hundred dollars toward the cost of the program, to a group of young pastors of the district who were ready and willing to work hard to develop the possibilities of the place as a summer center for Christian youth.

The Church Workers Conference The first institute at Riverside was held in 1912 under the leadership of the Rev. John Lowe Fort, then the new superintendent of Saratoga District. The institute was called "The Church Workers Conference," a name suggested by the Rev. Thomas M. Bishop as he and Dr. Fort and Dr. A. D. Angell were traveling home together to Broadalbin and Gloversville from the annual conference session in 1912. Mr. Bishop was made secretary of the executive committee, which included the three ministers already named and the Revs. Luther A. Brown, B. C. Dahms and J. E. Thompson. Mr. Bishop has been on the board ever since, serving as recording secretary or Life Work secretary all through the twenty-eight years and teaching a class annually. John Thompson also served on the board as member and on the faculty as teacher for twenty-six years.

Fifty delegates enrolled in the first institute, which was held for a full week, August 5-11, immediately following the camp meeting. Dr. Fort was chairman for two years.

For the next seven years, Dr. Luther A. Brown was the leader of the conference. For some years the institute followed the camp meeting, as did the first session in 1912. But interest in the camp meeting lessened, and finally it was discontinued. The Riverside Grove Association, however, continued to own the grounds and buildings, loan their use to the conference group, and help also with the program.

Attendance at the Church Workers Conference increased gradually, reaching 297 in 1920, Dr. Brown's last year. On the faculty from year to year appeared pastors of our conference and leaders from other conferences near and far. Among them were Bishops Quayle, Oldham, Burt, and Keeney; Dr. Sheridan, the secretary of the Epworth League; and Dr. Dan B. Brummitt, then editor of the *Epworth Herald.*

The Epworth League Institute In 1919, at the urgent request of the central office of the Epworth League, the leaders of the Church Workers Conference became affiliated with the league, accepting its offer of assistance in providing teachers, and assuming the name of the Riverside Epworth League Institute. Dr. Albert D. Angell, another of the founders of the Church Workers Conference, was chosen dean of the institute and served from 1921 to 1923. In 1922 the enrollment reached 387, the highest mark achieved even up to this time, 1938. To serve this host, double settings of the tables in the dining room were necessary. Student government was introduced in 1921. A demand for better lighting was also made, and in 1923 a Delco system of lighting by electricity was installed, replacing the use of kerosene lamps. The old and characteristic fire jacks were continued. About this time the custom of the sunrise service on top of Mt. Carpenter, which overlooks the institute grounds, was begun.

Dr. C. J. Miller, who had been associate dean with Dr. Angell in 1923, became dean in 1924 and served three years. During his administration, the surviving members of the Riverside Grove Association offered to give the property to the institute if it would assume a note for $1,200.00. After considerable discussion, the offer was accepted and the Riverside Epworth League Institute was incorporated, directors chosen, and officers elected, with Dr. Miller serving as president as well as dean.

With the reorganization, representation on the board of directors was granted to the leaguers of the Albany and Plattsburgh districts, to the conference at large, and to the student council. Rev. John E. Thompson succeeded Dr. Miller as president and dean in 1927. He filled both offices for two years when the duties were divided. Mr. Thompson continued as dean and Rev. Leon B. Randall became president of the board of directors.

In 1930, Mr. Randall became dean and Rev. L. A. Barker president of the board. Under this new arrangement, the president of the Board is responsible for the care of the property and the dean for the arranging of the institute program. That year arrangements were made with the New York Power and Light Corp. to furnish electricity to the institute. The institute sold some of the current to cottage owners, delivering the current by its own lines to the cottages, collecting the rental, and applying it to the total cost of the service supplied by the company.

Also in 1930, the gathering of offerings at the Sunday services was resumed. From the very beginning of the old camp meetings, the matter of financial support had been ever present. At first, collections were taken. Later, a fence was built around the campground, and a gate fee payable but once a year was required. This caused considerable resentment in the minds of the community. For those attending conferences, the institute paid the gate fee as an extra. Then the gate fee was included in the registration fee, which from the very beginning had been paid by those who enrolled in the church workers conference and in the institute. In 1927, the receiving of gate fees was abolished and taking of Sunday offerings was begun. Later this was omitted, but the income from this source was greatly needed to supplement that received from registrations, and annual subscriptions for underwriting the next year's program were always solicited on the Saturday evening of institute week.

Rev. Alan F. Bain followed Mr. Randall in 1932 as dean, with Charles Russell succeeding Mr. Barker as president. Two years later, Rev. F. J. Reid became dean and R. B. Cook president. In 1936, Dr. C. J. Miller was called back to serve as dean for a year, and in 1937 Rev. L. P. Ives was chosen to follow him. Mr. Ives also arranged the program for 1938, but having taken up special work outside of Troy conference, Associate Dean Rev. Paul Hydon was in charge for the 1938 institute and was chosen dean for 1939. The attendance for the last fifteen years averaged 247, with 179 as the lowest and 385 in 1933 as the highest.

Through the years, experienced teachers and notable preachers have been on the institute programs. Among them were Bishops Keeney, Waldorf, Thirkield, Dr. John Davis, Eugene Durham, Dr. Alderson, and Dr. G. C. Douglass, and many other pastors of our own conference.

Fun and frolic have been included in the schedules. We had events such as socials, hikes, rides, stunts, pageants, and municipal elections for the coveted positions of mayor and judge, and even dog-catcher of Riverside.

Inherited from the old camp meeting days, the Riverside Missionary Society is still maintained by the women of the campground, assisted by the institute folks. In fact, for this cause alone is a gathering of money allowed. Yes, there is one other. The collection taken at the institute Sunday School sessions is halved with the local church school. The missionary money given by delegations, faculty, and residents is solicited by the treasurer of the society. For years the Riverside Missionary Society has maintained a scholarship for a girl in India, helped support a school in South America, and aided many home mission projects.

Year by year the property has been maintained, repaired and improved. Roads, walks, a new dormitory, an icehouse, a bridge, and sanitary equipment have been provided. When the temporary equipment for supplying electricity to the cottages needed replacement, it was decided to discontinue supplying current to the cottages and grant the right of installation and service to the electric company, which now deals directly with the consumer.

Pastors' Conferences Under the leadership of Dr. A. D. Angell, then superintendent of the Plattsburgh District, the Board of Home Mission cooperated in the holding of pastors' conferences at Riverside. Several of these were supported by missionary funds, which were not channeled to their original purpose for a while. Recently these conferences have resumed under the guidance of Rev. Fred Vogel and others on this program. Many general and local church leaders have appeared, to the helpful instruction of those who attended the sessions.

The Managers Behind the scenes of Riverside events through the decades have been those who gave unstintingly of their time and talent to the housing and feeding of the hundreds who came to camp meetings, conferences, and institutes. With meager equipment, emergency help, few funds, and often insistent and unreasonable demands, these men and their staffs accomplished much. Always there was plenty, if not variety. To A. Edson Hall, L. E. Barker, R. B. Cook, L. P. Ives, D.T. Hill, and others, tribute is gladly paid for their share in the success of Riverside.

Riverside Results For years a feature of institute week has been the appearance of *Riverside Ripples*, a mimeographed daily, 8 & 1/2 x 11, printed on one side only but filled with news and notes and kept by many of those attending as souvenirs. But there are greater results and more lasting memories: of the woods, by the river, the walk to the bridge and down the lane. Recollections of the new light that came in class study and in worship hours, new visions on the mountain top and by the water, new inspirations that came in the class, moments of communion by candle light, new views of service for Christ in the home, church or in ministry abroad. New dedications, clearer declarations of belief, new ventures of faith, new acquaintances, rich friendships, fine companions, even for life. Only the recording angel knows it all. Nevertheless those who through the years have borne the burdens, guided the plans, undertaken the tasks, encouraged the folks, young and old, to attend, to serve, to help, have many satisfactions in remembering that they too, have been co-workers with God.

During the business session at conference in 1948, a motion noted that the properties at Missisquoi (Riverside Camp Meeting Association) in Enosburg Falls, VT; Skye Farm; and Riverside Epworth League Institute in Riparious, NY, were all necessary to an adequate program of Christian youth summer education and recommended the trustees purchase Missisquoi and Riverside. A substitute motion, which prevailed, asked instead for a study of the properties and a title search before proceeding with the purchases. The report coming back in 1949 was that the title of the Riverside Camp Meeting Association in Vermont was clear. The trustees were authorized to accept that property. The title of the Riverside Epworth League was not clear, so conference voted not to accept the title to that property.

For the occasion of the fiftieth anniversary of the Aaron Hall Tabernacle in July 1958, the Rev. Cassius J. Miller, one of the leaders during the Epworth League period, and Rev. Franklyn Wright prepared materials on the history of Riverside. They noted that the altar, cross, candlesticks, and lectern in the tabernacle were built by the Sea Bees during World War II and used in the north of France by Chaplain Taylor E. Miller, who had spent his boyhood summers at Riverside.

Missisquoi

The majority of the material in the following section comes from the research of Ouida Schwartz. We appreciate her willingness to allow its inclusion here. We are especially grateful for her first hand accounts of life in the camp during the summer institute period.

Sheldon Camp Meeting, which would become Missisquoi, began with the renting of about forty acres of wooded pasture from a farmer during the decade of the 1870s. The level ground provided ease for walking about, for pitching tents for the one or two weeks of services, and eventually for the construction of cabins and cottages. Not only was there a river for recreation, but natural springs provided drinking water. Roads and rail service, adequate for the times, made it easy for members of many churches to attend day or evening services. Nearby supporters were Saint Albans, VT, one of the larger churches of the conference, Richford, and a dozen or so neighboring churches. Yet the site was sufficiently removed from any village to afford privacy from hecklers and outside disturbances. Within a short while, barriers and a tollgate strengthened this seclusion. Even though it was well situated, the real survival test for the period was the ability to move with the changing demands of the time. This was the secret ingredient which clergy and laity provided here. Some other camp meetings lacked this flexibility, and that lack ultimately brought about their demise.

Missisquoi Tabernacle

By 1882, enthusiasm and attendance warranted the formation of a more permanent organization and the actual founding dates from that year. The Vermont Conference minutes reported in 1883, "Two camp meetings were holden last fall upon the [St. Albans] District, one at Morrisville and the other at Sheldon. Both of these were seasons of marked spiritual interest, and without doubt were largely profitable to our people. A goodly number of souls were converted, and a few attained unto the heritage of faith, or a blessing of a 'clean heart. '"

It should be stated that the site was known at various times as Sheldon, Missisquoi Valley, Riverside, and finally at the time of merging with Troy Conference where there was another Riverside on the Hudson, Camp Missisquoi. The meetings at Sheldon and at Morrisville became the prominent revival centers for the district by the 1890s. Dates were cooperatively arranged so that they would not be competitive but rather would allow people to attend both assemblies.

By the end of the 1880 period, Missisquoi had built a special cottage for the presiding elder for his "comfort and convenience." Ten years after the formal organizing, the grounds attracted a large attendance and reported numerous conversions and "the manifest presence of the Holy Spirit among the people." At this time the legal title for the association was The Missisquoi Valley Camp Meeting Association. A policy statement made the following year affirmed that "purely evangelistic services are best for camp meeting purposes, and while favorable to, and interested in benevolent and philanthropic organizations, [the members of the association] have put themselves upon record as declaring their purpose to adhere strictly to evangelistic work." The first indication of a missionary speaker occurred when the Rev. Dr. Edwin Parker, missionary to India, preached at meetings in 1896.

After the turn of the century attendance dropped a bit. The presiding elder admonished, "If the laymen in large numbers would cut loose from business and with their families attend these services, and the preachers all go for work and not for a picnic, our camp meetings might be and would be Bethels of Pentecostal power and the occasion of the conversion of many souls."

In an effort to reawaken enthusiasm after the state closed the public assembly for a season because of an epidemic, the association initiated a Bible School and a Sunday School Workers Conference. Teachers from local churches pronounced the sessions practical and useful. Clearly the decision to adhere to purely evangelistic services had been revisited, and the association rose to meet the needs for Christian ministry in a new day. The Rev. Charles Nutter wrote of this development, "Camp Meetings are not as much a necessity as in former years. They may be considered more as a luxury than a necessity; but if so, they are a luxury that can well be afforded by the common people. One of the sins of our fast time, and of our Christian people, is overwork. We work too many hours in the day and too many days in the year."

The Vermont Conference minutes of 1906 note that the site offered "the only summer Bible School within reach of the people of Northern Vermont." By the following summer it was agreed that instruction for church school teachers should become a fixed part of the program. The growth in interest was so broadened that the charter was changed (under action of the Vermont state legislature) to enlarge its scope and make additional membership possible. With this action, every Methodist pastor in a district church, all lessees of lots, and one layman from each church that rented a lot or paid the sum of one dollar a year could become a member. Thirty acres of land were paid in full and laid out into streets and lots—completely the property of the association by 1906.

The new name of the camp was the "Riverside Camp of the St. Albans District of the Vermont Conference." With considerable pride, the association announced improvements, a number of new cottages, and "improved sanitary methods," which visitors said were in advance of those found in any campground in New England. Newly elected Bishop W. S. Anderson formally dedicated the "large and convenient tabernacle" in 1908. The cost of twelve hundred dollars was raised before the dedication.

Attendance continued to mount, and speakers were brought from New York, Rhode Island, Illinois, Massachusetts, and various universities. Special services were planned for children and young people. Physical comfort and the ever-present considerations for health were priorities second only to spiritual needs. The Woman's Home and Foreign Missionary Societies held special meetings and raised substantial sums of money for their work. Bishop Theodore S. Henderson of Tennessee preached several times in 1913 to larger than usual audiences.

Notes of general information sent out ahead of the camping season are a reflection of the times:

» Good Board with lodging at the boarding house at $1.25 per day. Board without lodging $4.50 a week. Meals—dinner 50¢, breakfast or supper, 30¢; per day, $1.00. Horses fed and cared for at 25¢ a feed.
» Admission to grounds: single team by day 15¢; per season 50¢; automobiles by day 25¢; per season $1.00. Lot rents $3.00 a year; for tents $1.00; stall rents per season $1.00.
» Northern and New England Telephone connections on the grounds; daily mail by way of Enosburg Falls, Vt, R.F.D. #3
» Ask for tickets for Riverside Camp Station near South Franklin, Vt.; mark baggage plainly: Riverside Camp Station. Baggage to Grove House carried free; reasonable rates for tent baggage delivery; personal baggage delivered 5¢ each way.
» A good grocery will be run on the grounds of the Association where family provisions can be obtained for self-boarding at reasonable rates.
» Owing to great damage done in previous years by hitching horses to the trees, other hitching places have been provided. We hope all will take note of this and cooperate with the

officers of the Association in trying to preserve our beautiful grove. (From the program of St. Albans District Bible School and Camp Meeting, Sheldon, Vt., August 11th to 23rd, 1914)

The report of the Rev. W. B. Dukeshire reflects the general attitude toward camp meeting programs by 1915:

Beautiful for situation on the banks of the Missisquoi River, and in a grove that abounds in springs of water as cool and as refreshing as the Children of Israel found at Elim, is Riverside Camp Meeting of St. Albans District. The isolated nature of its location, the kind of people who attend its services, together with the fact that so many preachers must be employed who have no special training for their work, make it imperative that the work of our camp meeting be educative and inspirational for ministers and other Christian workers. At least one strong leader and teacher in Methodism is secured every season to give a course of addresses of practical value to the preachers on the District. Last year, Dr. Wallace McMullen of Drew Theological School gave five days of service that were of great value. During camp meeting week, which is the last week of the session, Dr. C. K. Jessess, of Easton, assisted helpfully in the work. The work of the Woman's Foreign Missionary Society and of the Woman's Home Missionary Society was represented.

For the next several years such sports as baseball, football, tennis, running, jumping, boating, swimming, and campfires were the order of the day. All available cottages were used, tents were pitched, hammocks swung, and some persons even had to go to adjoining villages to find lodging. The hotel (The Grove House) register showed guests from Montreal, Easton, Malden, Fitchburg, Worcester, Washington, D.C., Chicago, New York City, Ohio, California, Rhode Island, Texas, Connecticut, and Nebraska. All of this indicated the strength of the programs and satisfaction with the location and available accommodations. An electric generator was installed so that evening services could be held in the tabernacle. Both vocal music and a twelve-piece orchestra added interest to the services.

By 1922 it was announced that the campground was the authorized camp meeting for the Vermont Conference. A Governors' Day was held with addresses by the current as well as former governors and state officers. Sunday offerings were large, and the camp was in good financial condition. Porch conversations centered on the effects of radio and the automobile on Christian ministry; whether the entrance fee at the tollgate should be discontinued; and the influence of the camp as a Methodist Boys' Training Center, an institute for church school workers, and a training camp for serious Bible students.

By the 1930s the emphasis had shifted to a family-centered focus. Charles Chayer made the statement that the way was "now open for this camp to mean to Vermont Methodism what Old Hedding means to New Hampshire Methodists, and Ocean Park, Maine, means to the Christian forces of New England."

A Golden Jubilee, celebrating the fiftieth anniversary of the founding, was held the week of July 24 to 31, 1932. By this time the term "Missisquoi Institute" was commonly used along with the designation, "Riverside Campground at Sheldon, Vermont." Lavern C. Dibble described the Riverside influence at this time as "a departmentalized program with the aim of building Christian character to function effectively in the modern world." About 250 persons related to this program directly, in addition to hundreds of others who attended Sunday and special services, lectures, and other programs during the season. The goal was training for service in the local church and communicating a vision of devotional life, personal commitment, and the world mission of Christianity. Dean Dibble continued, "The challenges of social justice, race relations, and world peace are presented as essential parts of the whole gospel of Jesus Christ, nor are music, Christian art, and other life enrichment projects neglected. This year [1934] we will have parent education and home building groups." Meeting separately in this varied program were kindergarten, primary, and junior ages, intermediate and senior Epworth League institute groups, laymen's meetings and a newly offered innovation, the ministers' seminar. Attendance at the eight-day family week was about 250 for the entire time, with many additional persons attending for shorter stays. All of this activity, fifty years after the founding of Missisquoi, indicates a broad vision, a serious spiritual intent, and a sense of relevancy to changing conditions and times not found in most camp meeting associations.

A reevaluation came around 1940 spurred by the anticipated merger with Troy Conference. Should the focus now go to the Troy Conference center at Riverside on the Hudson River? Should Vermont's conference campground cease to exist? Or, should it continue with a different emphasis under a new name? The last suggestion prevailed: the Vermont Riverside became Camp Missisquoi, and the emphasis shifted to the development of a youth institute.

The Rev. Charles and Ouida Schwartz served on the staff of the new institute in August of 1941 and 1942 as persons in charge of music and Bible courses, respectively. Among other faculty members were the Rev. Fred and Winifred Engle (teacher and camp nurse, respectively), the Rev. George Butts (Congregational clergyman), Doris Kingsley, Stanley Moore (theological student), the Rev. Conrad Heins (missionary to India), and in 1942, a woman missionary from one of the Latin American countries.

The morning schedule included devotional times, Bible classes, and various aspects of local church youth work. Activities such as softball, swimming, choir practice, writing and rehearsing dramatic skits, and rehearsal for the talent night filled the afternoons. This writer recalls sitting on the piano stool for five straight hours of rehearsal with various individuals and groups for the music activities of the week. Students were encouraged to create original skits for the competition night. Judges were appointed, and first, second, and third place awards were presented. Remembering the struggle to decide the future of the campground, one enterprising group held a mock funeral as their entry in the competition. With teenage humor and confidence, they hid a small boy in a refrigerator-sized carton and with many moans and wails they bore the "coffin" to the front of the tabernacle and placed it on wooden horses to the tune of a funeral dirge. After a suitable period of mourning, the person popped from the carton and declared that youth would save the day for Riverside and secure its future with loyal service.

A number of visitors from neighboring churches, people summering on the grounds in their cottages, and the kitchen crew made up the audience for the evening performances and lectures. Good-hearted women from the Swanton church provided the food three times each day. In 1942, the Missions Banquet was prepared, with special attention to Latin American recipes under the direction of the missionary of the year. The class on Bible used the then popular "Ligon Course on the Beatitudes." Encouragement and opportunities were given for personal growth and in creative and practical leadership.

The work at Missisquoi continued to be affirmed, and yet there were underlying concerns. The report of the Board of Education to conference in 1950 recommended continuance of a summer program at Missisquoi "on a self-sustaining basis, pending development of a new campsite in that region of Troy Conference.

During the fifties, attendance of children and youth rose from around 250 to more than 350. With the addition of a swimming pool in 1956 and general improvements to the property, including the construction of new cabins, the purchase of new chairs, and the provision for weekend use, the camp could now meet the growing requests for retreats and conferences.

The sixties brought a trail camp to the list of summer offerings, which provided a different kind of outdoor experience. This decade also introduced the Missisquoi facilities and program to youngsters from the Albany Inner City Mission.

The Conference Board of Camps and Conferences reported in 1970 that, in cooperation with the Conference Board of Trustees, they had completed the purchase of the formerly privately owned cottages. The camp now had full use of all grounds, buildings, and facilities. In addition, they had a State of Vermont approved full water supply system, a new year-round retreat lodge, which doubled as a health lodge in the summer, and two new cabins. The decade of the seventies saw a new canoe camp for seniors, a limited canoe experience for junior highs, and an ecumenical bicycle camp jointly sponsored with the

Congregationalists. It was not unusual for Missisquoi to include Congregationalists in various programs through the years. Discussion of such mutual ventures had occurred in the latter part of the 1800s and was an extraordinary ecumenical feature for the times.

A hint of the commitment people showed to the camping program at Missisquoi appears in a statement in the 1979 Journal: "Following the death of her husband, Mrs. Dorothy Preston of Enosburg Falls, VT, Camp Missisquoi registrar for 26 years, decided that she could no longer hold that job as well as meet the duties she must now face alone. Camp Missisquoi was sorry to accept her resignation, and the camp's Board of Managers has recommended to the Board of Camps and Conferences that the Camp Missisquoi retreat lodge be named 'Preston Lodge' in recognition of the support that both Reuben and Dorothy Preston have given the Troy Conference camping program, and especially to Camp Missisquoi, for over a quarter of a century."

By the close of the seventies the camp leadership was grappling with increasing costs of operation and the effects of deferred maintenance. Although supportive of church camping and eager to have their children involved in its programming opportunities, parents and churches were reluctant to underwrite the increasing costs. Grove House was discovered to have rotted floor timbers and roof rafters. Still, programming on the site was sufficient to warrant having a part-time camp steward through the winter season.

In 1980, an appeal went out to the churches to finance repair or replacement of the tabernacle as part of a 1982 centennial celebration. The funding campaign was successful. Restoration was underway by 1983. The camp was solvent. Nevertheless, because of its off-center location, deterioration of other buildings, and lack of adequate water supply, all of which had plagued the work for more than twenty years, it was recommended in 1984 that a Master Plan Review Committee assess the strengths and weaknesses of the camp. Definite assets and possibilities were identified in the areas of elementary camping, summer programming for adults and families, and for intercultural camps, summer day camps, all-season retreats, and day ministry. The review committee also noted that upgrading would "take a major infusion of capital in the approximate sum of $350,000."

After sober reassessment of the facts, the committee concluded that a new location was the irrefutable answer to Vermont United Methodist camping needs. It was not that Missisquoi died! On the contrary, in its last year Camp Missisquoi accommodated 330 campers for a total of 1891 camper days. The very successful day camp set a pattern for a similar plan at Skye Farm in New York State.

A final statement appears in the 1989 Journal: "The trustees have proceeded with the sale of Camp Missisquoi according to the direction of the 1988 session of Troy Annual Conference. The property

Bad News

The Camp Missisquoi Master Plan Review Committee brought bad news to the Board of Camps and Conferences in October 1984. The following assessments are taken from their report.

1) Preston Lodge—above average condition but shower doesn't drain properly and no footers under the building
2) Pool—usable but needs to be sealed, painted and something done about tar coming up through cracks in the bottom
3) Water supply—inadequate and the spring house can be flooded with rain contaminating the supply
4) Toleroy—not usable as living quarters
5) Dugan—not usable
6) Grove House—unsafe, dry rot in dining hall floor, floor under freezer gave way

And after numerous additional repairs, replacements and upgrades, the camp would still be very small. So while it could continue to have an important and vital ministry, it would not be self-sustaining.

was put out to bid and an offer of $230,000 was accepted."

When Troy Annual Conference directed its trustees to sell Camp Missisquoi, it was more than the usual business transaction. The cross by the riverside, the bell, and items from the venerable tabernacle were incorporated into the development plan of a new camp, but the intangible legacy of spirit and tradition was of even greater value than these simple artifacts. Certain characteristic qualities were apparent from the official beginning of Missisquoi in 1882: traits of relevancy to the spiritual and temporal needs of people, a devotion to Christian belief, witness, and education, and a farsighted willingness to cooperate with other denominations. These distinguishing features set Missisquoi apart from other camp meetings of the era. No price could be placed on this legacy of spirit which was transmitted to the new Covenant Hills Christian Camp.

Tribute must be given to the continuous stream of volunteer support from local pastors and laity during 106 years of ministry at

Riverside on the Missisquoi. Faithful volunteers have made a long and determined effort to nurture a growing knowledge of God and a respect for God's world and other people. It is significant that ecumenical inclusiveness, which was traditional at Missisquoi, was continued with the United Church of Christ at the new facility. Rich in achievement, faithful in commitment, abundant in service, bold in venturing with visionary faith, the Missisquoi legacy now handed to the new camp, Covenant Hills in Cabot, VT, exceeds monetary value. The heirs have a worthy heritage to enjoy and noble standards to attain from over a century of loyal camp ministry in the cause of Christ.

For well over 100 years, camp meetings were a significant part of the ministries of Troy Conference. Pastors and laity, youth and adults alike, found refreshment, fellowship, and renewal in these settings. Even in what we think of as simpler times, it was important to have places that became holy ground because they were set apart. The 1962 Journal memoir for the Rev. Charles Porter Hogle notes, "For nearly 20 years Brother Hogle served as platform manager of the Mooers Camp Meeting, where he always presided with grace and wisdom."

Mooers camp meeting

Methodist Farm at Crooked Lake

In late 1910, several pastors of Methodist Episcopal churches in Troy and vicinity held a conference to think about ways of stimulating the work of their Sunday Schools. One meeting led to another, and soon they came to the idea of holding a Union Picnic to bring even more churches and people together. The event held in June 1911 at Tibbets-Warren Grove in Beman Park in Troy, was an amazing success. The churches—and the weather—cooperated to produce an attendance of six thousand.

This enthusiastic beginning encouraged plans for

Camping at Crooked Lake

Merle and Catherine Doud

In the early 1960s we found a camp available at Methodist Farm on Crooked Lake. It was a wonderful place for children to spend their summer vacation; they didn't lack for friends and things to do. One plus was having a lifeguard on duty. The lifeguard also taught children to swim.

Vacation Bible School was available all summer. On the weekends, a movie played each Saturday night in the enclosed pavilion, which also served as the chapel for Sunday night vesper services. Area pastors filled these spots on Sundays.

At the top of the hill was a little store that provided necessities and lots of candy choices. Across the road, a beloved camper, C. Malden Wells, had a "flea market" in a barn. We gave him our unwanted articles to sell, which brought in revenue for the farm.

Picnic facilities were available to anyone for a slight fee, but member churches of the association had free access. Each member church received a number of free passes to enter the grounds during the summer months.

The site was called Methodist Farm because part of the property originally was used for farming. Most of the camps, however, which began as tent sites and then became tent platforms before evolving into permanent cabins, were shaded by trees. Despite the rocky soil and lack of sunlight near the cabins, a few people tried to have gardens. Some flowers did fairly well, but one year a neighbor put in a couple of tomato plants. The plants struggled to survive through the summer, but near the end of the season several large ripe tomatoes could be seen in the foliage. It turned out that the fruits had come from the market and were inserted with a vain hope continued cooperation among the churches. A second picnic was held in September. This one drew not quite so many, but still over 5500 people attended despite the threat of bad weather all morning. This second success encouraged the Sunday Schools of Troy, Cohoes, Waterford, Watervliet, and Green Island to form the Methodist Sunday School Association of Troy and Vicinity. One of the things they wanted was a more permanent location for summertime activities. Around 1915, the Stiles Farm on Crooked Lake in Averill Park became available. The association soon incorporated and purchased the property.

One early improvement was the digging of a deep well to provide drinkable water. Some of the lake front property was sold on the open market to meet operating expenses. However, the association soon realized that this could lead to the loss of all desirable locations. Instead, tenting sites were rented on a yearly basis. This approach allowed families to camp on the site at minimal cost. The leases were available only to the members of the churches making up the association. In the course of time, tent sites were replaced, first by tent platforms and later by permanent camps.

Through the years the camps, though fairly rustic, were modernized with electricity and running water, including connections to the town sewer system. Many families got into the habit of spending the summer at Methodist Farm. For some, the commute to work from the farm was hardly more onerous than the trip from home.

Among other program offerings, in the summer of 1990 Methodist Farm held a series of day camps for elementary age children from kindergarten through third grade. The opportunities were published in the regular camping brochure, along with camp offerings at Skye Farm and Covenant Hills.

As of 2009, a dozen United Methodist Sunday Schools from Averill Park to North Chatham to Troy to Latham to West Sand Lake made up the association. The annual

> of fooling those who had rightfully doubted all along.
>
> During the time of Joel and Trudy Shippey's pastorate at Waterford, our very active Asbury Club for young adult couples would gather at our camp for the annual chicken barbecue. Trudy had a recipe from Cornell that we used. Imagine the confusion when thirty or more people packed into our little camp when it rained!

meeting, as required by charter, is still on the third Tuesday of April. The draw of camping as part of the religious and educational experience continues to thrive in our midst.

Skye Farm

The rich campmeeting tradition in Troy Conference brought numerous satisfactions. That style of ministry brought many people to a deeper appreciation for God and for the natural setting. Christian education, especially training in Christian education, flourished in the many institutes offered across the conference. Still, in the 1930s it became clear that a different approach was required.

The Rev. C. Walter Kessler, at that time with about ten years of pastoral experience, tells the story of how the call to a new kind of camp came to be broadly heard across the conference. Most of the description that follows, up to 1945, comes from Rev. Kessler, even though he modestly refers to himself in the third person.

The idea of summer camping for young people came to Troy Conference early in 1938. At a meeting of the Board of Education where it was discussed, everyone favored such a project, but since youth work had been confined to institutes and the conference had no such property suitable for camping, the usual motion was made to appoint a study committee. However, the younger people present proposed the idea of an experimental camp for that summer.

A committee was appointed to undertake the assignment. C. W. Kessler volunteered to be camp director and agreed to take a course of study on camping at Columbia and to attend a training conference on summer work for youth. Both experiences furnished excellent guidance in the theory of experimental camping.

The Warren County Boy Scout Council loaned its campsite at Skye Pond for one week in the summer of 1939. There, 26 junior high youngsters, four counselors—including a life guard, a cook and a nurse—plus the director spent six days studying, singing, hiking, swimming, and worshiping without benefit of electricity or plumbing, while sleeping behind a barricade of citronella and mosquito netting. Present were Olive Steward (Mrs. Roger Trombey), Beatrice Thompson, John Cole, Jr., Edwin Moses, Mrs. Frank Bevan and Mrs. Maggie Giles, the cook. The experience was evaluated and declared successful, in spite of a major casualty—the Galilean Service. Miss Thompson planned this worship service and explained its significance. The entire camp was seated near the edge of the pond as she walked, Bible in hand, along the narrow dock to the rowboat. John Cole was waiting, oars poised, as she stepped down near the edge of the craft, which tilted over, shipped water, and left her and the helmsman standing in three feet of water. That broke up the Galilean Service!

The second and third years of camp were held on Lake Pleasant at Camp Agaming (in Speculator, NY), which was rented from the YMCA. Most of the staff attended camp and institute training sessions in New York City to receive program tips and practical hints for their task. Registrations were limited to sixty young people each summer. The camp director planned both the program and the menu, enlisted his staff, hired the cook, recruited a nurse and a lifeguard, acted as registrar and business manager, and ordered the supplies and foodstuff. The sessions lasted ten days with outdoor activities including hiking, swimming and row boating on the lake for recreation. Sunday found the camp packing the little church at Lake Pleasant to hear the Rev. Clarence Winchell preach. Each year so many young people were turned away from these camps that the need was felt for at least two sessions each summer. Since no facility could be rented for such a period of time, the search began for other locations.

In 1942 three men—Luther A. Brown, H. Elliot Chaffee, and C. Walter Kessler—sat on a big boulder near the outlet of a beautiful lake that nestled among the majestic Adirondack Mountains and reflected the glorious green of the forest. They were sensitive to the Eternal Presence in this setting of natural beauty. What if such a place as this could be used to inspire boys and girls with the same awareness of God that they felt? Surely this was the ideal spot for a Christian adventure camp.

Out of their prayerful conversation, a vision appeared and a

Three Men on a Rock

The three men on a rock by the outlet of a beautiful pond were all pastors. Rev. Dr. Luther A. Brown served in Troy Conference from 1903 until his retirement from Round Lake in 1938. He had been active in the summer institutes at Riverside. Rev. H. Elliott Chaffee served in several other conferences before his appointment to Saratoga Springs in 1935. At the time of the meeting he was at First Methodist, Pittsfield, MA. He later went on to be assistant to the president of Green Mountain Junior College for several years. Rev. C. W. Kessler came to Troy from the Kentucky Conference in 1932. After Beekmantown and Point Au Roche, he served at Chestertown (1933-1934) and then Corinth (1935–1940) before his appointment to Cobleskill (1941-1949). In 1968 he became the first Troy Conference program director.

compact was formed. The eldest of the three, [Luther Brown] a silver-haired veteran of the faith, would give his land for the Christian education of young people, if his younger comrades would see the project through. And so, one hundred and forty acres of mountains, brooks, and lakeshore were dedicated to God, and Skye Farm was born. Numbers of willing hearts gave money, scores of willing hands built the dining hall and cabins, and a host of willing minds planned programs and sent their youth to camp. Christian stewardship made the dream come true.

Impressed by the zeal and mounting interest among this small army of enthusiastic workers, Dr. and Mrs. Brown additionally decided to deed to Skye Farm their twenty-acre lot with its cottage and buildings and eight hundred feet of excellent lakeshore. They drew keen satisfaction from the fact that their largess provided Troy Conference youth with an adequate camp property second to none in possibilities.

Edwin Moses, a student at Syracuse University, under the able direction of Professor Bradford G. Sears, designed the camp layout. The conference trustees loaned $1200 for building materials; a dozen people gave $50 apiece to build the small, waney-edge cabins that are still in use after over thirty years. The building now called the "Tepee" and the 12 other cabins were built by pastors and laymen who gave their time and labor. ("Tepee" is short for trading post and, among other things, is the location of the camp store. Many years later the Tepee received the official designation of H. Elliot Chaffee Lodge in honor of Rev. Chaffee's role in founding the camp.) Hands-on investors in the camp were the Revs. Leon M. Adkins Sr., Lloyd Olson, C. W. Kessler, O. F. Ireson, and L.R. Stapley, along with J. C. Jansen, Itsuzo Sumy, Irwin Shafter, J. L. DuMond, Herman Shafter, and many others. Baker & Sons sawed lumber. The Kessler Lumber Company of Wichita, Kansas, furnished prefabricated rafters at cost. Part of the difficulty in getting the camp started was due to the war effort, with the rationing of food and fuel, and yet rationing boards generously provided the necessary stamps for gasoline, meat, sugar and butter.

The entire operation began as a low-budget facility, but with the lake and the mountain setting how could it fail? The Revs. Orrin Ireson and Leon Stapley directed camp sessions and Walter Kessler was business manager. In 1943 a session of junior camp was introduced with Rev. Elburt Parkhurst, pastor at Schroon Lake, as director. Parkhurst's use of Indian lore at his camp was so thorough-going that one pastor sourly remarked he had not sent his kids to camp to become good Indians but better Christians.

Very early at Skye Farm, the hike around the lake and the climbs to the haunted house and to Buck Mountain overlook became annual activity highlights. Annually the splendid grove of Norway pines became the scene of a big get-together of neighbors and friends who came for miles for a gala picnic and chowder party.

A word about the old building used as a kitchenette for activities operating out of the Tepee. This was the original home of Lemuel Sherman, who owned the farm, cleared the land, tilled the fields, dug the old well on the hill, laid the massive stones for the cellar, and built the plank house. No wall studs supported this old building, which now wears a handsome plywood interior—just three layers of overlapping white pine boards, 1 and 1/4" thick. The well, fifty feet away, was dug by hand and beautifully lined with stone. The old plank house must have often rung with the laughter of children, for the Shermans raised their family there. Years later, he built a more pretentious house near the lakeshore where the dining hall now stands, the basement of which is still used for storage of food and supplies.

Mr. Sherman became a legendary figure, in part because of the stone fences he built and the rock plateau he filled in at the lakeshore at the brook outlet. Each spring he would load the rocks and boulders thrust up by winter frost and, using an ox-drawn stone boat, carry them to the rock fill or the fences. Because of these prodigious labors, it is said that he was simian in appearance, with arms stretched down until they reached his knees. But this is only a tall tale. Those who knew him say he was proportioned just like other Adirondack farmers.

Mr. Brooks, father-in-law of Luther Brown, acquired the farm, and the Browns inherited it from him. When Dr. Brown was a "Presiding

According to one line of evidence, the name "Skye Farm" dates back to long before the camp was established. Apparently, Mrs. Luther Brown used that title as she enjoyed the cottage beside the lake in 1918. The lake itself has had several names over the years—Long Pond, Daisy Pond, Sherman Pond and now, officially, Sherman Lake.

Elder", he used to use the lakeshore house as a place to spend the night when he was making his round of Fourth Quarterly Conferences by horse and buggy on the district. Daisy Lake, as it was then called, was advertised as a paradise for fishermen by the D&H Railroad, which ran excursions to Warrensburg.

As you climb the hill from the dining hall to the recreation hall, you now observe tall white pine trees halfway up the hill. Dr. Brown planted these when the entire hillside was an open meadow. The line of little trees reminded him of his nephew's children, who often spent a week's vacation with their parents in the old farmhouse on the hill, and who daily climbed the hill in single file after having had a swim in the lake.

The camp received the name "Skye Farm" after careful consideration of proposed alternatives. The chosen name was suggested by Mrs. H. Elliot Chaffee and represents the canopy of heaven above watching over all the activities and experiences that consecrated leaders, devoted counselors, and eager young people enjoy. The dream that came to Luther Brown and his two companions while they sat on a boulder in 1942 thus continues to inspire, encourage and stimulate today.

Leaving behind Kessler's narrative of Skye Farm, we most assuredly do not leave behind his influence. In 1943, annual conference presented Rev. Kessler with a purse to express appreciation for his work in developing and turning over to conference the property at Sherman Lake. He promptly contributed the purse to the offering for retired supply pastors. Some of the motives behind the push for a camping program may be glimpsed in the report from the Commission on Education in Social Action for the same year. The commission expressed great concern for the rising incidence of juvenile delinquency. Contributing factors to this rise were identified as the "high incomes of high school youth, child labor, easy accessibility of vice, of alcoholic beverages, of gambling opportunities, of relaxation in home disciplines and of indiscriminate movie going."

While pastoral commitment to summer programs was growing, so was a certain kind of tension in the local churches. Pastors were welcome to lead and attend camp but only by giving up vacation time. The 1944 conference addressed the situation by noting that "leadership for summer institutes, camps and caravans has been and is being furnished for the most part by ministers." So, local churches were asked to "release pastors for reasonable periods of time for their valuable conference service, provide pulpit supplies in their absence and in no wise lessen their normal vacation periods because of service to and participation in these conference projects." The matter was revisited in 1947 when, by motion of C. W. Kessler, conference voted that a minister serving on camp or institute staff be excused from a week of parish duties and on Sunday his pulpit, and further, that the church provide a pulpit supply and impose no penalty on his usual vacation.

In 1945, a special session of conference in Glens Falls approved the loan of $12,000 to build a recreation hall at the top of the hill and four pre-fabricated cabins on the meadow hillside. (Not too long after that, the recreation building was named Kessler Hall, in recognition of the contributions to the camp made by Walter Kessler and the Kessler family.)

The 1946 session of conference noted a broader concern. Some 600 youth had attended various camps and institutes the preceding summer. Following the recommendation of the Board of Education came a vote to "study the Vermont situation" (Recall that the Vermont and Troy Conferences merged in 1941) and authorize the Board of Trustees to advance up to $7,500 for the further development of Skye Farm.

Interestingly enough, the memoir for the Rev. Luther A. Brown appears in the 1947 Journal, with no mention of

Camping opportunities from "The Traveler"

The Traveler, the MYF conference newsletter, edition of May 1944, was written at a time when two ways of "camping" intersected. The lead article outlines the transition. "Troy Conference offers its youth a variety of summer camps and institutes. These programs vary in both setting and content. The camps major in an outdoor program: camp clothing is worn, and cabins provide sleeping quarters. Several of our institutes have traditional services and social events that highlight their programs. Accommodations are usually in dormitories and cottages. Some camps and institutes have exceptional facilities, which are used with maximum effectiveness. Others need to be developed; there you will find an opportunity for worthy service."

The list of summer programs shows just that mix of interests at a variety of sites. There are opportunities at Missisquoi, Claremont, Riverside, Lake Sherman, Teela-Wooket (run by the Congregational Conference in Vermont), Green Mountain (at the college), and an early June work camp for adults at Skye Farm. The Traveler advertised the then-new song book, "Sing It Again" (12 cents a copy), which contained music for diverse settings. "God of Grace and God of Glory," and "For All the Saints" are only pages away from "Waltzing Matilda" and "I'm Going to Leave Old Texas Now."

Lorraine Agan remembers

I think it was the summer of 1947 when I took a job at Skye Farm as assistant cook. I was engaged at the time and didn't like having to leave Bill for so long. We served meals in the old dining hall on the hill. One item I remember from the menu was prune whip. We served that very often. We stayed in a small hogan near the dining hall. It had a net over the door to keep some of his role in the establishment of Skye Farm. Though clearly significant and generous, his actions went unrecognized at his death.

The 1948 Journal makes specific mention of Camp Mohawk I and II held at Skye Farm, junior camps at Skye Farm and Missisquoi, and additional camps at Enosburg Falls, Camp Riparious, and Claremont Junction. More detail on "Skye Farm on Lake Sherman," the first full report of its kind, appears in the report of the Board of Education. The six-week program hosted 325 campers supported by 85 counselors, along with a full time lifeguard, full time manager, and full time commissary staff. The dining hall had a new aluminum roof. On the wish list was the hope "that a fleet of non-sinking row boats may be provided for the waterfront."

Responsibility for the conference camping program resided with the Conference Board of Education. That group accepted its obligation with great enthusiasm and sincerity. For example, in 1950 the board reported to conference, "For many years much of the most thrilling and encouraging Christian work in Troy Conference has been done through the program of Camps, Institutes and Conferences carried on each summer... The fruits of these summers have been gathered in our local churches—in unrecorded numbers of ministers, missionaries and laymen whose dedication in home, church and community has been as pillars of strength for Troy Conference Christianity." Yet, the report continues, "All of us are aware that the summer work has been carried out often under the handicaps of poor or makeshift facilities, inadequate funds and other adverse conditions... In the countrywide movement among Methodists to provide better facilities for what is increasingly recognized as a most important phase of Christian work, Troy Conference has lagged far behind other conferences. Secular agencies with modern facilities are offering increasing competition to our camps and institutes for our youth."

The response to this clearly perceived need was the

the bugs out. The program for the kids included taking hikes and preparing skits. We also had regular evening vespers. The bats were always flying around us at that time of day. Most of all, I remember it as a peaceful place.

Sustained Forestry

Dick Nason, Forester

Owning land in the Adirondacks naturally raises the issue of land management. When I first became active at Skye Farm in 1985, there were some who assumed that the best idea was to just let the forest be "forever wild." It took a while for me to convince people that real stewardship of the land involved sustainable care for the property. First of all, the Skye Farm site is not original wilderness. All of what we see now is second growth at best. When you find stone walls running through the forest, you can be sure that the land on at least one side of the wall, if not on both sides, was under cultivation. This is Skye "farm," so we know that years ago this land was harvested for timber and then used as open fields.

Another thing is that we don't actually use the land as wilderness. We have campers living in, and actively moving through, the woods. Dead trees are dangerous to people and buildings. Diseased trees can harbor pests that threaten our neighbors' livelihood. Underbrush on the forest floor can be a fire hazard. So it makes sense to keep track of how trees are doing and remove those that are threats.

There is also the issue of the carbon cycle and our carbon footprint. A large, healthy tree puts oxygen into the air, but as a tree ages it may not do that effectively anymore. The goal is to have a mix of young and mature trees, so that when the older ones are harvested the younger ones can take over the space and recruitment of Bradford G. Sears from Syracuse University, who had helped with the original planning of the camp in the early 1940s, to create a master plan that would include Missisquoi, Riverside, and Skye Farm. One of his key recommendations involved revising the specifications for Skye Farm to allow up to 150 persons to use the facility at the same time. The budget for this development was fixed at a maximum of $48,000.

The board continued to reflect on the nature of the experience they were seeking to provide. The central concept was that church camping was "an extension of the local church program of Christian education and fellowship." It was not expected to be a "carbon copy of private, Scout or public school camp." The goal was to help campers see "the world and the interesting life around them as part of God's created world."

Interest in and use of the camp continued to grow. In the summer of 1952 all the Skye Farm camps were filled to capacity. The site boasted a new boys' washhouse, a pressurized water system, a refrigeration unit for the kitchen, and many minor improvements. The organizational structure was changed, too, with the creation of a Committee on Camps and Conferences to facilitate all the aspects of camping from program materials, training sessions, and interpretation of church camps to overseeing the staff and supervising the care, insurance, upkeep and maintenance of the property.

The conference session of 1954 initiated the Rev. George L. Fox scholarship fund to enable more youth to attend Christian camps and institutes. The Rev. Fox was one of the "Four Chaplains" who sailed on the troop ship SS Dorchester in 1943. When torpedoes attacked the ship, the chaplains gave up their life jackets so that others might survive. Fox was a member of Troy Conference, and this scholarship was understood to be a suitable memorial, both to his heroism and to his active involvement in youth work.

The camping report noted that in the summer of

grow vigorously.

So, I began with a cruise of the property to see what trees were where and gathered data for a master plan. I found which trees needed to come out for firewood, which ones could be harvested and sold, and which ones could be cut into lumber for use at the camp. Through the years we've been able to keep the property in a dynamic balance—old, overcrowded trees came out and other trees thrived. Every few years a number of trees are ready, and they come down so that others can take their place.

Sustainable forestry is good for the camp and the environment. It shows campers a wise way to use our natural resources without abusing them and actually maintains the site for future generations. So when people hear my 18" chainsaw at work in the woods, they should realize I'm being very careful about what trees are coming down. They can sit at their campfire at night and enjoy it, knowing the wood came from a tree that had already done its part to make Skye Farm a special place.

1953 nearly 750 youth were involved in a variety of camping experiences. Specific mention is made of the fact that Skye Farm offered the Red Cross senior lifesaving course, among other camping opportunities.

In a plea that resonated through the years, the Rev. Al Strobel, then chair of campsite development, spoke to potential divisions between Vermont and New York camping interests with the comment, "Let us operate on a conference basis, as planned and previously ordered, rather than on a campsite basis." Generally through the years that small bit of wisdom helped conference to balance needs, sacrifices, support, and opportunity across a conference that otherwise might have become divided over state or site-oriented interests.

In 1954, conference voted to employ a full time conference director of youth work. In March 1955 Rev. Leonard Bass, coming to live in Glens Falls from the Northern New York Conference, began to fill that position. Howard Grout became the Skye Farm business manager, a role he filled until 1959 and then shared with Al Cederstrom in 1961. Al continued to serve as camp manager for some time after that.

The camping program was burgeoning. Reports in 1955 showed 100 campers turned away from the summer program due to lack of leadership or equipment. The following year saw over 1000 youth and children involved in summer programs. Typically about half of these would have attended Skye Farm and Missisquoi and the other half the various additional institutes and training sessions held at a variety of venues. Some 200 adult leaders were required to meet the leadership needs.

The report for the 1956 Skye Farm season celebrated the construction of a new health lodge, the purchase of a deep freeze unit for the kitchen, and the installation of "a much needed telephone." That same year, over 1200 youth were involved in the conference summer programs at Skye Farm, Missisquoi, Paul Smith College, Claremont Junction Campground, and Green Mountain College.

The "Sears" Master Plan from the early 50s continued to be relevant at Skye Farm. In 1957 plans for the "new" central washhouse began to take shape. In a hint of the kind of support always important to the camping program, it was noted that "some of the finishing work is to be done by work groups from local congregations." Preliminary plans had been drawn up for the new dining hall on the site of the Sherman family farmhouse overlooking the lake. Construction was set to begin as soon as the necessary funds became available. Central washhouse was completed in 1958, and the price of the new dining hall was optimistically set at $24,000.

Reports in 1960 noted that attendance at camp

continued to increase. The previous summer program involved over 1520 youth and nearly 360 counselors. Again, this number was spread across a wide variety of sites, but between them Skye Farm and Missisquoi continued to attract more than half the total number. Programming also included some specialty camps such as the fourth annual family life camp at Skye Farm. The total cost for that camp was the registration fee of $10.

International Counselors

One long-standing feature of Troy Conference camping is the recruitment of international counselors. As far back as the time of Leonard Bass, campers have had the opportunity to interact with people from other cultures. In 2007, we had ten staff members from places as diverse as England, Germany, Hungary, Poland, Russia, South Korea and Zimbabwe. They are described as "wonderful people" who bring both an interesting and uplifting aspect to the summer experience. Some of them struggle with English, but the language barrier turns out not to be a barrier after all as they go about their work of relating to the campers in a warm Christian way. This experience gives them a chance for language immersion, although we hope they can sort out standard English from what other things they might learn from interaction with the campers.

A young man from Australia served as a counselor at Skye Farm and enjoyed the experience so much that he has come back at his own expense for several summers. He got paid but probably not quite enough to cover the air fare from half-way round the world. Making the most of his involvement here, he also went on a VIM trip to Maine before heading back home.

One story of how connections are formed dates back to the late 1970s after a counselor from the Congo returned home. A year or so later, his daughter was

The summer of 1961 saw over 680 campers at Skye Farm. The camp made good use of the new dining hall, which came in at a cost of $36,500, including equipment. The trading post got a new freezer and stove, and four new tent platforms were built with two more planned. The old craft shop now offered staff living quarters upstairs (Bachelors' Hall) and a workshop underneath.

In 1962, the board purchased an additional 240 acres (the Robertson Property) to add to the program opportunities for Skye Farm. This land eventually became the site for Ogden Lodge and Shippey Lodge.

Skye Farm leadership worked to offer an ever- increasing range of camping opportunities. In 1963, the program included 45 different options for youth—including canoe camp and hiking camp, which were new choices that year. Family camp continued to attract attention with 150 attending one of the Sunday services. The Rev. Jim Rhodes and the Rev. Charon Denson teamed up to offer a safari camp (see Appendix B) to visit a variety of mission stations. Meanwhile, in April 1964, the Rev. George Miller became the director of youth work. He held this position until 1968.

At a special session in October 1966, conference voted to initiate a fundraising effort called the "For This Hour Crusade." The intent of the near-million dollar crusade was to raise money for church extension ministries, for the Saratoga Retirement Center, and $240,000 for the work of Camps and Conferences.

Meanwhile, the camping program continued to thrive in terms of the numbers of campers. At the same time, the shortage of volunteer counselors was becoming "very acute." Without additional lay and clergy volunteers, it would become necessary to use paid staff, which in turn would require either a subsidy by annual conference or an increase in the registration rates.

The crusade moved forward, eventually generating over $176,000 for the camping program. A portion of those funds went to the building of Ogden Lodge on a portion diagnosed with a serious kidney problem. He wrote asking if there was anything his Skye Farm friends might be able to do. Within a short time, George and Ann Voland, Rev. Steve and Joan Butler, and some others had made a number of remarkably helpful connections: Methodist Hospital in Brooklyn, Pan Am Airways, a ham radio operator in Essex Junction who was able to reach a missionary in Ghana, a hotel in New York, and others from Skye Farm who helped with monetary contributions. The trip soon came together. The girl and her mother safely arrived. The health issues now took a strange twist. On closer examination, the girl did not have a serious condition after all: the earlier X-rays were quite misleading. Thankfully, the anticipated surgery was not needed. But, someone along the way noticed that the girl's mother had very puffy ankles. The doctors checked the mother and found she was suffering from extreme congestive heart failure. They were able to treat that in a timely fashion, and a finally healthy family was reunited in the Congo.

A Letter from Ruben Jacobi

When I look back to the camp I think I never had such a good time in my life and made so many experiences in this short time.

Rubin Jacobi at home in the snows of Germany, 2009

In the beginning of the summer you know it was so difficult for me to talk and understand all the stuff I had to do. During the first weeks I learned so much English to talk a little bit like you guys and this would never happen if all of you didn't help me so much.

BIG THANKS for that!! I had a sooo good summer with the nicest American people of the world :)

of the Skye Farm property set off from the original main camp area. The lodge was named after the Rev. Dr. Terrance F. Ogden (1899–1962), a long-time youth leader of the conference, whose family gave generously to the project in his memory. Additional funds were given to the project in memory of Mr. Glenn Shanholtzer and through a bequest from Mr. Frank Palmer. This lodge, designed to be used year round, included central heating, a number of dormitory rooms with shower and toilet facilities, a kitchen, and large comfortable meeting area. The focus on amenities was intended to make the site more attractive to adults interested in a retreat atmosphere, rather than the more out-of-doors experience that was the usual thrust of the camping program.

Bishop Wicke dedicated the lodge on September 19, 1971. Just over five months later, on February 23, 1972, Ogden burned to the ground due to a furnace malfunction. Fortunately, the building was not in use at the time so no one was injured. It took a while for the insurance claims to be settled, but the rebuilt lodge

Retreat lodge fire, February 1972

was dedicated in September 1973. The stunning double-sided fireplace dominates the common room, which provides both dining space and meeting space for over thirty people.

Ogden Lodge, 1973

Meanwhile, work continued on the upgrade of the main camp. The year 1971 saw the construction of a junior washhouse, four new cabins, and the purchase of twelve canoes

Judy Palmer remembers

It is 1975 and we are driving in a fully loaded car up the Northway to get off at exit 24 and make the trip up the dirt road to Skye Farm. Our three children are with us: Tim almost 7, Christina 4-1/2, and Julie 10 months. We are on our way to camp to work for the summer for the first time. Dick was hired to be maintenance supervisor, and the family has come along. With great anticipation, we round the corner by the big rock on the upper dirt road, stretching our necks to see what is ahead. It is warm at the end of June and windows are open, allowing the scent of pine to be the dominant smell.

And for the succeeding thirty years Dick and I have followed much the same pattern as we worked for Troy Conference camping. For many years, it was with the children as they went through their childhoods at camp, for some years when they were also employed there, and now, for many years when Dick and I have made the trip alone to be part of the summer staff. The anticipation grows as we look forward to connecting with returning staff like ourselves, meeting new staff members, greeting campers who will spend a week or more at camp, enjoying the many extraordinary volunteers who give a week or more of their time to enhance the program, and, of course, smelling the smells of the woods and living in those woods for the summer in a simpler life style. For us and many others, the season allows a homecoming to a place that has become a peaceful "safe sanctuary," a place that feeds and renews our souls.

Skye Farm is in a beautiful setting of many acres of woods on a picturesque Adirondack body of water, Sherman Pond. But what makes this a truly special and remarkable place are the staff, paid and volunteer, who each bring their special gifts and talents to share, and the campers who come for a summer experience. There is a great passion for what happens in this outdoor to support a growing interest in off-site programs.

The next year at annual conference, on a motion by Dr. C. W. Kessler, the new dining hall was officially named the "Luther A. Brown Pavilion." This gave permanent memorial recognition to Dr. Brown, who had given the initial 140 acres and over 800 feet of shoreline on Sherman Pond to establish Skye Farm Camp.

As the years passed, supervision of Skye Farm was becoming far more complicated than it had been originally. With more buildings and more complex systems, the facility was generally in use year-round. So, to provide oversight of both the property and programs, the decision was made in 1975 to hire a full-time steward on an experimental basis. The Rev. Harold Shippey assumed that role beginning in 1976.

About that same time, work began on another major building—a combined health lodge and retreat center at the top of the hill overlooking Sherman Pond. The facility holds up to fourteen people. Volunteers constructed the huge trusses of the common room on site. In fact, most of the building was constructed with volunteer labor. This explains why the facility and furnishings cost only slightly more than $35,000. Retreats can be scheduled for seasons when camp is not in session. When summer camp is held, it becomes the nurse's home and the infirmary.

The building was named Bass Lodge at the time of its dedication in July 1978, in honor of the Rev. Leonard Bass (1921-1981), who had served as conference director of youth work from 1955 to 1963. Officiating at the dedication were Bishop W. Ralph Ward, and the Rev. William Cotant, who had recently joined the conference in order to become the director of camping.

Over the next few years much attention went to some specialized camps. For instance, one summer offering was hospital camp, a six-day tour of hospitals and health care facilities. Additional options included gymnastics, basic horsemanship, and adult canoe camp. A camp for those ministry. What a combination, a beautiful site coupled with multitudes of caring, loving people—children, youth and adults.

There have been many changes over the years that we have known Skye Farm. In 1974 and '75, Ed Osterhout was the summer camp manager. In 1976, Harold Shippey was hired as a full-time steward to care for the site year round. He continued in that capacity for nine years, followed by Kevin Wrigley for four years, Debi Paterson for nine years, Dee Lowman for two years, and then Harold Shippey found his way back for nine more years. On Harold's retirement, David Johnston stepped into the leadership role. The job of camp steward evolved into executive director and now includes program planning for summer camp and retreats. A caretaker has responsibility for handling the site work.

The registrar's job, which I have done for 27 years, has had some changes also. When I began, the registration form was a 4" x 5" triplicate form with minimal information about the camper. This form evolved to something much larger and more complicated that includes health information, dietary and other special concerns, picture and address sharing information, and a special area for office use for financial record keeping.

The health form took a similar path, evolving from a 6" x 8" index card kept in a file box to a very complete four-page 8.5"x 11" form with health immunization records, health history questions, and a doctor's signature giving the camp nurse permission to dispense prescriptions and over-the-counter medications. The New York State Department of Health established numerous regulations that the camp has had to meet.

I remember the way financial records used to be kept—on wide spreadsheets with information entered by hand. The registrar's records, also entered by hand, were kept in spiral bound notebooks for lists of campers over 60 was led by the Rev. David Lockwood and the Rev. Howard Hills, a retired pastor named the New York State Senior Citizen of the Year in 1979. Both Skye Farm and Missisquoi offered camps for young people ages 11 to 25 with special needs. The winter program included senior high snow camp, winter picnics, a November retreat for families considering ways to de-commercialize Christmas, and a clergy family ski retreat. By 1980, six cabins on the main camp were winterized with insulation and heated by wood stoves.

Special offerings for 1982 included an adult running camp, three-day mini camps for first-time campers, music camp, confirmation camp, and small-boat sailing camp. Under the title "Clearwater in the 80s," senior highs could participate in a Hudson River environmental awareness camp. The Rev. Newton Perrins led this camp, which started at Lake Tear of the Clouds, headwater of the Hudson River, and ended at Albany after three days of backpacking, canoeing, and white water rafting.

In the mid 1980s, clown camp, video camp, clown ministry, and computer camp followed. Options expanded later to include a Canadian fishing camp, Red Bird mission work, a ten-day worship caravan that toured the conference, drama camp, and a work camp in Washington, DC at Ram's Horn Urban Ministry.

Typically, new programs and camping opportunities were introduced without much ado. However, in response to the growing awareness of AIDS and HIV, a camp for AIDS victims, the "Quality of Life Retreat," was scheduled for the summer of 1987. This camp would provide an inclusive, hospitable setting and provide an opportunity to talk about needs and pain. Concerns over the wisdom of such an event led to the unusual step of a resolution coming on the floor of conference to cancel the offering. After considerable discussion the resolution was defeated, and the camp was held under the direction of the Rev. Richard W. Neal. The Board of Camps and Conferences later declared by church, and in 3-ring binders for lists of those registered at weekly camps and what had been paid on each account. This all changed with the introduction of the computer. Now we generate labels to send campers their own brochure each year as soon as they become available. Record keeping became more sophisticated, and computers gave us the ability to generate all kinds of reports.

Several additions have been made to the site since 1975, including Bass Lodge, Ms. Manor, two picnic pavilions, a new maintenance shop, Tucker washhouse, an equipment storage shed, a nature pavilion and camper cabins. Staff West and Staff Northwest have been replaced with newer buildings. The trading post and the dining hall have been upgraded. The waterfront has been improved with a terraced beach, a new canoe dock, and an improved swimming dock.

Amidst the upgrades and changes, some things remain as constant threads in the fabric of Skye Farm: no electricity in camper cabins, campfires at the end of the day, cookouts over the wood fire. This approach has contributed to a rustic atmosphere that gives campers a chance to experience a simpler, less complicated life at camp. Experiences in their daily lives may have become more complicated, but children come to camp with the same needs from year to year. They need to be respected, cared for, and cared about. They still wonder what cabin they will be in, who will be with them, will they be accepted and liked, and can they survive for a week away from home. Each camper sets foot on common ground. It is everyone's backyard, and each person is treated as a unique and special person.

It could be 1975 or 2009. The noise in the dining hall is the same: happy chatter as the campers come in their family groups to share a meal, singing after meals as their voices fill the air with joyful sounds. Sometimes the ministry a success and encouraged a continued commitment to that work.

The 1982 report of the board notes that the need for this style of ministry continued as strong as ever. Over 1300 campers enjoyed time at Skye Farm and Missisquoi—the best year yet. At a time when other conferences and other denominations were closing camps, Troy Conference facilities were busy. Indeed, "Skye Farm [was] looking at preliminary plans for another retreat lodge." The report went on to say, "Funding and construction is at least a year away." That "at least" turned out to be an astounding understatement, as it would be more than twenty-five years before the groundbreaking. Despite the delays, the dream continued to flourish.

The summer of 1982 saw the dedication of the Skye Farm nature pavilion in memory of Todd Barnes. The pavilion provides a place out of the sun and rain for campers to consider the natural world. It serves as a starting point for expeditions around the camp and functions as a mini-museum of natural history. Sometimes various wild creatures get temporary housing there, so that more campers can see some of the less obvious inhabitants of the woods and lakeshore.

That summer of '82 also gave the camp an opportunity to demonstrate the principles of Christian hospitality and care for others on which it is founded. Riding High Ranch, located directly across the lake, caters to tourists and vacationers. One night that camp suffered a serious fire that destroyed their dining hall. The permanent and volunteer staff at Skye Farm extended an invitation to the Riding High folks and provided them with meals while they got reorganized. One of the larger Riding High craft served as a nearly constant ferry, bringing people back and forth across the lake.

In 1985, conference approved a major camping fund drive with two main purposes: to build a new retreat lodge at Skye Farm and to address identified deficiencies at the hill leading to the lower part of camp is so quiet you can't imagine there are a hundred children on site. Then over the top of the hill comes a cabin group of kids, chatting, laughing, almost running, full of life as they head to the beach for a swim. The happy voices resound through the trees to say life is good at Skye Farm.

I love speaking with the moms or dads trying to schedule their children for camp. Again, it could be 1975 or 2009. They tell their story: why they need to schedule a certain week, their child's background and particular needs, and concerns that camp be a safe place and offer a good experience. And as best I can, I schedule them to accommodate their busy lives and listen to what they say about their child. I then proudly and honestly tell them that health and safety are the first priorities. On that basis, the program proceeds and individual needs are addressed up here at the end of the dirt road just off Exit 24 of the Northway.

Diane (Osterhout) Marino remembers

My parents worked all summer at Skye Farm starting when I was six years old. I was a "staff brat" until I was 17 and went to work as a dishwasher at Camp Missisquoi. It was a wonderful way to grow up and I would count down the days all school year anticipating the next summer at camp. There were always other staff brats to play with, but one of the greatest things about camp was the number of patient, kind, nurturing teachers we had in the adults and teenagers on the staff. We staff brats got swimming instruction from the lifeguards, made god's eyes and friendship bracelets at arts and crafts, were welcomed to music camp choir rehearsals before we were old enough to be campers, and the kitchen staff even let us help decorate the birthday cakes every Friday morning. The maintenance guys let

,Missisquoi. A funding request for $450,000 went to the churches for the lodge. Another $350,000 was requested for a new camping site in Vermont, because by this time the issues at Missisquoi were deemed impossibly expensive to correct, considering the type of program conference wished to offer. The next year, the campaign began under the title "People of Faith Building Places of Vision." Val Gray, a musician on the Board of Camps and Conferences, wrote a catchy song based on that very theme. Also in 1986, conference connected an Advance Special to the campaign and determined that 5% of the funds received, up to $50,000, would be paid to support "Campo Limpo," in the São Paulo Methodist Conference of Brazil.

As of April 30, 1987, when the pledge campaign officially ended, the results were that of the $1,000,000 requested, $668,553 was accepted by the churches and $63,087 received. A year later, the reported uses of the received funds were $23,000 for administrative expenses, $162,000 for Covenant Hills, and $14,000 for Campo Limpo, with $91,000 held in reserve to fund the new retreat lodge. Hopes continued to be expressed that the full $1,000,000 campaign goal would be reached. In fact, several churches and individuals responded with gifts and pledges beyond what was asked. However, over $225,000 of what was requested from the churches was unsupported when a number of congregations decided not to participate. By the end of April 1989, total pledges stood at $857,000 with $580,000 received.

In an effort to maintain interest and enthusiasm for the campaign, the cover of the 1990 Journal showed an artist's sketch of the proposed adult retreat lodge. Another view and outside elevations appeared on the next-to-last page. Clearly, though, funding the needs of Covenant Hills was of a higher priority. At the end of 1989, the full $350,000 sought for the new camp had been expended. Administrative expenses were $30,000, the camp in Brazil received $27,000, and the balance left for the retreat lodge us ride in the back of the camp truck to the dump and help throw the garbage bags into the landfill—a trip we always considered a treat for some reason. One year some of the college students who worked in the kitchen bought me a recorder and taught me how to play it. They sewed a red felt bag with a drawstring for me to keep it in. I learned how to play the guitar on an instrument borrowed from one of the cooks, using her chord chart and a camp songbook. It was as if I had a dozen mentors every summer. What amazing role models!

The other part of being a staff brat that made for a unique childhood was the amount of freedom we had. My parents were working, but they knew the 400 acres of Skye Farm were full of people who knew me and were looking out for me. The cardinal rule was that I had to appear at every meal and be in the cabin by dark. Otherwise, I was pretty much free to roam. There were camp rules, of course—the hardest one for me to obey was the "no bare feet" rule, which I tried to get around whenever I could—but I was allowed a tremendous amount of freedom while still being in a safe place. I feel sorry for children today whose parents are so worried about their safety that they never get to experience the independence I enjoyed.

1986 Camping Capital Funds Theme Song

Val Gray

People Of Faith Building Places Of Vision

People of faith building places of vision –
Children of God finding mountains to climb.
Working together, united in mission –
Serving our Lord all of the time.

was $210,000. This was less than half of the $450,000 hoped for at the start of the campaign.

Work on the lodge progressed even though the money for the actual building was not on hand. The well was drilled, and the architectural drawings were completed. The Town of Bolton signed off on the necessary approvals. At the end of the campaign in December 1990, the final report showed 55 churches had paid more than was requested, and another 57 had paid their asking in full. Another $190,000 was received under the heading of major gifts. Overall, a generous $626,000 was given to allow people of faith to build places of vision.

In the decade that followed, the Board of Camps and Conferences continued to make slow progress on the retreat lodge while keeping the rest of the Skye Farm program thriving. By 1993, they reported that all necessary permits were in hand. This was no small thing as building projects in the Adirondacks need multiple levels of approval, sometimes with conflicting and even contradictory requirements to be met. It can take considerable time and expertise to get all the agencies involved to agree, especially on a project of such magnitude and potential impact on the environment.

The permits were in order, but an additional $200,000 was needed before construction could begin. In 1994 the board hired a fundraising specialist. The following year a note appears in the Journal that the contract with the fundraiser was "completed." However, the funds to build were not in hand.

The board continued to wrestle with the problem of how to move forward and bring the dream of a retreat lodge to reality. In 1997 conference passed a resolution appealing for $7 per member. No substantial follow up occurred, and only an additional $19,000 resulted from the appeal.

In 1999, the Board of Camps and Conferences took on a new name: the Board of Camping and Retreat Ministries. The change signaled a move from what had been

New Year Staff Reunion

For many people, the Skye Farm New Year Staff Reunion was a high point of the year. For some of the children of permanent staff, that gathering was an even bigger deal than Christmas. The event typically began as people arrived at Ogden Lodge on a loose time schedule. The evening meal was certainly on the agenda along with games, perhaps skating on the lake if conditions were right, maybe a complicated puzzle, and lots of conversation. A communion service welcomed in the New Year. The early birds went to bed around 2 a.m. and as for the others—who knows?? There was a common breakfast and then conversation, skiing, and sliding when the snow cover allowed. After lunch on January 1, everyone helped clean up and headed home. The time together served to unify the Christian community that underlies the whole rich camping experience. It was a time away, a time for renewal, and time of looking ahead.

Weather Bomb

Debi Paterson
From the Skye Farm Annual Report, 1996

Looking back at 1995 reminds me of the blessings of our connectional church system. Our summer camp theme was "We are One Church, Many Members." This was modeled for our campers this July when Skye Farm was hit by a storm called a "weather bomb." We were left with a camp that looked like a war zone. However, we were blessed with no injuries and few damages to buildings. We had a camp full of children and staff. Volunteers appeared and took care of power needs with generators. More volunteers used chain saws to clear fallen trees. The Roberts family of Bolton UMC provided drinking water. We were able to operate through four and a half days without electrical power and running water. And, important since the early 1900s to what was anticipated to be important in 2000 and beyond. The board also took another look at the retreat lodge project, seeking alternatives to the original plan that by now was nearly two decades old.

In 2000, the Adult Retreat Ministry Task Force, convened by the Rev. Bill Lasher, issued their report. The report summarized some 17 years of effort and noted that the cost of the building as originally designed was now $1,200,000 more than funds on hand. The reality was that to build such an expensive structure in the hope that people would come would be a high-risk venture. On the other hand, if the retreat ministry were created first, then possibly a new building would be seen as necessary. Thus the recommendation, and decision, was to put the emphasis on program first rather than to seek more money at that time. That same year, the Rev. Harold Shippey came back on the staff as executive director of "Skye Farm and Retreat Center." Ogden Lodge and Bass Lodge would be the primary sites for the effort to expand the market for a retreat ministry.

Meanwhile, the main camp continued to mature and meet the demands of a new day. Tucker washhouse, for instance, given major financial support by Joan and Al Tucker, was completed in 1995. The facility, while fairly rustic, is handicapped accessible, which is not generally the case in that area of Skye Farm. Coincidentally, it also has a more open and airy feeling than the other washhouses with their concrete floors and more limited ventilation.

Shippey Lodge, 2009

The summer program flourished in many directions. The low ropes challenge course that came into being in 1999 got much use by campers and staff. The 2000 program included camps on circus arts, M.A.D.D., Christian

of course the campers thought it was a great adventure. They even praised the Lord for outhouses. What we had for those four and half days was the power of God's love. Our volunteers showed us the true meaning of our theme. We had the support of the many gifts of our Christian community—the gifts of the spirit—and we are thankful.

Grandfather-in-Residence

Rev. Art Hagy

Back in the late 1970s, a retired widower named Walter Nord came to Skye Farm and served through the summer on the maintenance crew. If you asked him how he was doing, he was quite likely to respond, "I've never been more tired and I've never been more happy." When he remarried, his new wife joined him at camp and often produced mounds of cookies for everyone. Just having someone of their age around the camp added a special dimension for the rest of the staff and the campers. So we knew that having an older, full time volunteer was an idea with merit.

When my own retirement approached, it struck me that after being involved with Skye Farm since 1958 I might have something to offer in that regard. I started out, with the blessing of Harold Shippey, as Grandfather-in-Residence. The kids typically were happier calling me "Grandpa Art" and that was fine with me too. I had no particular schedule so I rarely had to cut a conversation short because I was expected elsewhere. I did some handyman stuff, drove people who needed a ride, and picked up odds and ends as the need arose. One of my special concerns is supporting the homesick, or as I prefer to say, "lonesome" camper. I read stories to younger children and tell stories to the older ones.

I also end up doing some pastoral work through the summer. With our fifty or so employees facing a yoga, science, and Animal Crackers (with an emphasis on farm and more exotic animals related to the Heifer Project). The following year, offerings included water skiing, girls' volleyball, lifesaving, and emergency medical services. Music camp was in its 26th season. The old metal swimming pier, dating back to 1962, was replaced by a new design fabricated by volunteer Bud Jameson. It was partially in recognition of that effort that he was named 2001 Skye Farm Volunteer of the Year.

In the summer of 2002, Skye Farm offered a "Kids for Kids Camp" in support of children who had lost at least one parent in the September 11 attack on the World Trade Center in the previous year. A camp for "Web Weavers" addressed the World Wide Web (not Spiderman). In 2003, the acquisition of a fleet of kayaks added a new feature to the waterfront program. That year Skye Farm held its first whitewater rafting camp. In the years that followed, an additional pavilion was erected and a new storage barn constructed. Long-time camp volunteer Bud Jameson also fabricated a modular canoe dock, which moved the launch area away from the swimming and beach activities. One additional feature of the new dock was the easy access it allowed for a whole cabin group to paddle together in a 14-person peace canoe. The canoe, the Newton M. Perrins, was purchased as a gift to Skye Farm by friends of the Rev. Newton Perrins, in memory of his long ministry as a canoe camp director.

Meanwhile, the Board of Camping and Retreat Ministries worked to update the master plan that dated back to 1972. Usage of camp retreat facilities doubled from 2002 to 2003, with some 1,815 individuals enjoying the site due to a marketing effort that targeted school groups.

By 2006, it was abundantly clear that the original design for an adult retreat center was too expensive for any time in the foreseeable future. Interest turned then to the idea, typical of the Adirondack great camps, of proceeding with a series of smaller buildings. This approach would allow the project to begin with one facility and lead whole range of frustrations and struggles there are often those who need someone to talk with. I'm around every day, they know me, and the conversations flow. So, officially now, I have the title "Chaplain," but to most I'm Grandpa Art.

Harold Shippey

Reprinted from the Shippey Lodge Dedication booklet

Rev. Harold A. Shippey was introduced to Skye Farm through his family when his father, Rev. Joel Shippey, was a volunteer director. Harold became a Skye Farm camper, then a member of the summer staff. His leadership in youth ministry brought him to the Skye Farm Site Committee and in 1976 he became the first full-time Skye Farm manager, serving in the position which was known as Camp Steward at that time. He continued to be Camp Steward until 1986.

Harold returned to camp leadership as Troy Conference Director of Camping and Retreat Ministries, as well as Executive Director of Skye Farm, in 2000. He retired from that position, effective January 1, 2009.

During his professional career at Skye Farm, he brought a strong witness of social concerns and environmental awareness, along with a deep love of the Christian faith. His careful attention to detail and his thorough appreciation for the lives of those who shared the Skye Farm experience were evident to everyone. During the final two year as Executive Director of Skye Farm he shepherded the planning and building of the new resident lodge which bears his name.

to other buildings as interest continued and funds became available. The new design called for a main structure with the capacity to provide all utilities and fire suppression for itself and the other buildings anticipated in the design. The site chosen was near Ogden Lodge, which would allow access to the kitchen there. The new building was designed to be handicapped accessible from the start and would hold sixteen adults in its four suites—each with its own bath and shower. The final configuration would include three more buildings with sleeping and meeting space and a dining hall, for a total capacity of 60 to 70 adults.

Construction plans were finally in place. In the spring of 2008, a major new sewer system and leech field, costing $63,000, were installed at Staff Hill in the main camp. Meanwhile, there was a substantial delay in getting an excavator to start on the retreat lodge. Someone put two and two together and approached the sewer excavator about the other job. His response essentially was, "I can start right away." Shortly after that the cellar hole and the rough grading were completed at the new site. The main construction was contracted out, but while the finish work was being completed, the Thursday crew of volunteers went to work and built the two access ramps that lead from the parking lot to the entrances on either side of the building.

On an overcast and frequently drizzly day, June 27, 2009, Bishop Susan W. Hassinger dedicated and consecrated the lodge, naming it "Shippey Lodge" in honor of the Rev. Harold Shippey. The cost of construction was $635,000, which included the building, landscaping, and utility support for the additional buildings that for now are only projections in the current master plan.

In 2010 Ogden Lodge and Shippey Lodge were designated as the first two facilities of the Bruce Conklin Retreat Complex at Skye Farm. The initial vision shared by "three men on a rock" continues to spread, offering now a welcome to people of all ages who wish to enjoy the world our God has made.

Well My Dear, It's Time to Go

Words & Music by Dan Berggren based on stories from the Skye Farm family of friends. Reprinted by permission.

The setting sun means day is done
And I won't say that I'm tired
But it surely would do me some good
To put my feet up by the fire

For just an hour, maybe more
We'll forget our cares and worries
Who'll go first as we share this time
As we tell the old stories

You've heard about the pine tree limb
That broke the windshield accidentally
Remember when a whole tree came down
On the outhouse, coincidentally

Who's the man behind the winch
Who's the man behind the chain saw
You can depend upon this friend
The one behind that bearded jaw

He is the happy camper, negotiator, plumber
Mister safety first, a dust bowl driver having fun
A steward and a teacher, unconventional preacher
Harold is all of these rolled into one

Harold Shippey is the name
The one all Skye Farm campers know
He's famous for his fashion sense
Dressed in wool from head to toe

When a rooster crows from the lifeguard stand
When a bat flies in the dining hall
When an injured hawk needs sanctuary
Harold is the one to call

Who's beside this humble man

Who'll fix and save a dinner plate
Carol Shippey: nurse, companion
Fire poker, lifelong mate

Back in college, Harold took Carol
To a winter prom when snow was deep
He picked her up for the dance
With no top upon his Jeep

He'll squeeze moss to get water, squeeze a budget
  to get dollars
He'll fight fires and not give up until the job is done
He's mister hospitality, building bridges for community
Harold is all of these rolled into one

With tools of love and discipline
Taking care and giving worth
Offering lessons large and small
Walking gently on God's earth

Thank you for this campfire here
It's much more than light and heat
The stories could go on and on
We'll have more next time we meet

So my friends we all move on
And like the endless river, flow
Well my dear, well my dear
Well my dear, it's time to go

Well my dear, well my dear
Well my dear, it's time to go
Well my dear, well my dear
Well my dear, it's time to go

Buck Lake

In 1950 the Conference Board of Education, which then held responsibility for camping programs, called for "cooperation with two other denominations (Baptist and Congregational) in the search for and development of a new campsite in Vermont." The Vermont Church Council was to be the coordinating body. This innovative approach to siting and creating a camping program turned out to be effective, at least for the short term.

The search was successful as it found Buck Lake, in the Town of Woodbury, about a half-hour northwest of Cabot, VT. By 1953, the Vermont Church Council had ownership of 184 acres of land with a 56-acre pond. The property only cost $6,500 at the time, but Troy Conference found raising its $2,600 share of the investment a bit of an effort and had to borrow from Skye Farm accounts for a year until apportioned funds from local churches came through.

The report of the board in 1954 expresses great optimism over the plans prepared by a camp architect. The expectation was that the camp would be well built and a source of pride for years to come.

It was slow going. Rev. Leonard Bass, conference director of youth work, directed one of the camps there in 1958 and noted, "For the first time, Buck Lake had a rather extensive program ... serving over eighty campers." The hiring of a business manager for the camp followed in 1959, and the site hosted a full summer of camping.

The facility was used for training youth leaders in 1960 and hosted a spiritual life retreat in 1961. In 1963, the camp purchased an additional ninety acres to make possible greater use of the site.

The report on the summer of 1963, the last year Rev. Bass served as coordinator of youth work, has this to say: "...probably Camp Day Break at Buck Lake for emotionally disturbed children is the most outstanding project of the summer program. This two-week camp has brought national attention to Vermont. As a result of some of our learning experiences there, we have two mission camps with juniors. One was with boys and girls from the Albany Inner City Mission at Missisquoi, and at the end of the summer, another such camp was held at Skye Farm. Ministering with a much larger staff and fewer campers than the usual 60 has taught us some of the values of this type of camping with "special" campers."

Despite these affirmative words and the learning that still informs various camps for persons with special needs, the Buck Lake experiment soon ran its course. In 1970, Camp Day Break was transferred to Missisquoi. That same year, the Board of Camps and Conferences secured approval for a set of resolutions: that conference limit itself to ownership and development of two sites for camping, that the two sites be Skye Farm and Missisquoi, that funds on hand for a new campsite be allocated to present camp site development, and that money received as the Troy Conference share of the sale of Buck Lake be allocated to capital expenditures at either Skye Farm or Missisquoi.

With that, Troy Conference moved away from ecumenical camping—until Camp Missisquoi could no longer support the kind of program conference wanted, and the effort that led to the cooperative venture at Covenant Hills began.

The Camp That Almost Was

In late 1971, the Committee on Camps and Conferences began enthusiastic discussions with Keeseville UMC regarding two pieces of property in their community that might become suitable sites for church camping.

In the early stages of planning, things moved along quite well. The 1972 annual conference voted to accept the offered parcels for use in "Christian life and education." After that promising start, things began to slow down. A year later, the Board of Camps and Conferences was still waiting for the deeds to be finalized and the recommendation for use from the Adirondack Park commission.

In 1974, it was noted that one parcel was rugged mountaintop land that offered potential for some kinds of camping. The possible use of the other parcel, near the

Northway, was still in negotiations involving a New York State beautification project and the status was "unsettled." The following year, the state finalized purchase of some two and a half acres of land. This encouraged Camps and Conferences to anticipate that soon it would "come to terms with the development of the property."

But in 1976 came word that the Keeseville UMC had plans "outside the jurisdiction of Camps and Conferences" for the property by the Northway. That property was turned over to the Board of Global Ministries, who used it for the establishment of a retirement home, Keeseville Country Gardens. However, the hilltop property continued to be of interest, and the conference trustees held the deed on behalf of the camping interests.

The final word on the mountaintop property came in 1977. The resolution from the Conference Council on Ministries said, "After consideration, [the council] has concluded the potential use of the land is not feasible for Troy Conference." Conference then agreed to relinquish its interest in the property and returned it to the Keeseville church with appreciation.

So the camp that almost was became instead a place for the conference's risk-taking mission through the Geriatric Foundation.

Acampamento Betel

In 1986, Troy Conference was deep in the midst of a three-year camping capital funds campaign to raise money for the purchase and development of a new site for camping in Vermont, and for building a retreat lodge at Skye Farm. That year at annual conference, the Conference Board of Global Ministries offered a resolution, which conference passed, to use 5% of the proceeds of the capital funds campaign, up to a total of $50,000, in support of a camping related Advance Special, "Campo Limpo," in the São Paulo Methodist Conference of Brazil.

VIM team at Acampamento Betel, 1989

This new connection with Brazil came about largely through the influence of Flavio de Almeida. Flavio was from São Paulo and served as one of the intercultural resource persons who spent the summer of 1985 at Skye Farm. He related well to the campers and staff here in the Adirondacks. He also got people excited over the opportunities and needs of church camping in Brazil. The resolution in 1986 resulted from his influence.

The effect of the 1986 resolution was not only to raise money for a camp but also to raise enthusiasm for going to Brazil and making a hands-on investment. In 1989 a substantial team, including Bruce and Brooke Conklin, Will Chamberlin, Shirley and Carl Byers, Peter Elmendorf, Harold and Madeleine Robinson, and Bill Pattison traveled to São Paulo for a nine-day work camp at a place we now understand to be properly titled Acampamento Betel.

That first trip focused on building a dining hall. During a second trip a few years later a team worked on staff housing. There is a certain irony in that the work on the Advance Special was completed before one of the primary goals of the capital funds campaign. The Covenant Hills Camp property was purchased and the first camping season held there in 1989, and the major gift to Acampamento Betel, the dining hall, was also completed in 1989. But it took until 2009 before Shippey Lodge at Skye Farm became a reality.

Building a Camp in Brazil

Will Chamberlin

We flew to São Paulo and the camp staff picked us up in their bus, which had 6 bald tires and a flat on the inside dual. We kind of shook our heads, but it got us to the camp. The camp was not far out of town—more suburban than rural. It was a few years old with a swimming pool and a soccer field, and interestingly enough, electricity—at least a light bulb—in the camper cabins. This is in contrast to the more "old days" style of camping we offer in the cabins at Skye Farm.

When we arrived, the roof of the dining hall was already up on steel posts. You might describe it as butterfly shaped—high on the outside and low in the middle. It was designed to drain the rain to the center of the roof, rather than the edges, so it didn't drip on you as much when leaving the building in wet weather.

Once we arrived, they were able to purchase the concrete blocks we used to lay the walls. The blocks arrived the next morning and we went to work. A number of hard-working Brazilians joined us on the project. We used a small concrete mixer for the actual mixing, but then it all had to be carried bucket by bucket to the walls. We made the outside walls and a couple of inside partitions. They had an electrician ready, so the wiring was completed about the same time we finished up.

The kids there were very patient. Sometimes they'd have to wait in line for a half-hour for their meals, and they'd be there without the confusion we typically get up here around the dining hall. Early on we noticed that the kids were only getting beans and rice for their meals, while there was much more variety for the work team. We talked to the camp and arranged to pay a bit more for food so that the campers could have meals like ours.

Our trip was important partly because of the

building we did. Even more important were the friends and connections we made. That's why we were willing to go back again a couple of years later to work on the staff housing.

My Involvement with Brazil

Rev. Bill Pattison

The trip to Acampamento Betel was my first VIM trip. It came about like this: Bishop Paulo Ayres Mattos attended our conference session in 1988. As part of his presentation to conference, he showed a video. After viewing the video, I offered the bishop some suggestions on how to improve it. At the end of my critique, I rather carelessly wrote, "I'd be willing to come to Brazil and do training in video production." Later that year, I found out about the VIM team going to Acampamento Betel and wrote to Bishop Paulo saying, "I have a way to get to São Paulo, can you get me to Recife and put me up for a week or so?" Then, early one Sunday morning in December, I got a phone call from Eve Cain, a missionary working at the regional headquarters in Recife. She told me they would indeed fly me to and from Recife and lodge me in exchange for training. That trip grew into seven or eight over the next decade or so. Along the way, I've learned some Portuguese and have met some marvelous people.

Covenant Hills Christian Camp

The Vermont site of the Troy Conference camping program had for many years been in the northwestern part of the state on the Missisquoi River in Sheldon. The site was a former ground for camp meetings. The camp's buildings, except for Preston Lodge (the summer nurse's residence) and the recently renovated tabernacle, were in marginal condition, the water system was out of date, and additional acreage for programming was unavailable. After more than twenty years of struggling with the shortcomings of the site, the 1985 annual conference authorized the Board of Camps and Conferences to find a new location for United Methodist church camping in Vermont. The criteria were that it be central to Vermont, reasonably close to the main highway system, have more space, provide the opportunity for new programming, and have a sufficient water supply. The unstated criterion was that this hoped-for site had to be affordable. The capital funds campaign approved at the same conference would help to meet that challenge.

The first meeting of the search committee was in January 1986. The Rev. Larry Curtis served as chair with the Rev. Oren Lane; Art Doty, Debi Paterson, Hale Ritchie, and Betty Welch served as committee members. The Rev. David Murphy, conference director of camping, was also a member of the search committee. At midyear, an extended debate over the wisdom of purchasing and developing a new site arose at annual conference. Perhaps, some thought, it would be better to consolidate all Troy Conference camping at Skye Farm. After serious discussion, conference agreed that was not the way to go.

The search committee continued its work and by late in the year they were ready with a recommendation. On December 11, 1986, the board approved their suggestion to purchase a 139-acre property on a hillside in Cabot. This approval naturally required several additional steps before the deal could be considered closed. In due course, annual conference affirmed the purchase for the price of $139,000, the Town of Cabot selectmen approved the use of the land for camping, and the necessary environmental protection conditions were met. On December 29, 1987, conference trustees gave their approval, and the next day the land came into the possession of Troy Conference.

Even before the United Methodists had moved to purchase a new, more effective campsite, the Vermont Conference of the United Church of Christ had already gone through a reappraisal of their camping ministry. Their property at Camp Wihakowi in Roxbury spanned two steep sides of a valley with a highway running down the middle, and their buildings were outdated. They had sold that site and, being without a location for their camping program, were already cooperating at Missisquoi. This cooperation proved to be of mutual benefit.

So while in negotiation over land acquisition for a new site, Rev. Murphy continued in dialogue with the United Church of Christ in an effort to establish an intentionally designed cooperative camping program. The discussions were an experiment in ecumenical activity. The final agreement, prepared in the form of a legal covenant, committed the United Church of Christ to providing a level of financial and volunteer support for a UMC site and program. In return, the United Church of Christ would have ongoing input into, and use of, the programs at the facility. It was a friendly but difficult agreement to prepare, especially as so

Canvas Castles

Most of the camper housing at Covenant Hills is in cabins, but two "canvas castles"—very large tents on platforms—are permanently part of the facility. Environmental regulations require that the camp have both a septic system and place for a reserve system. The castles are in an area that has suitable contours and drainage for such a reserve. So, no permanent structures are allowed in that part of the camp, but until that indefinite future, the white billowing canvas walls and roofs serve as a summer home for a week at camp.

few precedents could be called upon to guide the outcome. In cooperation with the Rev. Hal Harrison, conference minister for the Vermont Conference of the United Church of Christ, the discussions were formalized in early 1989.

The new site needed a name. The winning submission was from Debi Paterson, Skye Farm steward. The name suggested, "Covenant Hills," turns out to reflect, affirm, and help memorialize the covenant of mutual respect and responsibility between the two denominations.

At the time no one knew how well this cooperative venture was going to work out. It was an act of faith for both parties. The UMC had the responsibilities of property ownership, while the UCC gave donations of cash, sent volunteers to work and serve on committees, and paid for the construction of Wihakowi Health Lodge, named in memory of their former camp.

Once the property was actually in conference hands, the development of the site began to move forward quickly. The last summer of camping at Missisquoi was in 1988. Two camp sessions were held on the new property that same summer. The first building on site, the washhouse, was completed by the United Methodist Men in October. This was part of what is aptly called the "Miracle at Covenant Hills." Some 450 persons volunteered their labor so that sixteen buildings (dining hall, health lodge, washhouse, seven staff cabins and six camper cabins) were completed in less than eight months. As the Rev. Murphy reported, "All these buildings were built without paying a single dollar for carpentry."

In the spring of 1989, Troy Conference and the Vermont Conference of the UCC issued their first unified camping brochure, listing all the summer opportunities at Skye Farm and Covenant Hills. The official opening day was July 2, 1989. Again quoting the Rev. Murphy, "The air was literally still ringing with the driving of nails as campers arrived but by nightfall the facilities were ready." Also that year, the old camp was sold for $230,000. Meanwhile, the tabernacle bell and the cross by the Missisquoi River were transferred to the Cabot site as a sign of continuity with

Covenant Hills dedication, 1989

the past generations of camp supporters. Bishop Dale White officiated at the Covenant Hills dedication service on August 19, 1989.

Reports in 1991 indicated that over $1,000,000 in materials and labor had been donated to Covenant Hills. Marion Sablon gave a generous donation to Troy Conference in her will. A second disbursement from her bequest led to the decision to designate a suitable memorial to her at Covenant Hills. In 1992 Sablon Meadows, running from Faith Lodge to the town road, was chosen for this purpose. This "space for programming, playing fields, reflection, conservation and agricultural activities, (is) all surrounded by magnificent views of God's creation."

Taking advantage of an opportunity in 1993, conference purchased an additional 35 acres of property at the top of Hooker Mountain on the south side of camp.

Nearly 500 youth attended Covenant Hills in the 1994

season. In addition to basic camps, additional offerings included soccer, African and Native American, horse, gymnastics, canoeing, hiking, biking, adventure, music, clowning, and beach camps.

The camp prepared a float for the Cabot 4th of July parade in 1997. All the staff and campers walked in the parade so the whole town knew Covenant Hills was an active part of their community.

Additional signs of the vigor of the program and the drawing power of the facility appeared through the years. More new buildings were added to the property. In 2000, the campers filled the site nearly to capacity so more space was needed. An additional 90 acres were added to the camp property in 2003, both to provide a buffer zone for camper activities and with an eye to possible future expansion.

Meanwhile, program innovations continued to enhance the summer experience. In 2001, "Harry Potter" visited the camp. The site also offered a family weekend for single parents. Camping options for 2002 featured high flyers, "Veggie Tales" for campers going into kindergarten and grades 1 and 2, "Christians in Action," and extreme sports, such as rock climbing and whitewater rafting. Offerings the next year included "Survivor," "Explore New York," and roller coaster camps.

One of the important contributors to the early growth of Covenant Hills was Bruce Conklin. Bruce was a builder from New York with strong ties to the United Methodist Church in Saratoga Springs, Skye Farm, the Volunteer in Mission program, and many other dimensions of church work as well. His support of the new camp appeared in a variety of ways. In the early days he brought his framing crew to the site for three weeks to help make Faith Lodge a reality. In 2003, he died after a long illness. At his request, his ashes were spread at VIM sites in Mexico and Brazil, Fern Lake, a cemetery in Jonesville, Skye Farm, and Covenant Hills. The camp flagpole at Covenant Hills, originally given in his honor, now stands in memory of his generous, enthusiastic support of the ministry there.

The female staff dormitory is named "Peg Moore Lodge" in honor of Margaret Moore (wife of the Rev. Dr. Stanley Moore), who among her other contributions brought volunteer builders to the site. She is credited with recruiting, coordinating, scheduling, and encouraging hundreds of volunteers during the first two years of construction, as many as one thousand the first year alone. Some days, one hundred volunteers shared the site at the same time.

Starting around 2004, the camp leadership began to give considerable attention to the process of obtaining certification from the American Camping Association. Camps in Vermont were not regulated as closely as those in New York, so the certification was an important way of showing that Covenant Hills did in fact meet high standards of safety and program quality. It took from then until 2008 for the process to be completed. Todd Marlow, executive director of the camp, is given credit for producing the required documentation through the years of bringing the process to completion.

Meanwhile, in 2006 Covenant Hills began to host a special camp for children who have a parent under the supervision of the Vermont Corrections Department. The camp is funded by a Burlington area Episcopal, United Methodist, and United Church of Christ ecumenical group. Each child in the program receives a prayer quilt, school supplies, a hat, and other gifts to show how much they are valued. Rev. Murphy and his wife Judy were the first to direct this offering, Camp Agapé.

A high point of 2009 was the August 22nd celebration of twenty years of camping at Covenant Hills. The event began with tours of the camp. The weather cooperated and those present got to walk the trails linking Vision Pond to the outdoor chapel, with its view of the cross (made from wood harvested at the camp) on the far side of the water, to various cabins and the "canvas castles" back in the woods.

The celebration itself was held in Taylor Barn. Completed in time for the 2008 camping season, the 2,700 square foot structure provides a large undercover area for camp activities as diverse as music, drama, worship, and games regardless of the weather. Taylor Vigne was a young, avid camper who died suddenly. High on the southern wall of the barn is a stained glass window featuring a rainbow that echoes the bow seen in the sky when the building was being completed. For those who knew her, the rainbow symbolizes Taylor's blessing on the building, its purposes, and all who are refreshed within its walls. Faith Lodge was the venue for the final part of the day's activities—a booster dinner featuring a 20th anniversary cake.

Back in 1987, part of the vision for Covenant Hills was that while it would be a place for camping and outdoor activity, a symbolic wilderness, it would also be handicapped accessible. The wisdom of that choice was underlined by the presence of the Rev. Oren Lane at the celebration. Oren was a pastor, camping enthusiast, and skilled photographer. He was active in all phases of the planning, purchase, and creation of Covenant Hills. While in the midst of his career, he contracted a debilitating disease that forced him into an early retirement, but he still had the strength and skill to work with his photographs. One key part of the celebration was a video he had created showing the camp under construction and the numerous volunteers responsible for buildings on the site. He could be present to greet his friends and receive their thanks for his efforts only because the grounds accommodated his battery powered wheel chair.

Covenant Hills is well placed for the new challenges of the future as it moves from the care of Troy Conference to that of the New England Conference. The hundreds of campers and volunteers whose participation have made the camp a special place will surely continue to support it and bring new people to the site. In the words of Rev. James McPhee, director of connectional ministries of the New

England Conference, offered at the twentieth anniversary celebration, Covenant Hills is "a space for us to connect with God and with each other."

Directors of Camping

Leonard Bass 1955-1963
George Miller 1963-1968
Joyce Giles 1975-1977
William Cotant 1978-1983
David Murphy 1984-1990
David Heberling 1991-1992
Judy Palmer-1992
Work handled by committee 1993-1996
DeeAnne Lowman 1997-1999
Harold Shippey 1999-2008
David Johnston 2009 -

Skye Farm Stewards

This job changed through the years. There were both summer and off-season camp managers until 1976, when the year round position of camp steward began.

Howard Grout- a year or two prior to 1959
Alan Cederstrom 1959-60
Alan Cederstrom and Howard Grout-1961
Alan Cederstrom 1962-1968
Bill Lasher 1968-1976 (off season manager)
Bill Lasher 1969-1970 (summer camp manager)
Laurel Weinheimer
Ed Osterhout 1974-1975 (summer camp manager)
Harold Shippey 1976-1984
Kevin Wrigley 1985-1988
Debi Paterson 1989-1996
David Hobbs 1997

DeeAnne Lowman 1998-1999
Harold Shippey 1999-2009
Tom Swift Creek Lee 2009 –

Covenant Hills Stewards

Cherry Gorton
Gary Larabee
David Hobbs 1992-2001
Matthew Conrick 2001-2003
Todd Marlow 2004-2009
Katie Taylor 2009–

Chapter 8

Stories Around the Campfire

For where two or three are gathered in my name, I am there among them. Matthew 18:20

One of the pleasures of a day at camp comes as darkness falls. We light the campfire, sit around, stare at the embers ... and tell stories. The tales emerge from a shadow land of happy recollections illuminated by the shifting light of an irregular, stick-fed fire. Around the campfire, we remember "back then." Back then might be earlier in the day, earlier in the week, or even decades ago. The stories come first from one person and then from another. They tumble out in no particular order. It is well to remember that typically campfire stories are enhanced by selective memory and often twists of humor. Parts of these stories are even true. Come into the circle, find a patch of ground, or sit on a log. Let the stories begin.

Fire Works

Even starting a campfire can be an adventure. One evening the present author and an even bigger, more robust leader were trying to get a flame going. We waved our hats at the dimly glowing remains of our tinder. We got as close to the fire pit as we could and blew until we were dizzy. A small, sad, curl of smoke was our only reward. Exhausted, we stepped back to get our second wind. Taking advantage of this break in the action, a slightly built, eight-year-old boy took our place. He gave a tentative puff in the general direction of the barely visible red center of our hopeless pile of wood. And before we could tell him he'd have to do better than that, the fire burst into flame with a roar.

Ah, the "Burn Pile." While sitting around the campfire, men are likely to let their attention wander from the conversation. Typically they are wondering, "Should this stick or that one go on the fire next?" "The coals are good but do we need more flame?" and "Is it time to move that big log over just a little?" So, it's no surprise that a favorite job for the Thursday crew is a controlled burn to get rid of the excess brush and scrap wood that piles up around camp. One December after the first snowfall, the camp manager sent us up to deal with the burn piles behind Shippey. We found three great snow-covered mounds easily enough and went to work. The manager joined us an hour later and asked how we were doing. "Well," we responded, "two of the piles are going well but we can't get this third one to start no matter what."

"I'm not surprised," he answered. "That one is a pile of dirt."

One evening we had a small fire going at the outdoor chapel. We each took a piece of paper, wrote on it sins of which we wished to repent and tossed the papers into the flames. As my paper began to burn, I realized that I had used my paycheck for this spiritual exercise. I grabbed it back and stomped it on the ground. When I took the charred remains to Bill Lasher to get a replacement, he gave me a new check and commented, "So Steve, you're not quite ready to give up the sin of acquisitiveness?"

In the "Don't Try This at Home Department," Al Cederstrom and Art Hagy were leading adult canoe camp late one fall. It had been raining so there was no dry wood. They took some sticks, added fuel from the Coleman lantern, and told people to stand back. One match later and "Poof!" they had a fire.

Olden Days

I remember my first trip to the site at Covenant Hills with David Murphy, who was program director in charge of camping at the time. The site had not been developed. All there was to see was a picnic table by the pond.

In the early years at Skye Farm, in the 1940s, the mattresses were just ticks stuffed with straw. The camp wiring, what there was of it, just ran from tree to tree in the woods. One of the first jobs each spring was to fix all the downed wires.

The early washhouses at Skye Farm were primitive. They were open sheds with tar-paper-lined troughs and cold-water spigots. At the time, there were outhouses scattered across the property. Regulations called for a pipe to run horizontally behind each lid so the covers could not stay open by themselves. The facilities were much more convenient to use when the pipes were removed. Still, when the health inspectors arrived, they always found the pipes in their proper place... and a maintenance worker catching his breath.

For some years as a camp improvement project, the rule at the beach was every day, every swimmer had to pick a few stones out of the wading area and toss them on shore to make the waterfront a better place for others who were to follow.

Grand Openings

Oren (the Rev. Oren Lane) was there at Covenant Hills from the beginning. He, Larry Curtis, and I (David Murphy) were the first people of Troy Conference to step foot on what is now Covenant Hills. Oren was on the search committee. He and I, with others, visited some fifty properties in search of the right place. Oren led the first work camp at Covenant Hills in 1988, the year before we opened the camp. His photo of "Vision Pond" was key to selling the conference on the purchase of the property. His photo essays of the camp are a legend ... and a legacy. (Oren died following a long illness about three months after he attended the Covenant Hills 20th anniversary celebration in August 2009.)

In the early 1960s the current dining hall was completed. We worked over the weekend to get everything moved down from the old kitchen on the hill to the new site overlooking the lake. Herman Schmidt was our gasman, and he worked until 2 a.m. on Sunday to get everything finished. We dedicated the new facility the next day, but alas, Herman was not with us. He was in Glens Falls Hospital having an emergency appendectomy.

Getting the necessary permits to proceed with the construction of Covenant Hills was a bit of a challenge in the face of environmental land-use restrictions that the State of Vermont and the Town of Cabot established as necessary concerns. Fortunately, Peg Moore was from Cabot. While waiting for the meeting of the zoning board she took us all through the municipal building, which was her old high school. At the meeting itself she had plenty of hometown credibility with board members. Things went well.

In the successful rush to get Covenant Hills ready for its opening season we had to build in all kinds of weather. One day we had to scrape the snow and ice off the floor so the builders could get in and start putting up the walls. In a few places you can see the chunks missing from the concrete where more than ice got chipped off.

When the first camping season at Covenant Hills was about to begin, they discovered the pond was infested with leeches. At my suggestion they stocked the pond with trout, and within a week the leeches were gone. At least as late as 2008 you still could find 12-inch trout in Vision Pond.

Bob Long and I (Clark Callender) shared a twenty-five year ministry as co-directors of family camp. Chet Vanderbilt gave me a ticket to a 1970 Family Ministries Conference in Chicago. When I returned we began Family Camp on Memorial Day Weekend in 1971. We had 260 attend family camp that first year. My wife Lucy was pregnant. We came home Monday and our baby was born Tuesday.

Name Tags

One year Jim Atkinson, Al Cederstrom, and I built a new cabin. For whatever reason, it didn't have a name. We christened it "Jimaled" in honor of ourselves. But when others wondered what the name implied, we told them it was a rare Iraqi word meaning, "The finest."

One of the early washhouses at Skye Farm went by the name "Pretoria." The full meaning of that name eludes us. "We are Marching to Pretoria" was a friendly and sociable folk song popular in the 1950s, quite fitting for a camp. On the other hand, Pretoria was kind of far away and the washhouse was set back in the woods. It may have taken a song to get campers motivated to head out there.

The first year I met Em we were in Eagle, and Linda was our counselor. Linda was fabulous. Our group that year bonded very quickly and strongly, and we were calling ourselves the "Eaglets," which became a running joke of sorts, mainly as a way to get under Linda's skin since it drove her nuts. By the end of the week, though, she caught herself also calling us "Eaglets." We wouldn't let her hear the end of it.

Up on the hill in the woods is the burned-out ruin of an old estate house. We used to call it the "Haunted House" but, fearing that title might be too scary for some of the smaller children we brought to it on hikes, we renamed it "The Castle."

Near one washhouse we were required to install a metal septic tank. We got it in the ground okay but weren't quite ready to hook it up at the end of the day. During the evening we got a heavy rain and the tank floated up. We never did get it completely back in the ground, so every now and then a curious camper would ask about this rusty metal tank off the trail in the woods. Our usual response was to tell them it was a sunken submarine.

Leading Men

Middle-aged and out of shape, I soon found the climb up Mount Ampersand to be more than a challenge. I would have given up on the climb but Ed Russell wouldn't let me. For every objection I made he had the answer. So with many breaks for rest and lots of patient encouragement I proudly made it to the top. The next year, as I got the story, my daughter was on the same climb with a fellow camper who wanted to quit. Her response to this was, "If my mother can climb this mountain, you certainly can." Thank you, Ed—I think!

Leonard Bass was the Troy Conference director of youth work from 1955 to 1963. His gentle and thoughtful style made an impact on many people, including several who are clergy today. When camp was in session he offered a spiritual presence. He could generally be found sitting on the hillside in the sun, reading but ready to listen, mentor, counsel, and offer direction. More than one camper having a bad week found sanctuary under his wings. On one occasion as a camp meal of spaghetti was being drained, there was an accident that put the pasta on the ground. "That's good," said Leonard. "That will make it taste better."

Off-site camping has been part of the programming for years. Ray Deming perhaps carried the "at one with nature" theme the farthest. He didn't bother with a sleeping bag. He'd just wrap himself in a blanket and sleep leaning against the trunk of a tree. Pat Bush remembers when Larry Curtis took a group of 36 ninth- and tenth-graders on an 87 mile canoe trip from Old Forge to Tupper Lake. The regulations on group size have been radically adjusted downward since those days!

Leaving Camp Missisquoi was not easy for people. Despite its shortcomings, it had the majestic tabernacle and a 106-year history of outdoor ministry. The Rev. Charlie Latimer, who almost single-handedly built the swimming pool there, was painfully disappointed when the site was sold. Later, Oren Lane took Charlie to Covenant Hills for a tour. Charlie said nothing the whole time. As they headed for the car he finally remarked, "Well, you got better than you deserved." His strong, deep support of the camping program through the years is remembered now in the Latimer Lodge director's facility, completed at Covenant Hills in the summer of 2000.

Leading Women

I arrived at camp a bit early one Saturday. Judy Palmer came by and asked in her warm, cheerful tone if I'd like to walk with her to get the mail. I readily agreed, not realizing the length, speed or bugginess of that "little walk" through the forest that she took every day. I needed a nap when I got back, and it took until Tuesday before my legs recovered.

Diane was our Covenant Hills lifeguard. One of the big events to end the week was the water carnival. After all the competitions Diane was to announce the winners. She asked, "Who had a good time?" They all responded with enthusiasm. "Then," she said, "You are all winners." After her announcement, one little boy started to cry. When we asked in an effort to comfort him what the problem was, he said, "I was never a winner before."

One year we had a new nurse at the camp. She was extremely conscientious. The rule she gave us was, "Come and see me every time you get a cut." After a couple days of seeing all the members of the maintenance crew a half dozen times and more, she raised the standard of injury required for a visit to her office.

I have a keen interest in wild eatables and when I took the campers on a nature hike, I had them try wintergreen, wood sorrel, Indian cucumber, bunchberries, and even made a beverage with the red sumac berries. I did worry that they would try things on their own and take something poisonous. Some of them would ask me about the mushrooms. I would tell them I didn't know which ones were okay, but if they wanted to try one, we'd watch and see if they survived and then we'd know if it was okay to eat. That kept them from making a mistake.

Oops!

The Bartlett Carry between the Upper and Middle Saranac Lakes is about as nice a portage as any—wide, level, and not too long. I used to include the carry on my route so if there were complaints, I could tell the campers this was just for practice and simple compared to others. I'd point to the sign beside the trail and tell them, "It's only a quarter of a mile." Then one year, one of the campers took a closer look at the sign and reminded me, "Point four miles is not the same as a quarter mile!" Well, that did explain why it seemed longer than it should have.

One day on canoe camp we had a girl who was too sick to paddle. That was all right because we had a passenger seat for her. While crossing the lake, we ran into a rain shower so we draped a tarp over her to keep her dry. We kept paddling and soon the sun came out, providing us with a glorious afternoon. About twenty minutes later we heard a sad little voice asking, "Can I come out now?"

It's not unheard of for bedwetters to attend camp. One year, a camper with this problem secured a place in one of the top bunks. Usually we supported the mattresses with a solid sheet of plywood. In this case, we happened to use two smaller sheets, one at the head of the bed and one at the foot, with a small gap in between. What the counselor said who slept underneath that arrangement is best left to the imagination.

Before we had a real forester connected with the camp we figured out how to take down trees ourselves. We preferred to call it "learning by doing," but perhaps "trial and error" would have been more accurate. Naturally we were careful. For instance, one day Harold hooked the winch of his truck to a tree and put tension on the cable to make sure it fell in the direction he wanted. That part worked okay, but the tree was taller than anticipated so it dropped in a perfect arc right through Harold's windshield. Now, having learned from that—uh—"doing," the next time we had a troublesome tree we used a pulley system so the truck was at right angles, far off to the side of the drop path. As the cut progressed, Terry Lasher, in his early teens at the time, raised a concern that the tree might hit a nearby outhouse. Older and wiser staff double-checked the angles and assured him that would not happen. The truck driver maintained considerable tension on the cable as the cut proceeded to be sure that everything was under control. In fact, when the cut was completed, he gunned the engine even a bit more. That pulled the trunk right off the stump and left the tree to veer in a "completely unexpected" direction, where it smashed the outhouse to kindling.

My buddy Jay Steele and I often worked on projects together. Once we were struggling with an electrical problem on the old camp truck. Somehow Jay got his head into the glove box and then couldn't get it out. I don't remember exactly how we managed to extricate him. Another time he was painting the washhouse and balanced the can of paint on the door. Shortly after that he reported, "Well, the door is white all over, and so am I."

Good judgment? It's not always in plain view. One of the fellows in Bachelor Hall got annoyed at the bats flying through his living quarters after dark, so he went after them with his bow and arrow. He didn't do any harm to the little creatures, but in the daylight it became obvious that he had sent several arrows right through the roof.

The third year I worked at camp, the Community Arts/Just-Foods person and I were assigned to be tepee assistants. Betsy Forsythe was the tepee queen that year. She trained us how to pack cookouts, run the store, and prepare evening snacks for the campers. That year the store had a new cash register, one that could calculate the amount of money a camper had left in his/her account after purchases were made. Betsy had not taken a day off for at least three weeks, but finally she felt we could handle things so she took off. We were sure of everything. We got the store items out along with the file box of camper credit records. The store opening was covered by a piece of plywood, which was secured by two nails. To get the plywood out of place, there was a rope running over a pulley. When the rope was pulled, the plywood swung in and up to a hook that kept it in place while the campers were at the store. We were ready!!! We took out the nails, pulled on the rope and ... WHAP went the cash register onto the floor, out of commission for the next three weeks.

Natural Highs

Most of the kids on canoe camp had not seen an eclipse of the moon, but there was going to be one in the middle of the week. As night fell we got heavy cloud cover. Still I suggested to them, "Pack it in early. I'll set my alarm for 2 a.m. and if we can see the moon, I'll wake you up." They took me up on that offer. At 2 a.m., the sky was completely overcast—except for a small break in the clouds where the moon appeared, already beginning to show the earth's shadow. I roused the camp, and we had a pleasant hour watching the eclipse move into totality through our little window in the clouds that amazingly continued to frame the moon.

I had a junior high group come to the Nature Center one afternoon and they were a reluctant bunch. They wanted to go swimming instead of tramping around in the woods. I took them down to the stream that comes out of the lake, with nets and scoops. They had a great time turning over rocks and splashing around. One young man from the Albany inner city found and captured a dragonfly nymph. It was a dramatic find, large and active. He wanted to take it home with him but relented after he agreed he couldn't duplicate the environment.

With all the confusion and exuberance of canoe campers you tend to see very little Adirondack wildlife up close. But one day, with the campers all in the canoes at the river, I went back up the hill for a last check of the campsite. As I turned to go, a large owl flew into the clearing and perched on a pine tree just a few feet away. I realized then just how quietly they fly; if I hadn't seen him I would never have known he had arrived. That interaction made my day, though I doubt it did much for his.

The staff kids brought a bullfrog out to the Nature Center. We put it in the 'water habitat' (a half barrel with water and rocks). I took my next group to the stream to hunt for things and we brought back small fish, nymphs and a pickerel frog. While we were sitting at the table discussing our finds, one camper yelled 'look' and we watched as the bullfrog devoured the other frog, not a lesson I had planned.

Part of the portage route on the Fulton Chain goes right through Old Forge. I'm sure the locals were used to seeing many people traipse through their town, but our group really got the guys' attention. It might have been because of our nice aluminum canoes, but more likely it was because of the twin girls in bikinis carrying their canoe overhead as they went down the main street.

Some sites in the Adirondacks are so perfect that they get totally overused. There was a lovely spot on one of the Saranacs that had a nice log lean-to and several huge boulders making a natural harbor. We'd stopped at this spot while canoeing many times. One year when we got there we found that firewood was very hard to gather. You had to walk several hundred yards into the woods to even find twigs to use as kindling. The last time we swung by, the state had "closed" the site by removing the lean-to and cutting trees to block the harbor. Hopefully, in a few years, or decades, the site will renew itself and be open for travelers again.

Love Stories

Several couples on site had spent the first summer, or even summers, of their married life together in Staff Northwest cabin. Eventually, though, the "Honeymoon Suite" had to be replaced. I was working on the demolition alone and got it ready for collapse. Then, when I knew everyone was gone for the day I used a cable and pulled it down with my vehicle. By the time they got back I had things pretty much cleared up, and they were spared the sorrow of seeing the site of their happy memories turned into a pile of scrap wood.

Skye Farm has seen the start or blossoming of more than one long-term romance. One year Ed Osterhout was a contented bachelor heading the maintenance staff. Carol True came to camp as part of the waterfront staff. Harriett Cederstrom, who knew them both, is reported to have said to Evelyn Bass, "His days are numbered. He just doesn't know it yet." She had that right, as they've already celebrated 44 years together.

Ed and Carol's daughter Diane and her husband Stephen chose Skye Farm as the site for their wedding and reception on June 8, 1991—the middle of black fly season and a time of year when the Adirondack weather can be miserable. Their day, though, went incredibly well—sunny but not too hot, a light breeze but not windy, and not a black fly or mosquito to be seen. Oh yes, they're still very much together.

Bill Lasher and Joanna Curtis met and courted at Skye farm before their marriage. Their son Terry also met his wife, Lori Scranton, in that place where vision and affection so often come together.

Terry and Lori (Scranton) Lasher

Sorry Plights

Part of our canoe route from one small pond to another led us to where a railroad causeway crossed the water. The causeway was pierced by a drainage conduit full of water and large enough for a canoe, except that somehow a twenty-foot telephone pole had gotten lodged in the pipe. Our choices were to remove the log or unpack the gear from our canoes so we could portage up a steep embankment and back down the other side. We chose to remove the log—which only took twice as long and three times the effort of the portage.

Among the issues that made leaving Camp Missisquoi desirable was the fact that the state condemned the maintenance shop. We redid a cabin and created a new shop—much nicer but not the ideal solution. The nurse's lodge had issues too. It often smelled of mildew and dead animals. Another problem we had was above ground waterlines. I guess it was good news/bad news. The bad news was they often got leaks in them. The good news was that when the waterlines leaked, they sprayed fountains in the air so we could locate the exact site of the problem.

At Missisquoi, the campers' cabins were in tough shape and more dangerous because they were electrified. It wasn't unusual for us to think that the power was off and then have a tool give off a spark and puff of smoke because the lines were still hot. The pump house and cistern were down by the river. We'd check that system every night because even one running toilet was enough to drain the whole tank by morning. The rule the maintenance crew often had to follow was, "Fix it but don't put a lot into it." When the tabernacle was rebuilt the ground inside was covered with a layer of new, white crushed stone. After we used that area to repaint the red picnic tables the floor looked like it was covered with blood spatters.

Perhaps it really is selective memory, but it seems that Tuesdays used to have more than their fair share of maintenance disaster. When the call came in, "Pretoria is stopped up," you could be pretty sure it was another "Black Tuesday."

Creative Solutions

We needed to install an outdoor electrical outlet on the side of the dining hall facing Sherman Pond. We ran the wire inside easily enough and made a small hole in the siding to locate the center of the electrical box. When we went off to get the right tool to enlarge the hole to create the necessary two-by-four-inch hole, Dick Nason happened by with his chainsaw in hand. By the time we returned, he had long since made the hole for us and was on to deal with more trees that needed felling.

Bob Long was the first full-time summer manager at Missisquoi. Money was very tight. He had enough money to buy food for camp, and if he shopped carefully there would be enough left over for one tool. One way he made it possible for the camp to run was by trading work and tools with the local farmers. If he gave them half a day baling hay, they could afford to let him borrow their tractor for a half-day in return.

We're not sure if it's necessary, but a frequent winter job is shoveling snow off the roof of the dining hall. One day we were shoveling while the thermometer outside the kitchen read 20 below. Steve Marino showed up to help. He unloaded his snow blower, hoisted it up, and moved that job to a quick completion.

We had a sickly birch tree near the Skye Farm parking lot. Actually, it was long since dead! With Bachelor's Hall in one direction, Sleepy Hollow outhouse in another, Garbage Gazebo #1 and the Flammable Storage Locker in another, and high voltage lines overhead, it was not an easy tree to take down. Techniques that might have worked on a sturdier tree were out of the question for this one. It was so unsteady that we didn't even want to put a ladder against it to climb up and attach a rope to use to pull it down. Maybe it was best just to leave it and hope that nothing important, like the camp truck, was underneath when it came down by itself. This tree required professional equipment we just didn't have. One day a tree-trimming crew happened to be at camp. Tom Lee, head of maintenance, asked if they'd be willing to take the tree down—a simple job with the truck they had with them. "We would," they said, "but all our saws are too dull and need sharpening."

"Now that's a problem I can solve," said Tom. Shortly after that, the tree was safely down and the crew headed off to their next job with five freshly sharpened chainsaws.

I guess it says something about the kind of person I am that I get such satisfaction out of being registrar. Forms, fees, faxes and photocopies—all that material needs to be in order so that campers can come to camp and have a good time. But the best part of my job is helping to find funds for kids who otherwise could not attend. It's pretty amazing sometimes. One year at annual conference I was standing in the lunch line with Art (Hagy) grieving over some children who needed major campership assistance. A lay member from one of the churches came up behind us and said, "We have about $1,000 to send kids to camp but don't have any to go this year. Any idea about what we can do with the money?" First, I gave him his answer. Then I let him have lunch!

Many of our cabin group continued together for the next few years. One member of our group had a reputation for being a bit of a troublemaker. One day, our counselor came into the dining hall to find the counselor of our neighboring cabin group chasing this kid around. "WHY are you chasing my camper?!" our counselor asked, only to be told "He pead in my shorts!" Indeed, after a battle that began with verbal teasing, our camper had taken a serving spoon of peas and put them down the back of the counselor's shorts. It sounds worse than it was because everything that was done, including the peas and the chase, was in good fun. And, if truth be told, the counselor had been egging the kid on. After all, this was creativity camp.

Bill Lasher was the Skye Farm manager for a period. One of his challenges as winter weather approached was replacing the furnace in the caretaker's house that served as the first retreat lodge. Working alone, he disconnected the old unit (a coal burner converted to oil), connected a cable to it, and used the camp truck to drag it across the cellar floor, up the stairs, and out the bulkhead doors. He eased the new unit back down the stairs using the same process in reverse as best he could and then hitched up the electricity, oil, and heat ducts. It's not clear if the town building inspector knew about any of this or approved the installation, but the furnace ran fine.

Many times prayers are answered at Skye Farm. One Sunday morning as we were preparing for the service in the chapel, our director Kevin asked us to pray. We did not have enough counselors for the coming week. While campers were coming in to register for camp, a couple stopped by who had been on the staff years ago. They had just been married and were traveling around on their honeymoon. They had nearly run out of money and were looking for a place to stay. Kevin asked them if they would be willing to fill in for a week, and they were delighted to do so.

Many times prayers are answered at Skye Farm. One

In the fall of 2003 we were working on Staff Northwest. The weather was getting worse and worse. The pressure-treated timbers were covered with ice. At one point someone asked, "What do we do next?" I said, "Let's cover it with a tarp and come back in the spring." Everyone seconded that motion in a hurry.

Weather Reports

On canoe camp we tried to protect ourselves against rain, but one night we had two very heavy storms come through and there was just no way to keep much of anything dry. Early the next morning we headed out in the rain, called Skye Farm, and asked Dick Palmer to come get us with the van. When we got to the designated pick-up spot it was still raining. The campsite was so wet that we didn't have to unload the canoes but just floated them a couple of hundred feet across the grass from the beach to the parking lot.

A "weather bomb" hit Skye farm in the summer of '95, knocking down numerous trees. Fortunately, there were no injuries and only minimal building damage. Still, the camp had no electricity for over four days. It was a bit of a challenge to keep things going but everyone got through it—and gained a real appreciation for the remaining outhouses!

One day at lunchtime a terrific lightning storm came across the camp. Several people in the dining hall, sitting at tables with metal edges, got disturbingly strong tingles as bolts outside induced charges on conductors inside the building. Once the storm passed, the maintenance crew went out to check the damage. Just down the road they found a tree blown apart. It was still steaming from the energy of the strike. And beside it, a six-foot-long "splinter" stuck out like a javelin in the road. In Bachelors Hall they found a hole in the roof and the cover blown off the fuse box by a cartridge fuse that exploded. Later someone brought a stereo over to the maintenance shop for possible repair. That piece of equipment was fried inside and had to be tossed in the rubbish.

One year, around 2004 or 2005, a group came to Skye Farm for a retreat and got more of a retreat than they bargained for. Extremely heavy rains washed out part of the Northway and part of the camp road. The camp itself and the people were quite safe though isolated. A woman needed to catch a flight, so she left her car behind and walked out to meet a friend who came for her. The next week she came back and rescued her car.

Somehow on a portage my daughter and her friend got separated from the rest of us. Although the trail was generally well marked, at one point they wandered a couple of feet astray and got well stuck in the mud. They were greatly relieved when my co-counselor returned for them, got them back on solid ground, and was able to retrieve their boots from the muck.

One very hot and humid day I crossed the volleyball court on my way to lunch, and one of the campers asked me about having it rain to make it cool down. I said I'd see what I could do. Much to my surprise and pleasure, it started to rain just about the time lunch was over, raising my status in that camper's eyes.

As a result of several heavy snows and a couple of winter rainstorms, the porch roofs at Kessler were thickly coated with ice. The Thursday crew clambered up on ladders and by much effort of chopping, shoveling, and grunting got the north, east and west sides of the roof mostly cleared off. When we got around to the south side, there was Bud chuckling at his clear, dry section of roof. "I got my part done quite a while ago," he informed us. Do you think the sun shining on the southern exposure had anything to do with his rapid success? We were suspicious but Bud wasn't saying.

Practical Jokes

In July 1979 we all knew that the unused space station, Skylab, was due to drop out of orbit. There was some concern about when and where the debris would land. It was big news at the time, and everyone at camp knew that the impact was on the night of July 11. Not everyone knew that the impact zone was the Indian Ocean. On the morning of July 12, camp awoke to find a scorched piece of machinery on Staff Hill with the "NASA" logo hand-lettered on it. Some thought it might really be space junk. Others saw right away that it was only the compressor from an old refrigerator, thoughtfully battered and placed there by the ever-helpful maintenance crew.

As a prank, person or persons unknown put a bucket of frogs in the cooks' cabin. The resulting confusion when the young women discovered the invaders in their bedrooms was exactly the intended reaction. We got most of them out easily enough, but one large frog got under a dresser. Now frogs try to escape by giving a mighty leap. Unfortunately, every mighty leap only caused this poor creature to whack his head. We finally collected him, dazed and covered with dust bunnies. I carried him outside and brought him to a swampy area where he could recover.

One day the noon lunch was a bit delayed. Ed Osterhout turned to me and said, "Let's bang our cups on the table the way we did when we were in jail." A woman sitting nearby quickly went to the camp director to warn him about the felons who seemed to have the run of the place.

In the early 1990s camping leaders were agog. "Agog" is not really too strong a word. The news was that an anonymous donor was preparing to give millions of dollars to United Methodist camping programs across the country. There would be a national conference center and $1,000,000 for each annual conference. The Board of Camps and Conferences went to work preparing to spend this gift, scheduled to be received early in the 21st century. Sigh! That news, which bounced around for several years, turned out to be a hoax or possibly a scam. The camping leadership never sent any cash to a post office box in Nigeria, but it was a similarly tempting and exciting offer while it lasted.

Snappy Comebacks

The maintenance crew always tried to be as helpful and cooperative as possible, but one year we had a cook who asked more than we could deliver. We were told that the flame on the gas stove was too hot. "Sorry," we replied, "but we are required to maintain the laws of physics."

When the Canadian Royal Mounted Police decided to get rid of two sixteen-person "peace canoes," they found a willing buyer at Skye Farm. Steve Marino was detailed to transport the boats across the border. Once the extensive paperwork was reviewed and found in order at the checkpoint, the customs officer commented, "Those are big canoes." "They are," replied Steve, "and you should see the guys who paddle them."

Shifting Viewpoints

It's wonderful how a canoe trip can be a great leveler. The status differences in a group of girls disappear in a hurry once they all get dumped in the water.

More than once while canoeing, as we enjoyed tuna on Rye-Crisp we commented on how good that food tasted at lunchtime. We tried them one time at home and found them—well, let's say we only tried them one time at home.

Coming into our campsite one hot afternoon, we had finished off all the beverages we had with us. Fortunately, there was a well with a pump at the site and we drank many cups of that delicious cold water. Then, as suppertime approached we went back to the well for more water and found it was so strongly flavored of sulfur that we could hardly drink it without running it through a filter. We hadn't noticed that flavor at all when we were really thirsty.

At one point the Board of Health mandated that each cabin at Skye Farm have a second exit in case of emergencies. That reminded me of when I was a camper. The counselors used to say that if an emergency exit were required they'd toss the smallest camper through the window screen. I thought they were kidding, but since I was often the smallest kid in the cabin I always wondered.

Canoeing is a great way to travel—on the water. Portaging is much less enjoyable. One day as we were finishing up the long portage around the falls on the Racquet River, we met a group of inner city kids at the landing going the other way. All their gear was in sturdy wooden boxes, carried on the back and supported by rope straps. As one young lad squished up the soggy trail struggling with his load, he remarked to his companions, "I don't see how this is so fun." It's an acquired taste, I suppose.

One of the neat things about church camping is the "family style" mix of boys and girls together. That point was brought home one day on canoe camp when our mixed crew entered the lake from a creek. We were laughing, colorful, and headed in pretty much all directions at once. Crossing in front of us came a camp of Boy Scouts—solemn, quiet, in an orderly row of canoes. Their leader glowered a bit (maybe he was just squinting in the sun), but I think the Scouts were more than a bit envious of our traveling companions and us.

Full Circles

One of the pianos at Covenant Hills belonged to Peg Moore. It was hers when she grew up in the town of Cabot, traveled with her and Stan to many locations during their years in the active ministry, and then came back home to continue to make music at Covenant Hills.

When Diane Marino attended the 20th anniversary celebration of Covenant Hills, she wore her old tee shirt saying, "Covenant Hills Opening Staff." Which is more amazing: that she still has it, that she can still find it, or that it still fits her?

Diane (Osterhout) Marino

In the early days of Skye Farm, Lemuel Sherman moved large stones to create his fields, walls, and pastures. In 2007, adventure camp moved small stones to build a labyrinth, thus adding another dimension to the devotional and spiritual possibilities of the camp experience.

Happy Endings

At clown camp we encouraged the campers to experiment with their faces and try something new each day. One young woman apparently was struggling with some issues because every day she created a sad face. We were pleased that finally, on Friday, she appeared with a happy one.

One of the counselors came to me with a problem. Her campers were not coming together and it was Wednesday already. Her co-counselor was a volunteer who couldn't go on hikes, and she asked me to take them on a challenging trail. I had an idea that we could go up a trail, and then bushwhack our way to Lookout Trail, a different route from the usual back way up to Lookout. We got deep into the woods. I was using a compass and topo map. We went down hill and up hill until I had no idea where I was. We'd been gone for more than an hour when we finally came to the road that goes to Alderbrook Lodge. Now I knew where I was but we were a long way from camp. We hiked to the highway that goes to Bolton Landing, down to Ogden Lodge Road, and back over the Orange Trail to camp. We arrived about 6:30, well after suppertime, but the staff gave us a cheer and fed us. We came through that hike without a scratch, thank the Lord, and that cabin group and I were now the best of pals.

It was the first year I worked at Skye Farm. I had been at camp for four weeks, not going home to visit my family, and I was experiencing what many campers have—home sickness. It was Sunday afternoon. The new campers were at Kessler for registration and I was in my cabin with nothing to do and feeling sorry for myself. A knock on the door! "Come in," I said. A friend entered who had decided to have a drive in the Adirondacks for the day and stopped in to see how I was doing. He and his friend invited me out to lunch and a scenic drive. That was the best thing that could have happened to me that day!

Sweet Afterglow

In camping it is important to remember that we are in this for the long term. I had a terrible time at sailing camp with one 16-year-old who just did not like the rules. That experience was so bad that I lost interest in directing. A few years later that person spoke at UMW Day and said the time with me was the "best camp ever."

I recall one youth who was a terror as a camper, but years later he came up to me and said, "Thanks for not giving up on me."

It was interesting when clown camp and creative writing camp shared Ogden Lodge together. The writers tended to be quiet and introspective. The clowns typically were, let's say, more dynamic and happy with confusion. So to accommodate the writers we were forced to take some time each day in thoughtful contemplation. That was good for us. And the rest of the time, the writers saw us bouncing off the walls. That was good for them as they got material to stimulate their writing.

I remember that creativity camp was almost always the same week as the special needs camp. We got to know those campers and looked forward to seeing them every year. When one of the regulars was not there, we would ask what happened.

Some of my favorite times at camp were at bedtime, when the counselors often read to us, usually either stories from *The Way of the Wolf* or *Winnie the Pooh*. I kept up that tradition the year I volunteered as a counselor for junior high aquatics camp. I read all the water-related Pooh stories to my girls. I have since bought a (now very dog-eared) copy of *The Way of the Wolf* just so I could read those stories again and again, largely to remind me of the nights at Skye Farm.

Without Skye Farm, I would not have so many special memories, so many friends, and such a firm foundation. My mom and uncle went there. One of my best friends to this day is someone I met as a camper there when I was 14. We both went back year after year. I am so proud that my daughter loves going as much as I did. I was, as any parent might be, a little nervous about her being away from me the first time. She was afraid she'd be homesick at mini-camp. When I picked her up, however, she begged to know when she'd be old enough to stay for the whole week. That was when I knew the third generation had come home to roost.

Storytellers

Al Cederstrom
Art Hagy ("Grandfather Art")
Bill Lasher
Bob Long
Bud Jameson
Cherry Gorton
Clark Callendar
David Murphy
David Osterhout
Dick Palmer
Ed Osterhout

Jackie Marino
Judy Lott ("Mother Nature")
Judy Palmer
Hale Ritchie
Harriet Cederstrom
Paul Dufford
Ralph Marino
Sarah Weber
Steve Butler
Steve Marino
Todd Marlow

And others, whose voices we heard but whose faces were obscured by the flickering logs and our flickering memory.

Chapter 9

Tending the Fire

... a dimly burning wick he will not quench. Isaiah 42:3

From 1982 to 2010, Troy Conference was deeply involved in maintaining continuity and easing transitions. While the five practices of fruitful congregations were playing themselves out at the conference and local levels, other things were happening in a rather "by the way" manner. These are actions and changes undertaken to build and maintain the active core of church and conference life. The implications of these events are perhaps not as obvious, but a review of their history and impact helps to give a fuller picture of what was going on through the years. Three particular areas deserve attention:

- location—of the conference center and of the conference archives;
- technology—the potential and possibilities in the ministry of the church from 1981 to the present;
- conferencewide fellowship—the contributions of United Methodist Youth Fellowship, United Methodist Women, and United Methodist Men in support of the ministry of conference.

Finally, by the way, it is important to look at how the approaching dissolution of Troy Annual Conference was experienced, confronted and interpreted. As hymn writer Natalie Sleeth put it so well, "In our end is our beginning."

Archives and History

*A*Flame of Fire* recounts how, once upon a time, the archives of Troy Conference resided in an old trunk stored under the stairs of the Fifth Avenue-State Street Methodist Church in Troy. In the 1950s, most of the historical records of the Troy Conference and the former Vermont Conference were brought together at the New York Historical Society building in Ticonderoga. The old building had a solid, rock of ages look to it, but control of temperature and humidity were difficult. In addition, our historical materials quickly overran the space available to us there. Soon other options came under consideration.

Finally, one snowy Saturday in the winter of 1972-73, the books and records were transferred in a rented U-Haul to a much larger space in the new library of Green Mountain College in Poultney, VT. This was a better location for storage and for research because the climate was under closer control and individuals had room to spread out. Further, the long historic connection between the college and Troy Conference made the site a natural choice.

The Commission on Archives and History upgraded the protection of materials with the purchase, in 1982, of two locked files. That was the year that the Rev. Charles Schwartz became archivist for the conference. He and his wife Ouida began the work of cataloging the archives. Charles prepared a typewritten copy of the very fragile handwritten diary of Mattias Swaim, one of the early circuit riders active in Troy Conference. In addition, 1982 was the year the commission published *A Flame of Fire.*

By the end of 1983, the Schwartzes had cataloged over 2,500 books and an equal number of documents and manuscripts. In 1984, the bicentennial of American Methodism, conference approved an archival policy that clarified issues of storage and recordkeeping. To help connect local churches with the history of Methodist work, the commission prepared "bicentennial place mats." Intended for use at church suppers, each mat pictured a map indicating sites of historic interest across the bounds of conference.

The Journal for 1986 notes that the collection at Green Mountain College now numbered over 10,000 books, letters, journals, and other items. The commission published *A Spreading Flame: The Story of the Churches of Troy Annual Conference* to coincide with the dates of annual conference. This book, also by the Schwartzes, provides a one-page history, a short list of historically important events, and a photo for each United Methodist church then active in the conference. Further, the commission began to gear up for the "long-term project of locating and marking the graves of all Methodist pastors buried within the boundaries of Troy Annual Conference." "Long term" was the right word to use as year by year, even to the present, the commission continues to locate pastors' graves and mark them with an appropriate symbol and ceremony.

In 1988, the commission published a booklet entitled *Access to Heritage*, to help local churches successfully maintain their historical documents and artifacts. The group assisted the Commission on the Status and Role of Women with materials for the celebration of the centennial of Georgia Harkness's birth in 1991. In 1990, the commission made application to the General Commission on Archives and History to designate places in Troy Conference as Historic Sites. In 1991, Bishop James Matthews led the services assigning marker #251 to the grave of Philip Embury in Woodlands Cemetery in Cambridge and marker #252 to the Ashgrove Cemetery. These were the first Troy Conference landmarks to gain this level of official designation.

The 1993 conference petitioned the General Commission to designate Christ Church, Troy as a United Methodist Historic Site, and in 1994 that marker, #296, was dedicated.

In 1995, Troy Conference hosted the annual meeting of the Northeastern Jurisdictional Commission on Archives and History at Pine Grove UMC, Albany. The Rev. Charles and Ouida Schwartz, the Rev. James Fenimore, and the Rev. Ralph Marino each presented a paper to the gathering.

The 1997 Journal includes a conference resolution that established a ten-year program to more carefully administer and use the growing body of material under the supervision of the conference archives. That same year, conference was given the chair used by Bishop Asbury during the conference held at Ashgrove in 1803.

The report of 1999 notes the inadequacy of storage, workspace, and security at Green Mountain College library. Meanwhile, Erica Burke, archivist, was preparing a database of material, with the hope of making the records searchable over the Internet at some future time.

Suddenly the storage issue at Poultney took on added urgency when a leaking roof made it necessary to package and relocate all the holdings. The commission then rented a van in November 1999 and moved all materials to the basement of the conference center in Saratoga Springs. The first major task then was a re-inventory of material to be sure the collection was intact. Meanwhile, the commission brought to the 2000 conference a resolution calling for a study of the feasibility of an addition to the conference center to hold the archives.

In 2002, the conference trustees were empowered to spend up to $75,000 to "create a suitable space for the conference archives." After due consideration, the trustees undertook a major renovation of the basement area of the conference center. The new space was deemed suitable for "processing new materials, preservation, security, and usefulness." With an expanded heating system, the facility was made comfortable for year-round archival work. The Charles and Ouida Schwartz Archives were formally dedicated during the 2004 session of annual conference.

At the 2007 session of conference, the "Methodist Cemetery" on the former site of the Barnard, VT meetinghouse was approved as an official historic site of the United Methodist Church. The site received marker number #430 and was dedicated on August 18, 2007.

The 2008 report of the commission noted that one

Ouida Schwartz remembers

Merle Doud phoned my husband Charles, saying there had been a water leak on the upper floor of the library where our archives were housed. The leak had destroyed the protective air controls. While none of our holdings were damaged, the library had boxed everything up and moved the materials into storage on a lower floor until we could make other arrangements for the archives.

Meanwhile, work on the conference center was progressing with the promise that space would be allotted us within its walls. We asked many questions along the way—about dampness, lighting, stairs, railing on stairs, a table large enough for research study, a locked area where we might store our most valued items, and adequate shelving. The final result was not quite everything we had wished, but we were thankful for a safe space. We have a fine collection. It was put together with thought, added to with selective care, and preserved with archival approved storage containers for our best holdings.

major project involved comparing what was on the shelves with a previous card catalog, thus producing a list of what was missing. Some of the missing materials were found at the Green Mountain College library, but not all items were recovered. During conference session the Wolcott, VT, UMC was designated the seventh historic site of the Troy Annual Conference, in part because the Rev. George S. Brown, the first African-American pastor in Troy Conference, oversaw the construction of the building there in 1856.

One major display at the 2009 session of annual conference was a timeline prepared by Karen Staulters, conference archivist. The display gave a year-by-year chronology of events and church foundings. Most members of conference found it important to stop by that display and see just when their church became an official part of conference life. The report of the commission that year indicated that on August 16, 2008, the Wolcott church received the United Methodist Historic Site marker # 439. Also, under "Projects Underway," the report lists "Updating the Troy Conference history from 1982 to the present day and publishing this with a guide of churches." The present volume resulted from that decision.

Through the years, the Commission on Archives and History has worked to engage conference with a thoughtful recollection of the past. Grave marking ceremonies were held in many locations across the conference, and the announcement of special church anniversaries in the form of "Historic Minutes" have been part of daily conference sessions. The commission has kept the "Ministry of Memory" alive.

Conference Center

When the conference administratively reorganized in 1972, the Program Administration Council (similar in function to the Council on Ministries which followed it) rented office space on the second floor of a former home at 175 Lake Avenue in Saratoga Springs. This location, while very small and non-handicapped accessible,

served the conference for a number of years. The Rev. C. Walter Kessler and then the Rev. Royal B. Fishbeck Jr. oversaw their responsibilities from that site. Paula Hanlon Carr, secretary and administrative assistant, joined the staff there and remained with the office until her retirement in 2005.

Then in 1980,

Conference center on Route 9 in Gansevoort, NY.

conference purchased a small piece of land on Route 9 north of Saratoga. On that site the trustees constructed a single floor ranch style home. The Rev. William A. Lasher became executive director of the Council on Ministries in 1981 and had his office there.

By 1986, it was clear that the initial land purchase was too small for long-term growth. Conference gave the trustees permission to purchase an additional 12 acres of land adjacent to the facility. This was far more space than was needed, but the trustees felt the excess could easily be sold.

By 1990, it became clear that both the office space and the parking lot of the conference center were over-crowded. The trustees were authorized to study the situation and either add on to the existing building or relocate as seemed best.

Already by 1991 the new offices were a reality. Conference received a gift of two parcels of land near Exit 15 of the Northway. A large handicapped accessible office building was built at 396 Loudon Road before May. The Rev. James M. Perry, who had been council executive director since 1989, moved into the new facility.

Finally in 2001, after years of leasing the Route 9 facility, the trustees reported, with an almost audible sigh of relief, that the old conference center had been sold.

The no longer quite so new conference center continues to serve its intended functions well. In addition to housing the office of the conference minister (the Rev. Barbara Lemmel from 2000 to 2007 and the Rev. Holly Nye from 2007 to the present) and staff, the building also is the worksite for the conference treasurer and staff, the conference director of communications, the Adirondack district superintendent and staff, the conference administrator, and the conference archives. The building also has additional storage space and rooms, which given its central location, make it a frequent site for a wide variety of meetings.

Technology

It is not much of a stretch to say that Methodists have been interested in technology from the beginning. John Wesley followed the early experiments in electricity with great interest. And when you say "Cokesbury," you may well be referring to the United Methodist Publishing House, founded in 1789 for the purpose of using technology to spread the Good News. Changing technology has also had its impact on Troy Annual Conference. The coming of the railroad made the great camp meetings much easier to organize. When the Vermont Conference met in Richford in 1913, the closing resolutions had this to say: "We are very grateful to the Northern Telephone Company for the installation of an instrument in the vestry and the gratuitous use of the same. May prosperity attend this company in all its undertakings." In 1922, invitations to the institute offerings at Round Lake included the opportunity to order free stereopticon slides to use in stimulating more people to attend the sessions.

In more recent decades the automobile has transformed the travel experience. Part of the appeal of Skye Farm Camp, and especially the adult retreat lodge, is its easy access by car. When choosing a site for Covenant Hills, a good location near major highways was a critical factor.

In 1982, Donald Waterfield, chairperson of the Communications Committee, reported on four uses of technology that at the time were innovative but now are all but taken for granted. While videotaping as a communications tool was just becoming available on the consumer market, "Reverend William Pattison ... used video tape recording of a Christmas pageant ... to produce an attractive tool for congregational and community learning experience. It demonstrated a more professional use of video than prior attempts." The Rev. Asa Sprague used multimedia displays to demonstrate that forms of inter- and intra- church communication can be enhanced. The conference newsletter, NEWS

After the request to write the history came, we went to the top store for computers in Portland. When we were asked the purpose and they heard "writers," they showed us a Brothers Word Processor for Writers. It was a dream machine for our work. We enjoyed it, but two books wore it out.

We knew most of the older generation personally and well enough to either arrange to see them (preferably) or write to them. We were holding and using four library cards in Maine and one in Boston, not counting three sources that we tapped many times in Vermont and several in New York. We used interlibrary loan, which gave us adequate time to extract information or take notes.

Charles chose the Industrial Revolution up to current days. I preferred Colonial through the Civil War so we divided chronologically. For fun we finally counted the number of printed pages each of us had written and we were within two or three pages of each other, by coincidence.

& NOTES, was being produced with computers, and Plattsburgh UMC demonstrated "application of a computer as a communication tool as well as an administrative aid in church operation."

It is very hard to recall from today's perspective just what a personal computer was like in those days. The technically minded may be interested to realize that the most affordable

This is a computer! (Or should that be: This is a computer?)

machines then were from Radio Shack. The largest amount of memory the typical microprocessor, the Z80, could address was only 64 thousand bits with an eight bit bus. That 64 K included the operating system, the keyboard matrix, the video display, the program, and the random access memory. Floppy disks were, in fact, very floppy and most home computers used the 5 ¼" size, which held around 100 kilobytes of data or programming. The displays were monochromatic, usually white on black. But, for just a couple of dollars one could get a plastic screen overlay to produce a nice green on black effect. Despite these modest specifications, as the Rev. William Lasher, council director, noted in the 1982 report of the Enlarged Cabinet, "The computer has proven to be a valuable tool." Publishing was much easier, as the ability to produce at least a simple version of "camera ready copy" was no longer restricted to professionals.

The impact of new technology appears in several places in the conference of 1984. That was the first year that videotapes were made of conference sessions. Bishop Nichols encouraged churches to find ways to use this "exciting tool (video equipment) to enhance ministry." In his episcopal address, he made extensive references to religious programming—what was out there and what United Methodists should think about offering. In a demonstration of the available technology, video highlights of annual conference were made available for viewing following the ordina-

Videotaping at conference

tion service and lunch on Sunday. In an example of new technology meeting the old, at one point the conference film photographer was focusing on camera 1. Camera 1 was looking at camera 2. And camera 2 was getting a picture of the conference photographer. The report of the council director noted that about $5,000 was invested in computer equipment for the conference and used for, among other things, "electronic mail" from General Board offices.

Again, the Journal of 1985 showed the growing awareness of the impact of technology on the church. Bishop White, in his episcopal address, noted how commercial television can be a positive source of information, as when it showed disasters where the response of UMCOR was needed, and a nega-

tive influence as when only part of a story is told. Conference was held at Winooski, VT, that year, and Bishop White got to experience the pluses and minuses when he was interviewed by television Channel 5, Plattsburgh. Meanwhile, the Commu-

A reporter interviews Bishop White

nications Committee reported the offer of computer workshops to help churches get started with the new technology.

In 1985, the conference office received a technology

Chet Vanderbilt

upgrade with the installation of a 12' satellite dish. The dish allowed the taping of "Catch the Spirit," a weekly program designed to run on local cable networks. Through the diligent efforts of Chet Vanderbilt, conference communications coordinator, conference had the satisfaction of placing "Catch the Spirit" on half a dozen cable systems. In part because of that effort and in part because of his long-term efforts in developing contacts with print media, the United Methodist Association of Communicators named Chet the Outstanding Communicator of 1986.

The 1987 report of the Communications Committee

notes with satisfaction the growing use of the media center. What once was mostly a collection of filmstrips had now grown to include several other types of media. Videotapes by now were much more readily available. By the end of the year, over 700 video titles were available at the conference center. Three video libraries were set up around conference—each with a VCR, a 13" monitor, and a small library of tapes available for loan to local churches. The Interpretation Committee also prepared videotapes for use in stewardship workshops through the year. The tapes were in lieu of slide sets or filmstrips that had been used in similar, previous efforts.

At conference in 1988, the representative from Cokesbury reported on the creation of the Cokesbury Satellite TV Network (CSTN) and the Ecumenical Youth Television Ministries Network. These attempts to use technology eventually faded away but were a clear sign of the desire to use technology effectively. The Division of Education of the Conference Board of Discipleship noted that several persons attended training events made possible through the use of CSTN. By 1989, the conference center had two satellite dishes in place, making teleconferencing a potential vehicle for training. In further search of the best use of technology, a coalition of mainline Protestant, Orthodox, Roman Catholic and Jewish groups launched the cable network channel, VISN, pronounced "vision." Annual conference in 1989 urged pastors and churches to build local interest in having this channel on cable networks. Cable television was understood to be a potentially significant way to keep the message of faith before the general public.

Perhaps the leader in the prescience department would be the Rev. J. Edward Carothers. His memoir printed in the 2000 Journal puts him clearly in the forefront of those who anticipated what new ways of communication would mean. He had a radio program on the major station in the New York Capital Area in the early 1940s and in 1948 wrote in the Christian Advocate, "We MUST get ready for television." In 1972 he wrote, with Margaret Mead, Roger Schinn, and Daniel McCracken, a book titled, *To Love or Perish: Technological Crisis and the Churches.* He had a far-sighted vision indeed.

The 1990 report of the communications coordinator recorded the honors given to two pastors with long-term involvement in public media. The Rev. James Beskin was the on-camera moderator of an ecumenical television program, "Good News," from 1962 to 1989. He also did extensive radio work through a connection with key New York Capital Region faith groups. The Rev. Walter Taylor had served for many years on various church media related organizations and also was the long-time host of a program called "Word and Music," which aired on an Albany radio station.

The 1991 session of annual conference brought two technology resolutions to the floor. One related to Telendow, a firm offering discounted long-distance service to users and financial aid to the conference. The resolution asked that local churches supply Telendow with the names, addresses, and phone numbers of their members so the company could solicit their business, with the generated income to be used at the discretion of the Council on Finance and Administration. After some discussion over the moral and ethical aspects of fundraising in this manner, the resolution passed. In addition, with the encouragement of the Communications Committee, conference passed a resolution calling for strong, coordinated efforts to place VISN programming on local cable networks across Troy Conference. Telendow never lived up to its hoped-for potential and, in the face of other more commercially successful long-distance services, it soon disappeared from use. Similarly, VISN programming, while attracting a small audience, never gained the community-wide support necessary to pressure cable companies to purchase its shows. VISN also, to the disappointment of its advocates, disappeared.

Among many other items the General Conference delegation reported back to the 1992 session of annual conference was an explanation of the electronic voting system in use there. This was considered a noteworthy innovation at the time. And at the 1995 conference session, Donald Watrous, chairperson of the Board of Discipleship, encouraged all with modems, fax machines, or email addresses to register, so that the innovative technologies could be used to communicate within conference.

An email directory appeared as a new feature of the 1997 Journal. From among all the clergy, laity, and churches of the conference, fewer than 200 names made up the list. The comment from the Rev. Thomas Shanklin, conference secretary, was, "These addresses are very complicated. In some cases it was difficult to tell if they were case-sensitive or not." This was, of course, the leading edge of a major transformation in the way information would be exchanged across the connection and around the world.

The conference web site was launched in the late 1990s. The whole concept was new enough that in 2001 the Communications Committee presented an explanation to help conference recognize the value and usage of a presence on the World Wide Web. In 2002, the committee was pleased to announce that the entire catalog of the media center was now available and searchable on the conference web site. By 2008, the committee was able to report that the news section of the site received over 21,000 hits in a twelve-month period. The church locator directory was activated over 10,000 times during that same period. It only took a few short years for the web site to move from being a curiosity to a reliable tool for communication and ministry.

Open hearts. Open minds. Open doors.
The people of The United Methodist Church

Meanwhile, in the early 2000s, the national "Igniting Ministry" campaign was moving forward. The slogan, "Open Hearts. Open Minds. Open Doors." began to appear in various forms, with the goal of using modern media to help the church better understand itself and to help those outside the church better grasp the vision of The United Methodist Church. Troy Conference located $32,500 to fund a television buy in the markets of the New York Capital District and in Burlington/Plattsburgh. The two-week campaign ran in 2002.

In 2004, the conference keynote address was given by the Rev. Tim Coombs, a Presbyterian pastor who extensively demonstrated some of the ways technology can enhance Sunday morning worship. Part of his presentation dealt with the evolving digital culture and the importance of finding good ways to relate to the generation growing up in that culture, its view of the world, and its music. In another presentation, he talked about the equipment necessary to bridge the gap from past to present. He noted, "It may be helpful to consider how much the families in our churches already spend on digital culture for their homes—because they are part of this culture."

Meanwhile, several other groups used video presentations at conference to raise issues of significance and importance. After thoughtful discussion, Internet access to the pastor's office became one of the minimum compensation requirements. The Communications Committee offered to assist local churches presently without a computer to obtain one. At that same session of conference, the Board of Church and Society brought forward a resolution noting that technology in the form of video lottery terminals was making inroads. The resolution referenced the traditional Methodist anti-gambling stance and also encouraged support of ministries of healing, including groups such as Gamblers Anonymous.

In 2005, Church of the Covenant in Averill Park proposed, and conference voted to approve, a petition stressing a new use of technology on behalf of very traditional Methodist goals. After noting the dangers created by drivers operating vehicles while under the influence of alcohol, the petition called for the installation of an ignition interlock to prevent those with a second conviction for DWI from starting their cars after using alcohol.

The local churches of Troy Conference moved into the digital age at varied rates. Some small churches borrowed equipment from time to time and made use of systems that were just barely adequate. Some churches, having access to members with expertise in the field, proceeded with more elaborate and expensive systems. Conference itself, in 2005, gave out over $20,000 in grants from the Critical Issues Fund to help nine local churches secure digital media equipment for worship.

In a major use of technology, Troy Conference joined with the Western New York, North Central and Wyoming Annual Conferences in October 2007 to have a simultaneous session in four locations. Creating the live video linkage taxed technical skills and resources, as well as presiding bishops who had to act within strictly planned time limits in order to have the feeds going in the right direction at the right time. This video conference allowed independent but coordinated debate on a variety of resolutions, to prepare the way for Jurisdictional Conference to make changes in conference boundaries in ways that honored the decisions made in the four locations. The actions taken at those simultaneous sessions were historic and were possible only due to the modern technology that had impacted the church in so many ways through the years.

Technology brought many changes to church work. The 2008 memoir of Jean Eleanor Beatty, a pastor's wife, noted with some amazement that when she assisted her husband in the early years of his ministry by typing the bulletins each week, "There were no computers then so everything was typed on a small electric typewriter without Word Perfect and with a lot of 'white out.'" A few people still remember when upgrading from a manual to an electric typewriter was a wonderfully liberating experience. The transition from hiring a printing house to do weekly bulletins, to running them off on mimeograph and then copy machines was no less astonishing.

Another 2008 memoir illustrating changing technology within a single lifetime concerns Muriel Richardson Chatterton. As the daughter of a Methodist preacher, she moved in 1924 from Williston, VT to Esperance, NY by horse and buggy. In 1949, as the wife of a Methodist preacher she moved again to Esperance, this time by automobile. And before she returned to Esperance again in 2008 to be buried, this mother and mother-in-law to several United Methodist pastors served as a director of the General Board of Global Ministries and traveled extensively around the world by jet plane.

Groups Linking Laity

The Conference Council on Youth Ministries (CCYM), United Methodist Women (UMW), and United Methodist Men (UMM) all have long, though very different, histories. They each have their own goals and ways of operating. At the same time, they share a common intention of linking people together for fellowship, work, mutual encouragement, and the sheer joy of being in ministry and in mission together. Through the years, they have each made a positive impact on the life of annual conference in a variety of ways.

In 1981, the CCYM offered a number of programs for youth. Thirty-nine attended the 22nd Annual UN Seminar in New York City. Large rallies were held on each district. Senior High Week was held at Castleton (VT) State College. Leaders from the group were part of a national Youth Ministries convocation in Sioux City, IA. Youth Annual Conference (YAC) was held at Calvary UMC in Latham, with a hundred youth in attendance. That same year, the Youth Service Fund raised and donated nearly $600 to programs benefiting youth in need.

Meanwhile, the UMM sent 53 men to a national event held at Purdue University. In addition, the group, through its connection with the national UMM, supported programs of prayer ministry with the Upper Room, boy scouting, and "Moving Members" (which was designed to reconnect people with churches following job or retirement related moves around the country).

Also in 1981, the Troy Conference UMW sent 145 women to the UMW Assembly in Philadelphia. UMW Day at annual conference brought 650 women together. The mission pledge plus supplementary gifts totaled just shy of $100,000. The annual meeting was in Rutland UMC with Ruth Nichols, wife of Bishop Roy C. Nichols, as keynote speaker. Four officers attended the Jurisdictional World Development Seminar. They sponsored leadership training on all the districts as well as at the conferencewide Summer Learning Fellowship.

These various gatherings were typical of the regular efforts made to teach, inspire, and encourage the diverse ministries of laity. Through the years the details changed and programs evolved, but the constant theme was the connection of local ministries and local churches to shared ministry and encouragement for greater involvement.

CCYM

Beginning with the session in 1982, youth at annual conference were highly visible in their roles as pages, serving as "gofers" during sessions and as worship leaders (typically handling one morning service each session). With the growth of technology, they also began to run the video cameras and related equipment used to make first videotapes and then DVDs of the proceedings.

Youth also operated the message display system, which used a small projection screen to give visual announcements of meetings and advise members of incoming phone calls. (The latter need declined when vibrating cell phones became common.) Interestingly enough, the technical means used to project the messages also changed. Handwritten transparencies gave way to typed video projected images with automatic scrolling through the announcements.

Through the years the youth worked hard and were highly visible in their efforts to raise money for the Youth Service Fund. In 1984, the CCYM raised $2,000 for the support of four community service agencies around the conference. Some of their fundraising methods were traditional, such as selling wrapping paper, while some of their other methods were, let us say, "unorthodox." For instance, at the 1985 session, spirited bidding for the privilege of throwing pies at various lay and clergy leaders raised over $1,500. That year they also "kidnapped" Bishop White and raised $425.16 for his return. In 1987, they got in meal lines early and then sold their places to others. Conference sessions were often held at Green Mountain College, and one complaint about conference hall was that the seats were hard. Youth came to the rescue with seat cushions for sale starting in 1987. Typically at least half of the members present advertised the YSF as they carried their cushions to and from sessions. That same year, conference raised $270 for the YSF by taking up a collection to encourage the bishop, district superintendents, and council director to remove their ties.

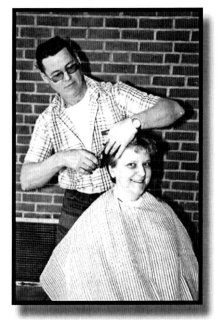

Merv the Barber

In 1988 the goal was to raise $4,500 for the fund. In 1989, the youth of conference were ranked thirtieth in the nation in YSF giving.

Starting in 1991 Merv Spooner, a lay member of conference with barbering experience, began offering haircuts in the lobby with proceeds going to the YSF. The youth also raised well over $600 by bussing tables after meals, and they auctioned off the last of their seat cushions for $350. They also began an attention getting "Penny Challenge" among the districts. The goal was to collect pennies for each district, but coins other than pennies were subtracted from the total. So having run out of pennies to support one's own district, one could put larger amounts in another district's receptacle to reduce the other's standing in the challenge. Regular reports to conference session kept everyone alerted to the current standings. The report the following year had Troy Conference youth second in the jurisdiction and twelfth out of 72 conferences across the nation in fundraising success.

In 1994 perhaps the most important and enduring legacy of the youth fundraising efforts began. Art Doty, a layperson from Vermont, having recently completed a term as chair of the conference trustees, proposed an "OOPS Fund Bottle." Anyone using an acronym was to make a contribution to the bottle. The goal was to make conference sessions more user friendly to new members and to help clarify debates and discussion. Bishop William B. Grove suggested that the proceeds should go to the Youth Service Fund, conference agreed, and the "OOPS Fund Bottle" became the Acronym Jar. Visitors speaking to conference were frequently taken aback as their first sentence, "I'm from GCFA" or "Greetings from AUMS" triggered a roar of protest from the members. People speaking from the floor of conference got stopped in mid-sentence, as did even bishops from time to time when they tried to shorten one of United Methodism's many complex titles. Each year after the jar's first appearance, the youth would bring it forward and explain its operation to the amusement of conference. It was especially delightful when one of the youth giving the explanation would say that funds collected went to the "YSF" instead of the "Youth Service Fund."

The interesting thing was that the influence of the jar extended to conversations and meetings all across conference. Everyone was much more attentive to using the longer, clearer, and more complex real names of things rather than verbal shortcuts. A few made the use of the jar into more of a game. One pastor deliberately spoke of YAHWEH and then paid his fine with a grin. A layperson speaking for the Council on Finance and Administration simply said, "Here's my contribution to the jar in advance." Then he launched into his report and used acronyms with abandon.

At conference in 1995, Bishop Grove gave money to NOT receive a wake-up call from the youth. Visiting Bishop Ruediger Minor also made a contribution so the youth got $150 for their non-efforts. That year the YSF total reached $3,000. National awards were given for the greatest per-capita giving and for the overall amount raised. Troy Conference youth won both.

Contributions to the YSF continued to grow. In 1996 the total was $3,138, in 1999 it reached $5,000, and in 2006 the Youth Service Fund grants to a number of agencies across conference were up to $7,950.

Youth programming was not static either. The annual visit to the UN came to be less appealing so other trips were planned. For instance, in 2004 the Mission of Peace trip was to India. Three youth and one adult from Troy Conference took advantage of that experience.

In 1997 the youth added a junior high rally to their annual program schedule, with the intention of getting more youth excited about what conference level programming offered. The Youth Annual Conference morphed into Youth Autumn Celebration in 2000, and despite the Acronym Jar, pretty much everyone called it YAC (pronounced YAK). The first session of the new YAC drew 215, the gathering in 2004 brought out 275, and the next year a total of 301 youth and adults attended.

The clear, strong presence of youth contributed much energy to annual conference through the years. They brought excitement and energy in a variety of ways. They often spoke from the floor of conference on issues of social and spiritual concern. More than once the business of conference was arranged so that members gathered in small groups. On those occasions, youth were included and usually spread across the gathering so their input would impact as many people as possible. Youth had every reason to consider themselves as valued and respected members of the conference community.

UMW

The United Methodist Women always had a strong presence at annual conference. Typically, UMW Day immediately preceded the opening session of conference. For many years that session was nearly as large as annual conference itself, so there was always a high level of energy as the two groups interacted.

The United Methodist Women, operating on the basis of their long tradition, tended to focus on the programs that worked well for them. The rounds of district meetings and Summer Learning Fellowship took considerable time and effort to plan and continued to draw enough response so that continuation made good sense.

One highlight of their programming was the 1991 visit of Dr. Dorothy Brown to the annual meeting held that year on the Embury District. The inspiring story of Dr. Brown is told in *A Flame of Fire,* pp. 350*ff.* As a black orphan in Troy she struggled to obtain an education. The women of Troy Conference helped fund her medical education in the 1940s, so her return home was always a special event for her and the UMW.

In 1995, the UMW contributed over $106,000 in support of the work of the General Board of Global Ministries. That same year, 74 women traveled to the UMW General Assembly in Cincinnati.

The women celebrated the fact that in 1997 there were twenty-six local church UMW honor units. To achieve that recognition, a local unit had to make a major commitment to social justice, as well as to mission, prayer, study, and action.

In the elections of 1999, two officers of the UMW, Shirley Readdean and Kay Washbourne, were chosen as delegates to General Conference.

In 2000, the conference sponsored the attendance of 13 teens and young adults at the national gathering, "Young Women, Rise UP!" held in Chicago. The next year, the UMW collected 330 children's books for the Red Bookshelf Program and gave 85 handmade baby quilts to the ABC Project for infants compromised by AIDS/HIV, alcohol, drugs, or family abandonment. Continuing involvement in broader interests is shown by the 45 women who attended the General Assembly in Anaheim, CA, in 2006.

The UMW consistently provided spiritual, personal, and financial leadership to Troy Conference. Fellowship across the conference, educational opportunities for men and women, and genuine support for mission work outline the impact of the UMW through the years.

UMM

The United Methodist Men of Troy Conference have always been an enthusiastic, though much smaller, group than UMW. In a typical year, the men would hold one retreat, do one work project, have a rally, and hold their annual meeting. They also advocated for, and encouraged men to attend, the quadrennial national gathering held for forty years at Purdue University. (The event was relocated to Nashville in 2009.) The men raised money to support camperships and work projects.

To give just a sampling of their efforts: In 1984, UMM gave four camp scholarships; in 1985, during a work week at Skye Farm they put a new roof on the tepee craft building and trimmed and painted Bass Lodge; in 1987, they raised money for seven camperships; and in 1988, they assisted in the construction of the conference's new camp, Covenant Hills, in Cabot, VT.

The UMM took on an ambitious project in 1992—raising money to purchase a station wagon for a teacher's college in Zimbabwe. They also undertook the considerable expense of shipping the vehicle there.

The unit sent eighteen men to the Purdue gathering in 1994 and began to take on a scouting ministry that included Boy Scouts, Girl Scouts, Campfire Girls, and 4-H. The next year, they completed a new washhouse at Skye Farm Camp, and the year after that built a new camper cabin there. In 2000, they took on the Little Red Bookshelf project, which collects and recirculates "gently used" children's books and even allows children to take home a free book.

In 1982, the national organization of United Methodist Men established the Society of John Wesley Fellows as a way of recognizing distinguished service to the church by men. Fellows who are recognized must demonstrate service and commitment and show witness, vision, and stewardship that enhance the mission and ministry of the church. In addition, the nomination to the fellowship requires the gift of $1,000 to endow the UMM scouting program and /or the men's ministry.

The first John Wesley Fellow from Troy Conference was Joe Civalier in 2001. Others followed with Joe Almeida chosen in 2005, Bruce Conklin in 2006, Will Chamberlin in 2007, and Rick Zitterling in 2008. Each of these men made important contributions, both to the work of the church and to the UMM.

Troy Conference UMM has made an impact on the conference that is disproportionate to the actual numbers of men involved. Few congregations have their own units, but the wider organization has established a setting for men to gather for fellowship and to coordinate mission efforts.

Through the years, conference level organizations offered youth, women, and men the opportunity to broaden their horizons and to discover and use leadership potential. Of course, the official work of CCYM, UMW and UMM did much good, but the additional opportunities for growth and service meant much to all individuals involved.

Troy Conference: From Independence to Integration

Troy Conference, originally part of the New York Area, came into being by action of the 1832 General Conference and held its first session August 28, 1833, in Troy, NY. The churches involved, loosely speaking, were those in New York from just south of Albany, west to Cobleskill, and north to the Canadian border. Also included were a few churches in western Massachusetts and all those in western Vermont. The connection with the Vermont churches changed several times through the years, but in 1941 all the Vermont churches became part of Troy Conference. In 1962, the western Massachusetts churches were assigned to the New England Conference, and the borders of Troy Conference remained generally stable for the next forty-eight years.

Even when Troy Conference was geographically stable, the question of conference viability continued as a major issue. The Conference Council on Ministries chose the program theme for bicentennial year 1983–84, "Strengthening our Ministries of Evangelism," because local churches clearly needed assistance to "identify, reach, embrace, assimilate, shepherd, and 'make' new disciples." In 1985, conference readily passed a resolution with several specific ideas for reversing membership decline during the next two quadrennials. Signs of the difficulty of the task were clear. The Journal reported that at the end of 1984, conference had 76,888 members, with an average local church attendance of 21,934 on Sunday morning. The report for 1992 showed 66,158 members and an average of 20,692 attending worship.

The Enlarged Cabinet in 1987 gave strong emphasis to the need to get the church message out in ways that would resonate with the contemporary world. Concern for the financial pinch of fewer people supporting the greater church budget appeared in the form of a petition asking the Council on Finance and Administration to consider a progressive rate schedule for conference apportionments.

In 1989, a proposal to reconfigure the area came under discussion. The plan linked Troy Conference, which straddled the New York—Vermont border with the Wyoming Conference, which reached across the New York—Pennsylvania border. That change took place in 1991, with Bishop James K. Mathews coming out of retirement to lead the newly created Albany Area.

In support of greater evangelism efforts, conference voted to endorse the 1990 Billy Graham Crusade in Albany. Queensbury UMC in Glens Falls was one venue for the pre-crusade training sessions, and a number of Troy Conference clergy were part of the team involved in supporting the crusade meetings themselves.

On the other hand, in 1989 the Conference Board of Discipleship brought forward a petition, which conference supported, to study the feasibility of appointing a full-time elder as conference evangelist. When the affirmative recommendation to create such an appointment came back the following year, conference chose to refer the resolution back to the board, which had begun the initiative in the first place. In 1991, the resolution calling for a conference-approved evangelist was not recommended, and the resolution was defeated. This came in the face of the report from the Enlarged Cabinet that noted concerns about being "an aging congregation where there are often too few people to do adequate programming. Everything becomes a struggle and all is focused on survival." Another major resolution that same year called for initiatives on all four districts to help revitalize congregations over the coming four years. Regrettably, most of these initiatives brought only temporary improvements at best.

In many ways, the "handwriting was on the wall" as far as changes to Troy Conference were concerned. In 1992, conference voted to extend an invitation to the New Hampshire Conference to conduct a merger feasibility study. Meanwhile, conference approved involvement in the AC 70 Project, which sought to raise $70,000 per year for three years in support of the Foundation for Evangelism and the Division of Evangelism. Active response to this project seems to have ended when Bishop Mathews returned to retirement in 1993.

Also in 1993, at the urging of the Committee on Strategic Planning, under the title "A New Creation," conference agreed to invite local churches to undertake a planning process to create a specific vision of ministry for the next century. The report of the Cabinet in 1993 notes that responses from the churches affirmed the need for local churches and annual conference to work in close cooperation.

More ominous was a comment in the Cabinet report in 1994: "At our present rate of shrinkage, even the continued existence of our conference can be questioned. We are spending too much effort rooting around in the debris of institutional programs, finances, and structures. The band-aids, patches, chewing gum, and bailing wire will not hold this tattered tent together much longer." Even so, it was difficult to spell out the steps needed to correct the visible problems.

The report of Council Director Rev. James Perry recorded more discouraging news in 1997. In the preceding year 40% of the local churches took in no new members on profession of faith—and that was the best record at least since 1987. Conference lay leader Julius Archibald, in his report, repeated a theme from his report as chair of the Council on Ministries the year before—evangelism. The need was glaring: "We have lost thirty percent of our membership and fourteen percent of our worshiping attendance in the last twenty-fire years; we cannot afford another twenty-five years like the last twenty-five." One response of conference was approval of a petition that allowed the creation of Mission Congregations, essentially giving designated struggling churches additional support, with the hope that they might return to healthy and effective status. Another response was a commitment to conduct a five-day academy for spiritual formation under the direction of the Upper Room.

Five churches were closed by conference action in 1998. A resolution from the Council on Ministries called for the holding of a second five-day academy for spiritual formation, if the evaluation of the first one was effective. The Board of Discipleship brought, and conference accepted, a resolution listing thirteen practices churches might use in support of discipleship renewal. Each local church was urged to add at least one new practice of spiritual formation each year. In addition, the conference treasurer was authorized to establish an ongoing fund to be tapped for spiritual formation education projects, as determined by the Board of Discipleship.

A major restructuring of the conference was implemented in 2000 under the leadership of Bishop Susan Murch Morrison. The explicit mission was spelled out in the report of the Implementation Team: "The mission of Troy Annual Conference is to provide, equip, and resource lay and clergy leaders for the purpose of helping churches make, nurture, and send forth disciples of Jesus Christ; and connect congregations with ministries around the world." This effort failed to completely fulfill its promise. For instance, Faith, Mission, and Evangelism, one of the defined critical issue ministry teams dealing with areas considered crucial to the life of the conference, made its last report in 2002. In 2003, that ministry team, along with the Board of Discipleship and several other agencies of conference, were put on "Sabbath rest," with the hope that some spirit of renewal might emerge. That did not happen, and the responsibilities of those entities were dispersed among other bodies of conference.

The Communications Committee tied into the national Igniting Ministry media campaign in 2001 with three resolutions. One sought funding to participate in a television buy, another encouraged all congregations to participate in welcoming training, and the third called for an "Open House Month" to connect local churches with the nationwide denominational effort.

Conference began to take a proactive stance with regard to possible changes in boundaries. These changes were by now understood to be necessary and inevitable. A resolution passed in 2003 called for exploring the possibility of adding parts of Massachusetts and some churches from the New York Conference to Troy. Some informal conversations were held as a follow up, but that proposal did not gain significant support.

Bishop Morrison formed a Boundaries Committee in the fall of 2004 to network with neighboring conferences, with the hope of having some control over the future disposition of Troy Conference. The urgency of their work is clear from their initial report: "Changing demographics and the requirements of the Book of Discipline make it likely that the Northeastern Jurisdiction will lose one of its ten Episcopal Areas in 2008." Troy, being the smallest of the thirteen annual conferences, was highly likely to be involved in any transitions. Changes were sure to come, and the Boundaries Committee continued to be active in seeking to formulate a plan that would give the people of conference a voice in suggesting what those changes would be. Maintaining the status quo simply was no longer an option.

Underlining the weakness of the situation were actions taken in 2006. Three more churches were discontinued, with a total of one remaining member between all three. Another church, First UMC, Bennington, became a Mission Congregation with the hope that their ministries might be able to continue, even though they could no longer support all their connectional responsibilities.

The situation in Troy Conference was serious, yet a new strand of self-understanding and meaning began to emerge. The Rev. Henry Frueh, chair of the Troy Conference Boundaries Committee, noted in his 2006 report that new boundaries were going to be required, but that better reasons beyond necessity could be discerned. He named five benefits: becoming a conference with increased racial and cultural diversity; broadening the base of appointable clergy for our churches and providing more churches to our clergy; increasing programming staff resources; offering our strengths to others and in turn receiving the gifts of other conferences; and contributing to a reconfigured strategy of mission for the entire jurisdiction. These reasons for change were not uppermost in the minds of most Troy conference people, but, taken seriously, they pointed to the reality that God's hand could be seen at work. Responses other than dismay over the uncertain changes were possible.

Meanwhile, the Council on Youth Ministries had taken the vague future as an opportunity to develop new and creative programming. Under the title *4Word'05*, over 600 youth from Troy, North Central, Western New York, and Wyoming Conferences met in Rochester, NY for an inspirational celebration. No decision had been made that those four conferences would become one, though that was a frequently suggested possibility. Even so, the youth chose to act in faith and began to make connections across the state. Without delay, *4Word'06* was organized and held in Liverpool. The youths' enthusiasm for a larger conference relationship continued strong. The *4Word'07* gathering was held in Binghamton, while the '08 and '09 events met in Syracuse.

In 2007 the tentative discussions began to take on greater clarity. One major issue was the options facing the Vermont churches. The two choices were that the Vermont churches would remain in connection with the New York churches of Troy Conference and become part of an Upper New York Area or, instead, connect with the New England Area. A glance at the map shows neither of those choices is clearly better in terms of travel. Vermont, being unique in many ways, was not an exact demographic match for either the New York or New England conferences. Early on, it was made clear that the Vermont churches would have to make the decision about where to place their allegiance for themselves. The New York part of Troy Conference felt ties with the Vermonters, and, after a joint history of over 65 years, many found separation hard to imagine. Yet, change would bring both distress and opportunity. The Boundaries Committee began a series of meetings to allow the Vermont churches to meet, consider, caucus, and express their feelings about the choices ahead. Naturally, the Wyoming Conference (which with the Troy Conference comprises the Albany Area) had some similar issues with churches in two states as well. The ties linking the Albany Area were going to be stressed no matter what decisions were made in the days ahead.

During 2007, a series of discussions held in Vermont made it clear that the Vermont churches were strongly in favor of forging a connection with the New England Conference. On that basis, the Boundaries Committee prepared the resolution for presentation to a special session of annual conference.

In October 2007 the Troy, Wyoming, North Central, and Western New York Conferences met in a teleconference-mediated joint special session. Technically, for Troy Annual Conference it was the adjourned 175th session. Bishop F. Herbert Skeete presided. Following presentations, both in person and via video link, the conferences voted to affirm a common resolution which concluded, "Therefore, be it resolved: the people of the North Central New York, Troy, Western New York and Wyoming (Conferences), in order to revitalize the mission of The United Methodist Church in the region to make disciples of Jesus Christ, agree to request the Northeastern Jurisdictional Conference to create a new Episcopal Area and a new Annual Conference from all or portions of these and/or other contiguous conferences with the Pennsylvania churches of the Wyoming Annual Conference considering alignment with the Central Pennsylvania Annual Conference and the Vermont churches of the Troy Annual Conference considering alignment with the New England Annual Conference, to be implemented in 2010." The vote in Troy Conference was 248 for, 12 against, and 6 abstaining. Similarly, solid majorities affirmed the resolution in the other conference sessions as well.

At the 2008 session of annual conference, the previously voted resolutions came before the body again so that all the technicalities might be properly observed. Again the votes were strongly in favor of recommending to the Jurisdictional Conference that the Vermont churches become part of the New England Conference and that the New York churches become part of an as yet unnamed upper New York conference.

The Northeastern Jurisdictional Conference confirmed the actions of the four participating conferees in the summer of 2008. Bishop Marcus Matthews was selected to lead the Western New York Episcopal Area and become the bishop of the new area that was coming into being. Then came the push to get everything in order for the transition. One key body in the process was the New Area/Conference Team, which generally became known as New ACT. Each of the four conferences involved chose leaders to this team and empowered them to provide vision, leadership, and organization through the coming months. Another body, the Joint Distributing Committee, required by the *Discipline*, was appointed by the bishops to deal with pensions, health insurance matters, and the allocation of resources under supervision by the trustees. Conversations began at once to provide the input and agreement needed to make a smooth and legal transition from six conferences to three.

The Vermont churches of Troy Conference would enhance the New England Conference, while the Pennsylvania churches of the Wyoming Conference would go to the Central Pennsylvania Conference. The Rev. Brigid Farrell, superintendent of the Green Mountain District, since July 2009, became in July 2010 the superintendent of the Vermont District in the New England Conference. While all the Vermont churches had been part of the Troy Conference since 1940, this was the first time since 1945 that all of Vermont was united in a single district. Meanwhile, the

New York portions of Troy and Wyoming united with North Central New York and Western New York to become a new single conference area.

With leadership provided by the General Board of Pensions and Health Benefits and the advice of legal counsel, all the steps forward were taken as they needed to be. After a thoughtful analysis of membership, apportionment payments, and related measures, it was agreed that the undesignated assets of Troy Conference would be divided, with 30% going with the Vermont churches to New England Conference and 70% going with the New York churches to the Upper New York Conference.

Another issue involved equalizing the pre-1982 pension annuity rates. The basic rule was that no one would receive less under the new arrangement than they did under the old. For Troy Conference, this involved increasing the amount per year of pre-1982 service from $465 in 2009 to $552 in 2010. Similar comparisons related to health insurance were more difficult, due to substantial differences among the plans. Active pastors in Troy Conference, for instance, had not been paying any part of health insurance. That benefit helped to compensate for the lower minimum salaries. Our retirees, on the other hand, had only a modest subsidy for their health insurance, where some of the other conferences paid for retiree coverage in full. All these issues needed to be handled with considerable compassion and attention to legal detail.

The bishops determined that the new conference would come into existence on July 1, 2010. In order to maintain legal continuity, some preliminary organization would have to begin ahead of time for signed contracts to take effect on that day. Many individuals, used to a more relaxed and grace-oriented approach, found dealing with important legal realities a difficult change of pace. Bishop Matthews began to exercise his leadership. A calendar and timetable helped clarify the new directions.

July 2008: Northeastern Jurisdiction affirms the reorganizational plans and names the new Upper New York Area under the episcopacy of the Rev. Dr. Marcus Matthews

January 2009: Conversations begin concerning pensions, property, finances, and administration

March 2009: Work begins on 2011 budget, inventory of assets and liabilities, development of information technology, and area-wide communication tools

May 2009: Interim report to the annual conferences

May 21, 2010: Final clergy session of Troy Conference, Saratoga Springs UMC

May 21, 2010: Evening memorial service at Christ UMC, Glens Falls

May 22, 2010: Closing session of Troy Conference, Christ UMC, Glens Falls

June 17, 2010: Vermont becomes part of the New England Conference Session meeting at Gordon College, Wenham, MA

June 19, 2010: Uniting session of the Upper New York Conference, Syracuse

September 11, 2010: Business Session of Upper NY Conference to plan for 2011, Empire State Plaza, Albany

Communication between Vermont and the New England Conference began early in the process. Vermonters needed to know how things were done in New England. New England needed to be introduced to their newest churches. Since the New England Conference had previously united with the Maine and New Hampshire Conferences in 1996, they already had experience in building new connections. The Rev. John Blackadar, district superintendent of the New Hampshire District, said the New England Annual Conference would "practice radical hospitality." His hope was that this effort might translate to increased hospitality on the part of local churches as well.

Fewer efforts were made at easing the transition for the New York churches because they would be part of creating the new conference. The call went out for volunteers to help shape the new creation: "The Interim Nominations Committee will be working to invite open-minded, energetic persons to serve in the new conference. Beginning with the essential structure we will be starting with the Board of Trustees, Conference Finance and Administration, and Conference Council or Connectional Table (body is yet unnamed). As we look forward to the future to the 23rd Century we will be looking for persons with new skills, new ideas, new hopes and dreams rooted in our tradition and faith."

As always, the future unfolds one step at a time. What began with the tentative steps of Philip Embury seeking a new life for his family, and the efforts of numerous early circuit riders, blossomed into Troy Annual Conference and the Vermont Annual Conference. Those conferences struggled, grew, and blessed the communities they served.

On November 7, 1940, the Vermont Conference met at the Waterbury Methodist Church for its final session. The welcome extended there by F. C. Lamb, the church treasurer, expressed the hope that as the Vermont Conference ended, "great things may happen for the Kingdom of God." With the actions taken that day, the new, larger Troy Conference began. Sixty years later as familiar relationships end, we live in that same hope that greater things may happen for the Kingdom of God. The wonder of those new things lies ahead.

Appendix A

Timeline

1760 Phillip Embury and Barbara Heck, his cousin, come to U.S. from County Limerick, Ireland

1765 Capt. Thomas Webb preaches in Albany, NY

1766 Phillip Embury preaches first sermon in NYC, starts the Wesley Chapel in NYC at urging of Barbara Heck

1770 Barbara Heck and Philip Embury move to Cambridge-Ashgrove area, form first Methodist society north of NY City. George Whitefield preaches in Albany, NY

1773 Mary Margaret Appleton Peckett ("Mother Peckett"), formerly John Wesley's housekeeper, emigrates to America

1774 James Dempster, Wesley's last missionary to America, arrives in NY

1776 Dempster preaches in Mohawk Valley and Montgomery Co., sets up churches in Sacandaga, Mayfield, Canajoharie, Galway, Underhill. First services held in Dempster's log meeting house.

1780 Margaret Peckett moves to Bradford, VT, organizes a Methodist Class

1782 Dempster preaches in Scotia, NY

1787 Freeborn Garretson named elder of 4 circuits

1788 Ashgrove Meeting House, first one north of NY City, erected in Cambridge

1789 Grooms Methodist Society organized in Clifton Park

1790 Jason Lee preaches in VT
North Hartland, NY church built

1791 Garrettson Station Church erected on corner of Pearl and Orange Streets, Albany
William Losee sent to Canada as first missionary to go outside bounds of Troy Conference
Saratoga Circuit organized from part of Cambridge Circuit
Johnstown church built
1792 Wells, VT church built
Pittsfield Circuit organized
1793 Vershire, VT church built, first Methodist Meeting House in VT. As of 1982, oldest church still standing.
1794 Vershire Circuit becomes first circuit in VT; soon divides into Vershire and Barnard circuits
1796 Embury organizes societies in West Camden, VT, Arlington, VT, and Shaftsbury, VT
Nicholas Snethen becomes first circuit rider of Vershire Circuit
Jason Lee starts Barre, VT Circuit
Richard Jacobs sent to upper NY State, drowns trying to cross Schroon River
Lorenzo Dow receives license to preach from Bishop Asbury
1798 Elijah Hedding replaces Lorenzo Dow in Essex Circuit, later in Plattsburgh Circuit
Martin Ruter boards with Margaret Peckett while attending school
Vergennes, VT Circuit organized
1799 Windsor Circuit organized in VT
Plattsburgh, Essex and Whitingham Circuits organized

1800 Lorenzo Dow visits Margaret Peckett
Albany and Pittsfield (MA) Districts started with 22 itinerant preachers
1801 Brandon and Fletcher circuits organized in Vermont
Laban Clark, "The Father of Wesleyan University," admitted to NY Conference

Martin Ruter admitted to NY Conference "on trial" at age 16, goes on to be missionary in Canada, president of two colleges, and founder of Allegheny College, PA.

1801 First Methodist class formed in Newbury, VT

1802 Grand Isle, VT and Adams, MA Circuits organized

1803 Danville Circuit organized
NY Conference held in Ashgrove, NY
Albany District has largest membership, 927, more than NY City

1804 Barre, VT and Magog, VT Circuits organized
James Dempster dies May 10
Montgomery Circuit holds first quarterly conference in July

1805 NY Conference held in Ashgrove, NY
First camp meeting held at Stillwater, attended by Asbury and Waitcoat

1806 Stanstead, VT Circuit organized

1807 Margaret Embury Lawrence, first preacher's wife in Troy Conference, dies
Schenectady and Rochester, VT Circuits organized

1808 Jason Lee preaches throughout Troy Conference
Pownal, VT and Charlotte, VT Circuits organized

1810 Middlebury Circuit organized

1811 Tobias Spicer married
New England Annual Conference held in Barnard, VT

1812 NY Annual Conference held in Albany
General Conference begins raising funds for missionary efforts

1816 First bishop married in America
First Methodist Episcopal Church of Albany holds first Sabbath School

1819 Missionary and Bible Society of ME Church started
Laban Clark introduces resolution to organize The

Missionary Society of the Methodist Episcopal Church in NY City

1820 Saratoga District formed
General Conference approves formation of Mission and Bible Society of Methodist Episcopal Church
General Conference enables a bishop to appoint a minister as president of an educational institution
1821 Society for Giving and Receiving Religious Intelligence starts with Elijah Hedding president
Plans made to publish *Zion's Herald*
1823 First issue of *Zion's Herald* printed
1824 Elijah Hedding elected bishop
1827 State Street Methodist Church in Troy dedicated
1828 Methodist Protestant Church formed
1829 VT and New Hampshire Conferences divided

1832 Troy Conference set apart from NY Conference with 98 preachers across Saratoga, Troy, Middlebury Districts
1833 Troy Annual Conference meets for first time, passes resolution to provide parsonages
Elijah Hedding, eighth American bishop, becomes first bishop to preside over newly formed Troy Conference
First parsonage in Troy Conference area built in Ashgrove
Troy Conference Temperance Society and Troy Conference Missionary Society formed
George S. Brown, first African-American pastor in Troy Conference, receives license to preach
1834 Daniel Chandler admitted to Troy Conference, first to receive mission appointment
Newbury Seminary, later to become first school of Boston University, opens in VT
1835 East Stone Arabia organized by (German) Evangelical Association

1836 Troy Conference Academy, later to become Green Mountain College, opens in Poultney, VT
1837 Female Benevolent Society started
Betsy Dow becomes first teacher of ministerial students at Newbury Seminary
1838 George S. Brown ordained deacon and elder by Bishop Elijah Hedding, John St. Church, NYC; returns to Liberia for four more years

1840 Newbury Bible Institute (VT), first American Methodist seminary and forerunner of Boston University School of Theology, founded
1841 Troy Conference passes resolution to have furniture provided in parsonages
1842 Radical abolitionists exit to form Wesleyan Methodist Church
1844 Methodist Episcopal Church, South, formed due to slavery issue
Bakersfield (VT) North Academy started
1845 VT Conference, consisting of Montpelier, Springfield, and Danville Districts, established by order of General Conference, holds first annual conference
VT Conference starts Sabbath Schools
VT Conference starts collecting funds for mission purposes
1846 Newbury Seminary (which becomes Boston Theological Seminary in1867) moves to Concord, NH
1847 Springfield Wesleyan Seminary and Female Collegiate Institute opens
1848 Longest session of Troy Conference on record—12 days!

1850 Nearly all preachers (seven-eighths of them) stationed at appointments
Phoebe Palmer, holiness evangelist, holds revivals in St. Johnsbury and Lyndon Center, VT and in Troy,

Albany, Hudson Falls, Plattsburgh, NY
1852 Elijah Hedding dies, Poughkeepsie, NY
Newbury Seminary has 538 students
1854 Only a few churches in Troy Conference have an organ
Ft. Edward Collegiate Institute built
1855 "The Great Debate" over which conference contains the Burlington District begins
George S. Brown starts church in Wolcott, VT
1859 Troy Praying Band organizes Jan. 29 with Joseph Hillman, leader

1861 Preachers Aid Society of VT Conference started
1864 General Conference establishes four German-speaking conferences. Troy Conference has German churches in Albany, Amsterdam, Troy, Ft. Hunter (started by Dempster), and Schenectady (started in 1848)
1865 Troy Conference Academy becomes Ripley Female College
1866 Preachers Aid Society of Troy Conference started
1867 VT Conference refuses to admit anyone who uses tobacco in any form
Troy Conference Historical Society formed
Montpelier Seminary (VT College) opened
1868 Land for camp meetings purchased in Round Lake; first ten-day meeting held
1869 Women's Foreign Missionary Society formed March 23
Women's Foreign Missionary Society auxiliary society formed Nov. 9, Troy, NY

1870 VT Conference organizes a Women's Missionary Society.
1874 Troy Conference Academy reopens under conference ownership
National Woman's Christian Temperance Union organized

Troy Conference passes resolution declaring that no member should lend his influence to its use, by making, selling or using alcohol

"Great Fraternal Camp Meeting" held at Round Lake

1880 Women's Home Missionary Society formed June 8

1881 Troy Conference Home Missionary Society formed April 20

1884 "The Great Debate" ends with Burlington District becoming part of Troy Conference

1885 VT Conference Home Missionary Society formed

1887 VT Historical Society formed

1888 Office of Deaconess formed

1892 General Conference approves "Epworth Leagues"

1897 "VT Preachers Wives Association" meets

1900 Millie Martin Dodge, first VT Conference deaconess, consecrated

1904 Women admitted to General Conference, VT Conference elects Mary Webb as lay delegate

1905 "Troy Conference Ministers' Wives" begins

1907 Board of Home Missions and Church Extension started

1908 Troy Conference establishes Committee on Evangelism
Fire at Troy Conference Academy April 18

1909 Troy Conference establishes Commission on Social Service

1910 Ft. Edward Collegiate Institute destroyed by fire

1912 VT Conference starts North Barre Mission for Italian marble cutters

1913 Schenectady German Methodist Episcopal Church has largest membership in U. S.

1915 Lillian Rember becomes first woman supply pastor in VT Conference

1916 Spring Grove Camp Meeting site in VT closed

Troy Conference Layman's Association formed

1920 VT Conference sends seven-point memorial to General Conference, asking for legislation that would "at least grant Quarterly Conference the right to license women, and the District Superintendents authority to appoint them as pastoral supplies with the hope that this act may be a way station toward complete ministerial equality of the sexes in the near future."
Mabel H. Whitney appointed supply pastor to Pittsfield Circuit, Mrs. C.F. Aldrich appointed supply to Williamsville, VT

1921 Layman's Association formed
Wesleyan Service Guild started
Troy Conference licentiates include Millicent Corps, Eliza Duffield, Mrs. I.D. Van Valkenburg, Mrs. E.W. Gould, Margaret Coleman, Mrs. Eleanor Ryder, Harriett Wells, Mrs. Eva Palmer
VT Conference licentiates include Ellen Wagner (Milton), Mabelle Whitney (Pittsfield), Amy Rogers (Waterville), Ruth G. Barr (Greensboro Bend), Sarah Aldrich (Williamsville)

1922 Conference pushes to have bathrooms in parsonages
Williamsville Home for Children opens
Georgia Harkness granted license to preach
VT Conference Rural Preachers Association formed

1923 St. Timothy's of Schenectady organized by Italians

1925 Ruth G. Barr becomes first VT Conference woman ordained deacon as a local pastor
Troy, 5th Ave. and State St. churches merge to serve Italian community with new name, St. Titus.
Laymen admitted to conference by vote

1926 Georgia Harkness and Eliza Duffield become local deacons. Between 1926 and 1956, Harkness is primary spiritual leader in struggle for full clergy rights for women.

1928 Eliza Duffield becomes first woman local pastor ordained elder
1929 Troy Conference Board of Education formed

1931 First Troy Conference seminar in religious education held in Amsterdam
Troy Conference Academy becomes Green Mountain Junior College
1933 World Service and Troy Conference Benevolences adopted
1934 St. Titus (Italian) closes
1935 Ellen Van Buskirk ordained local deacon in VT Conference
Student Pastor Fund started
1939 Georgia Harkness becomes local elder and professor of applied theology at Garrett Biblical Institute, first woman to hold such a position at a major seminary
Methodist Youth Fellowship begins
1939 Woman's Society of Christian Service formed

1940 Troy and VT Conferences merge
Board of Lay Activities formed
Troy Conference Woman's Society of Christian Service started
1941 Round Lake Institute merges with Green Mountain Institute
1942 The Rev. Luther Brown donates land for Skye Farm Camp
1943 East German Conference dissolves, Schenectady and Ft. Hunter churches join Troy Conference
1944 Doris Hartman ordained local deacon in Troy Conference
Rev. Earl Ledden from Troy Conference elected bishop
1946 Evangelical Church merges with United Brethren Church to become Evangelical United Brethren Church
1948 Troy Conference Rural Life Fellowship becomes

Commission on Town and Country Work
Conference Commission on Christian Vocations formed
Conference Board of Missions joins with Board of Education
The Advance for Christ and His Church adopted by General Conference

1950 Missisquoi emphasis on youth summer camping begins
1951 Troy Conference and VT Conference Historical Societies merge, locate archives in Ticonderoga
1953 St. Timothy's (Italian) Church closes
1955 Dr. Dorothy Brown, VT Conference, becomes first African-American member of American College of Surgeons
1956 General Conference approves full clergy rights for women
1959 Doris Hartman becomes first woman admitted "on trial" to Troy Conference

1961 Albany Inner City Ministry becomes Albany United Methodist Society
First Methodist Church of Albany merges with Trinity Methodist
1963 Doris Hartman becomes first woman received into full connection in Troy Conference
1967 Embury's grave and monument made Methodist Historical Landmark by NEJ Association of Methodist Historical Societies
1968 Evangelical United Brethren Church merges with Methodist Church to form United Methodist Church. The four EUB churches in Troy Conference are West Sand Lake, Amsterdam, East Stone Arabia and Calvary on Delaware Ave. in Albany.
Conference Center opens on 157 Lake Ave., Saratoga Springs, NY

General Conference creates Commission on Archives and History

1970 Summer Learning Fellowship started
1971 Ogden Lodge at Skye Farm Camp dedicated, burns down five months later
Alice Trost becomes first president of Troy Conference United Methodist Women
1972 Embury Apartments opens
Conference Archives moved to Green Mountain College, Poultney, VT
1973 New Ogden Lodge at Skye Farm Camp dedicated
Wesley Nursing Home opens
1975 Troy Conference Theological Academy begins
"Troy Conference Ministers' Wives" become "Ministers' Mates Fellowship"
1976 The Rev. Harold Shippey appointed camp steward
1978 The Rev. William A. Cotant appointed Director of Camping/Local Church Youth Enabler
Ruth Harlow becomes first woman to serve as conference lay leader
1979 Calvary UMC merges with St. Luke's in Albany
Glens Falls District renamed Adirondack District

1980 Crusade for Mission and Ministry begins with $3.2 million goal
Keeseville Country Gardens, Inc. opens
Winter Olympic Ministry held, Adirondack Community Church, Lake Placid, NY
1981 New conference center opens on RT 9 in Gansevoort, NY
Troy Conference hosts NEJCAH meeting
1982 *A Flame of Fire: The Story of Troy Annual Conference* published
Conference begins funding World Service at 100%
1983 Three thousand from Troy Conference worship at

Colonie Coliseum
1984 Major expansion of Wesley Facility at Saratoga begins
1985 Marion Moore-Colgan, Native American, ordained deacon, received as probationary member
First Troy Conference Walk to Emmaus held
1986 Troy Area Urban Ministry inaugurated
1987 Troy Conference votes to become a Reconciling Conference
Chester "Chet" Vanderbilt, conference communications coordinator, named UM Communicator of the Year
Burlington District renamed Green Mountain District
The Rev. Art Hagy named first Camping Volunteer of the Year
Exit 8 Ministry initiated
1988 Conference votes to support Billy Graham Crusade in Albany
First Howard and Reba Stimmel Peace with Justice Award presented to James and Pearl Campbell
Camp Missisquoi holds final season of summer programming
UMM construct first building, camper washhouse, at Covenant Hills
1989 Covenant Hills Christian Camp in Cabot, VT holds first season
Marcheta (Peebles) Townsend, first woman district superintendent in Troy Conference, appointed to Green Mountain District
First Small Membership Church Awards presented to Karen Haley, Waterford; the Rev. Jeff Matthews, Schuylerville and Quaker Springs; and Brownsville,VT

1990 VIM teams go to Saint Croix, Puerto Rico, Montserrat, SC
1991 Albany Area links Troy and Wyoming conferences
Marion Moore-Colgan becomes first woman of color received into full connection and ordained elder in

Troy Conference
Conference center on Louden Road in Saratoga opens
Bennington-Troy District renamed Embury District 1992
Committee on Health Insurance Plans reviews twenty
proposals before choosing carrier
1993 First VIM trip to Mozambique
1994 Denman Evangelism Award goes to prison inmate
Major time spent at conference considering human
sexuality
1995 Covenant with Brazil established
AUMS holds largest CROP Walk in NY, raises $125,000
Exit 8 Ministry, People of Christ UMC, unites with Waterford UMC
1996 Bishop Susan M. Morrison becomes first woman bishop to preside over Troy Conference
Elisabeth Burbank, Chelsea, VT consecrated as diaconal minister
1997 Vision Team formed to aid reorganization of conference
1998 VIM team from Mozambique visits Troy Conference
Vision Team reports on conference reorganization
1999 Construction of 60 housing units begins at Woodlawn
in Saratoga

2000 General Conference calls for Act of Repentance for
racism by annual conferences
Implementation Team reports on conference reorganization
2002 Operation of Keeseville Country Gardens passes to
National Church Residences
2003 Peter and Janet Huston become paid VIM Coordinators
2004 Charles and Ouida Schwartz Archives dedicated
2005 VIM purchases "Mission in Motion" trailer
2006 Bishop Susan M. Hassinger becomes second woman
bishop to preside over Troy Conference

2007 Troy Conference holds Act of Repentance
2008 The Rev. Melvin McGaughey celebrates 70 years as ordained minister

Emmanuel Faith Community wins NEJ Kinmouth Jefferson Award for Urban Ministries
2009 Albany United Methodist Society celebrates 50th anniversary

Covenant Hills Christian Camp celebrates 20th anniversary

Adult retreat center dedicated at Skye Farm

Shirley Readdean becomes first person of color elected to conference Board of Trustees

2010 VT churches of former Troy Conference join with New England Conference July 1. For the first time since 1945, all VT is one district.

NY churches of former Troy Conference join NY churches of Wyoming, Western NY, and North Central NY Conferences to create Upper NY Conference.

Grateful appreciation goes to Karen Staulters, conference archivist, for her major research and input.

Appendix B

Safari Camp

A long with the more traditional on-site camps, conference camping leadership has often experimented with "camps" of very different natures. Safari Camp was one of those experiments. This story of Safari Camp was edited from the original version that was dictated en route and later transcribed by the Rev. C. Walter Kessler.

On Sunday evening, July 13, the 1970 Safari group (Christine Mason, Lee Shippey, Maribeth Zimmer, Evelyn Woodmansee and C. Walter Kessler) met at Skye Farm. After supper, plans for the next ten days were discussed and sandwiches prepared for Monday lunch.

The next morning at 5:30 a.m. the suitcases and a box of groceries were packed into the trunk and the sleeping bags in the car-top carrier. After ample French toast in the Skye Farm lodge, washed down with steaming cups of coffee, Bill Lasher provided $360 in funds to finance the trip.

On the road at 7:30, the one-car caravan reached the Metropolitan Urban Service Training office in New York City four hours later. There we received a forty-five minute briefing on MUST activities. We were stunned when we were charged $3 for 1 ¼ hours of parking in the garage across the street. At 1 p.m. we drove to Hammarskjold Plaza and had lunch in the shadow of the United Nations. By 2:30 we were at the Church of All Nations and the young ladies spent an hour seeing the activities of the Settlement House. When the girls returned we took the Brooklyn Tunnel to Methodist Hospital where we were to spend the night. After supper in the cafeteria we took the subway to Times Square and walked for an hour before returning. When we unloaded the car we made the dismaying discovery that one of our sleeping bags had either been stolen or blown off. I can hardly believe the latter possible because the bags were securely tied on. It must have been a theft.

The next morning we got an extended tour of the hospital from the computer section in the basement to the blood bank, X-ray room and cobalt machine. At 11 a.m. we took off again after repacking our bags and gear. The new Verrazano Bridge into New Jersey provided easy access to the turnpike heading toward Philadelphia. We reached Emmanuel United Methodist Church in good time and unloaded our gear. We had time to run downtown before supper. The girls visited Independence Hall, the Liberty Bell, the Mall and the old congressional chamber where the First Continental Congress met and George Washington was inaugurated as first president. We had fifteen minutes for the quarter hour drive back to the church. I got in the wrong line of traffic and was headed out of town, but the toll collectors at the bridge were very understanding so we got turned around and reached the church without further mishap. A wonderful dinner awaited us—real southern cooking enjoyed by five white travelers and twice that many cordial Black hosts and hostesses who joined us. After supper, the associate minister, Rev. Jones, and his youth group took us to Willow Grove Park, a carnival affair, and the young people spent an hour and a half trying games of skill and various rides. We got to bed at 10 p.m.

On Wednesday we spent time at the Methodist Midtown Mission. Then we had a session that outlined the problems of the Black churchmen of the city. Before leaving we visited old Saint George's Church. Then it was on to Baltimore, where we visited the mother church of Methodism, Lovely Lane Chapel. We drove south to Cedar Grove United Methodist church.

Thursday, July 16, found the Safari motoring to Washington DC for sightseeing. We drove to the Dumbarton Methodist Church where we were scheduled to spend the night and found that there was no place to park. So we made arrangements to return to Cedar Grove for a second night. We visited the White House in passing, drove to the Washington and Lincoln memorials, had lunch at the Supreme Court cafeteria ($8 for full dinner for five), and visited the Lee-Custis Mansion, the Tomb of the Unknown Soldier, the Kennedy graves and the Smithsonian Institution. Back in Cedar Grove we cooked dinner in the church kitchen. After the girls had a swim in the neighborhood pool we inflated our mattresses for another comfortable night. The girls were in the nursery upstairs and the driver in the basement!

We began each day with devotions using the Upper Room. Friday we left Cedar Grove at 10 a.m., having slept late to recuperate from our exertions of the previous day. We drove through Frederick, MD, and turned off for a side trip to the Antietam Battlefield where 23,000 men died on September 17, 1862. We took several pictures including one of the old Dunkard Meetinghouse, around which the fighting began. Ironically, Dunkards are pacifists but the fighting left their church completely pockmarked. Because of heavy traffic and crooked West Virginia roads, we arrived an hour late at Scots Run Settlement House, near Morgantown, at Osage. We were quartered in two rooms of the settlement nursery school.

Saturday, driving through the mountains and trees along winding roads, we traveled toward Pittsburgh, also built on hills. We got lost in the city but arrived only 15 minutes late, for a wonder! A crowd of attractive Black youth met us along with the director of music, who invited us into Bethany House. After a spaghetti lunch we were treated to a tour of the city. Resuming our journey, we headed for Youngstown, Ohio via the Pennsylvania Turnpike. We arrived early, got the key and were shown where to bunk. We drove out to Oberlin College, had dinner at the inn, toured the campus and returned to the Community House in Youngstown. We were greeted when we got there by a group of little boys who were very eager to carry in our luggage and when I offered to give each one a dime, they said, "Oh, no, mister, we don't want any pay." Then one little fellow, looking at the girls, piped up, "Mister, are these your daughters?" I assured him that in a way they were after the experiences of the past few days.

We attended church on Sunday at the Monongahela UMC, then drove to Niles, Ohio, birthplace of William McKinley, then on to Warren, Ohio. With three hours to spare we went to Packard Park to watch the people at their picnicking and games, read the Book of Esther and a story in the Atlantic Monthly. Then we went to the Rebecca Community House for an hour's conversation about the work being done in the community. We drove to Cleveland and had a good dinner at the Howard Johnson's restaurant. Then we headed for the West Side Community House, where we were scheduled to spend the might. En route, however, in a long line of stalled traffic, the man behind us started up all of a sudden and jammed into the back of our car, causing a bad backlash and leaving Maribeth with a pain in her back. We got the insurance information, called the police and made a report to them. Then we went to the community house where I left three of our contingent to meet with the VISTA volunteers. I took Maribeth to the Lutheran Hospital, just two blocks away, for x-rays and examination. The doctor indicated that it would be okay to continue our trip as outlined. Unfortunately, all our luggage was packed in the car trunk which could not be opened after the accident. We were grateful that the VISTA people shared some of their beds and bedrolls with us.

On Monday we contacted the East Side Community Ministry. We conversed with them about the work four United Methodist churches are doing cooperatively and with considerable success. Their greatest concern is with the local junior and senior high schools, where racial riots have occurred during the past year and the community remains tense. One of the things that has impressed me all along the road has been the attitude of resentment and animosity toward the police departments in various cities. This attitude has been aggravated by treatment meted out to some of the Black Panthers and the failure of the police departments to defend the Black community when the latter felt they were being unjustly treated by certain white elements in various cities. We drove then to Rochester, where the young people were housed at Asbury-First United Methodist Church.

Tuesday morning we visited the campus of Rochester University, then set out for Hogansburg and the Saint Regis Indian reservation. We arrived at the reservation at 4:15 p.m. A group was at the church awaiting our coming. Dr. Frisch of Wayne University spoke to us for an hour on the history of the area. The Indians had moved up from the Mohawk Valley of New York to settle on a 23,000 acre tract on the Saint Lawrence River. When the War of 1812 ended and a boundary was drawn between Canada and the United States, it followed the river, splitting their community. The Indians' citizenship depended upon which side of that dividing line they lived. It turns out that to get to Saint Regis Village in Canada you have to go by way of U.S. territory. The Canadians built a bridge on Indian land and erected their Customs Office at the end so "Canadian" Indians who shop for groceries in the U.S. sometimes have to pay duty on their purchases. We went to the church for a tasty supper prepared by the ladies. The menu included several items of Indian food, including corn, which tasted much like hominy. We stayed in the home of the Smoke family and we enjoyed beds – a reprieve from the air mattresses. Many of the men on the reservation are high-steel workers.

Mrs. Woodmansee has a brother who lives near Massena, so she left the Safari to spend the week visiting relatives. At Plattsburgh Maribeth bade us farewell. Driving south we took Christine Mason to Reber, and this left the driver and Lee Shippey to complete the trip back to Skye Farm where her folks were awaiting our arrival. The trip covered 2,350 miles and we had about $20 left in our kitty.

I undertook this assignment with some misgivings, being the only male in the crowd, but the generation and gender gaps were no barrier to congenial fellowship, good conversation, much singing, occasional witticisms, gales of laughter, and a bond of Christian goodwill that left feelings of nostalgia as we parted at journey's end.

Appendix C

Camping Volunteer of the Year Award

The first award was made in 1987.

1987 Rev. Art Hagy (Art's comment on receiving the award: "This clearly demonstrates that camping is not just for the young and thin.")

1988 Saratoga Springs UMM (accepted by Bruce Conklin and Bill Hunter in memory of the Rev. James I. Borden, pastor, murdered by one to whom he was offering hospitality)

1989 Peg Moore (accepted in the name of over 200 volunteers involved in building the new camp at Covenant Hills)

1990 Rev. Harold Robinson

1991 Mildred Keays and Alan D. Cederstrom

1992 Richard Smith

1993 Elton (Stubby) Borden

1994 Muriel & Barry Williams

1995 Phyllis Burbank (Covenant Hills)
    Charles Pemburn (Skye Farm)

1996 Kenneth Wright, United Church of Christ (Covenant Hills)
    Rev. Bob Long and Rev. Clark Callender, for their long time leadership of Memorial Day Family Camp (Skye Farm)

1997 John Chase (Covenant Hills)
    Ed Osterhout (Skye Farm)

1998 Judy Badger and Jan Harrington, United Church of Christ (Covenant Hills)
John Schuyler (Skye Farm)

1999 Betsy Searle-Schrader

2000 Wesley Bristol and Lindsay Townsend (Covenant Hills)
Lauri Nair, long-time director of music camp (Skye Farm)

2001 Merv Spooner (Covenant Hills)
George "Bud" Jameson, Roman Catholic (Skye Farm)

2002 Leslie Desrosiers (Covenant Hills)
Val Gray, author-composer of "People of Faith Building Places of Vision" (Skye Farm)

2003 Mike and Susan Burns (Covenant Hills)
Barbara and Paul Wiley (Skye Farm)

2004 John Schuyler (Covenant Hills)
David Schlansker (Skye Farm)

2005 Maurice Rathbun (Covenant Hills)
Joan Butler (Skye Farm)

2006 David Orr and Wanda Locke (Skye Farm)

2007 Irving (Bud) Geerey (Covenant Hills)
David Smith (Skye Farm)

2008 Michael Moore (Covenant Hills)
Mike Davis (Skye Farm)

2009 Dave McGowan (Covenant Hills)
Oakley Neitzer (Skye Farm)

2010 Richard Nason (Skye Farm)

Appendix D

Denman Award

The first award was made in Troy Conference in 1988.

The Foundation for Evangelism uses the Denman Award to encourage recognition of United Methodist laity and clergy who excel at helping others experience God's transforming love through Jesus Christ. Harry Denman was renowned for his preaching, frugal lifestyle, and passion for sharing the Gospel with everyone he met. Persons nominated for the award should have a personal spiritual discipline and demonstrate personal conduct that creates an effective witness to Jesus' love. The Cabinet and the conference and district lay leaders select the award recipient.

1988 Rev. Charles Warner
Eleanor Leggett

1989 Rev. Jeffrey Stratton
Grace Morehouse

1990 Rev. L. Philip Dann
Janet Watt

1991 Rev. Dr. Lawrence Curtis
Raymond Peacock

1992 Rev. Dr. Kenneth Parker
Ione Keenan

1993 Rev. William G. Vigne
Janice and Loren Mills

1994 Rev. Maurice Drown
Willie Bates

1995 Rev. Carrol Newquist and Rev. David Lefurgey
Allan Clarke

1996 Rev. Donald Aiken
Peggy Abbandondalo

1997 Rev. Ted Ruggles
One Achord, a musical group from Round Lake UMC

1998 Hank Coghill

1999 Rev. Barbara Dwyer
Gilman Ford

2000 Rev. Clark Callender
Ruth Bostock

2001 Rev. Don Wheeler

2002 George Herrick

2003 Paul and Barbara Wiley, on behalf of Heifer Project

2004 Rev. Patricia Girard
Dr. Julius Archibald

2005 Karen Bryant

2006 Rev. Myron and Wanda Ducharme
Robert Jaccaud

2007 No award given

2008 Sandra Allen

2009 Rev. David Schlansker and Robert Bower, on behalf of
the Emmaus/Chrysalis community

Appendix E

Peace with Justice Award

The first award was made in 1986.

The United Methodist Church has a long history of involvement in social justice, seeking to make real the biblical vision that all persons might live in harmony, wholeness, peace, and well-being in relationships with humanity and all of creation. This award honors persons who make excellent and concrete contributions to this biblical vision of social justice, as interpreted by the United Methodist Social Principles, and who make justice visible to society.

This award is given to one person, lay or clergy, who lives within the bounds of Troy Annual Conference. Activity in church work is not a prerequisite for nomination, and applicants will be considered regardless of religious affiliation, race, age, occupation, or national origin. The Troy Conference Peace with Justice Awards Committee selects the award recipient.

1986 Rev. Walter Taylor
1987 Rev. Joyce Giles (posthumously awarded)
1988 James and Pearl Campbell
1989 Rev. Dr. Stanley Moore

1990 Kenneth Bollerud
1991 Stan McGaughey
1992 Rev. Dr. Don Washburn
1993 Rev. Leon Adkins
1994 No award given

1995 No award given
1996 Elaine Cooper

1997 Rev. Angelo Mongiore
1998 Jerry Oliver
1999 No award given

2000 Rev. Marcheta Townsend
2001 No award given
2002 Rachel Graham
2003 No award given
2004 Judy Ayers

2005 No award given
2006 Gary Geiger
2007 No award given
2008 No award given
2009 Alan Randall

Appendix F

General Church Leadership

Through the years Troy Annual Conference has provided a number of persons for church leadership at the national and international levels. Some were in volunteer positions on General Boards, and some were chosen to provide General Church leadership in paid positions. This chart is included in an attempt to honor the service of those listed and those inadvertently overlooked.

Troy Conference, though small in numbers, has been eager to support connectional ministry not only with apportionment dollars but also with human resources. The list below is incomplete. It includes only some of the many persons who have served. A more complete list might also have mentioned those elected to the episcopacy, teachers and administrators at seminaries and other institutions of higher learning, and those who served in the military chaplaincy. For a listing of Troy Conference related missionaries, see Appendix G.

Note that the Boards listed below are all General Boards of the denomination.

Name	Board Involvement	Volunteer or Paid	Years of Service (when known)
Archibald, Julius (Partial listing of general church involvement and leadership roles)	Council on Ministries Board of Discipleship President, Association of Annual Conference Lay Leaders	Volunteer	1985-1992 1997-2004 2000-2002
Barney, Rev. William	Church and Society	Volunteer	
Bollerud, Ken	Church and Society	Volunteer	

Name	Board Involvement	Volunteer or Paid	Years of Service (when known)
Byers, Shirley D.	Discipleship	Volunteer	1989-1996
Carothers, Rev. J. Edward	Global Ministries	Paid	1964-1971
Chatterton, Muriel	Global Ministries	Volunteer	
Conklin, Brooke	Global Ministries	Paid	
Cooper, Earle E.	Council on Ministries	Volunteer	
Farmer, Marilyn	Church and Society	Volunteer	1976-1984
Fishbeck, Rev. Royal	Council on Ministries	Paid	1981-1992
Heleine, Rev. Fred	Global Ministries	Paid	1976-1985, 1995
Kirk, Rev. John	Global Ministries	Paid	1988-1998
Lasher, Rev. William A.	Discipleship Council on Ministries	Volunteer	
Lerrigo, Rev. Charles	Global Ministries	Paid	1985-1987
Nugent, Rev. Randy	Global Ministries	Paid	
Readdean, Shirley	Religion and Race		
Robbins, Rev. Bruce	Christian Unity and Interreligious Concerns	Paid	1986-2004
Thompson, Rev. Nehemiah	Christian Unity and Interreligious Concerns	Paid	1989-1993
Trost, Alice	Global Ministries	Volunteer Paid	Prior to 1976
Van Gorp, Dirk and Carol	UMCOR Coordinators	Paid	
Walser, Ilah S.	Global Ministries	Paid	
White, Gail	Global Ministries	Volunteer	Prior to 1976
Wilbur, Rene	Global Ministries	Paid	
Wiley, Paul	Global Ministries	Volunteer	2005-2008

Appendix G

Troy Conference Missionaries

The Missionary Society of the Methodist Episcopal Church was founded in 1819. From early on, Troy Conference shared in that great outreach. The following list seeks to include the names of all those connected with this conference who have gone into the field.

The thought is to be as inclusive as possible. So "related to Troy Conference" includes world and national missionaries who were raised within Troy Conference, came to Troy Conference after their mission assignment, served in special mission projects within Troy Conference, or are listed in the annual Troy Conference Journal because of close ties here through an Advance covenant relationship with one or more churches. Clearly, with an effort this broad, some names may have been inadvertently omitted. More information on most of those listed below, including books written by or about them, can be found in the Schwartz Archives of the conference.

Barber, Edward Earle
Barber, Natalie Clapp
Barberi, Joy Ruth
Barberi, Mario C.
Barney, Stephanie Dawn
Bauman, Mrs. Ezra
Bauman, Rev. Ezra
Beaudry, Rev. L.N.
Blount, Allison R.
Bonaventure, Lucille
Boots, Nora
Boots, Wilson
Braman, Diane
Brunk, Jameson
Brunk, Susan

Brownlee, Rev. James A.
Brownlee, Sara Elizabeth Holt
Brown, Dr. Dorothy
Brown, Fred Richards
Brown, Mrs. Fred R.
Brown, Rev. George S.
Brooks, Cynthia H.
Burdock, Rev. George M.

Calhoun, John
Campbell, Donna Kay
Carl, Dixie E.
Case, Rev. William
Chandler, Rev. Daniel
Chase, Duane

Chase, Karen
Chikwaira, John
Clark, Emma
Clegg, Maria
Cleveland, Rev. Joseph Gilbert
Cleveland, Mary Ella
Crawford, Louise
Crawford, Carol
Crawford, Timothy
Crosier, Jean

Day, Joan
Dearstyne, Eleanor
Derby, Marion
Dewey, Glenn H.
Doane, Matilda Draper

Franca, Jeremias
Fry, Anita C.
Fry, Rev. Stanley A.
Fulton, Rev. Robert

Goodrich, Elizabeth
Griffith, Bruce
Griffith, Kathy

Hanson, Elizabeth
Hanton, Rev. Marjorie E.
Hartman, Rev. Doris
Henderson, Muriel
Henderson, Terry
Herjanic, Dr. Barbara Moss
Hoskins, Charlotte
Hoskins, Robert
Houser, Rev. Otto
Hyde, George Byron

Johnson, Lillian

Kayij, Kona
Kayij, Mutombu
Kim, Sun Sook
Kitchin, Fanny Carlotta
Kitchin, Rev. William Copeman

Langlais, Jennifer Elaine
Lee, Irene Emily
Losee, William

Mairena, Miguel
Mairena, Nan McCurdy
Martin, Charles Roscoe
McGaughey, Grace T.
McGaughey, Rev. Melvin R.
Miller, Charles Edward
Miller, Ellen Girton
Moller, Peter G.
Moller, Sharon Chickering
Moore, Helen
Morris, Frieda
Morrison, Bishop Susan Murch
Moss, Hatsumi Ishii
Moss, Rev. John A.

Olmstead, Helen
Onwu, Jackie
Onwu, Samuel

Pak, David Uhnkyn
Pak, Susan Chatterton
Parker, Edwin
Parker, Lois
Perry, Constance
Pinder, Helen
Pinder, John
Proctor, Caryl
Proctor, James

Rea, Rev. Julian
Rea, Mary Porter
Reese, Paul A.
Reimer, Dr. Marvin
Reimer, Dr. Sylvia Jean
Rickard, Rev. Harold
Rickard, Margaret B.
Rogers, Lois
Rogers, Jack
Ruhl, Martha P.
Ruter, Martin

Severance, Rev. Roy B.
Skinner, Achsah
Smalley, Rev. Ray L.
Smalley, Ruth E.
Snedeker, Gladys
Snedeker, Rev. James H.
Sparks, Fern Holcombe
Stevenson, Rev. Thomas
Stone, Edith Robinson
Strawn, Dwight J.
Strawn, Sonia Reid
Sturtevant, Abby Lucille

Taylor, Lyman Palmer
Taylor, Marian B.
Terhune, Hazel Bissell
Terhune, Rev. Robert M.
Thoburn, Dr. C. Stanley
Thoburn, Pearl
Titus, Julia
Trost, Alice M.
Trost, Rev. Robert F.
Tynan, Rev. Irving M.

Tynan, Florence

Wachs, Sylvia Allen
Wachs, Victor Hugo
Warnock, Carla
Warnock, Ted
Wentworth, Erastus
Whitaker, Rev. Meridith K.
Wier, Rev. John
Wier, Mrs. John
Wiley, Barbara
Wimble, Helen
Winans, Rev. Edward J.
Wood, Grace Hannah
Woodruff, Mabel A.
Woodruff, Frances E.
Woodworth, Kate
Wrisley, Winifred

Yambasu, John

Zimmerman, Deirdre
Zimmerman, Dr. Mark

Thank you to Alice and Bob Trost, Doris Hartman, Karen Staulters, Patricia Roeser, and Hatsumi and John Moss for the research and preparation of the archival material that underlies this listing of conference related missionaries.

Appendix H

Conference Sessions

Troy Conference
Methodist Episcopal Church 1833-1939

Year	Location	Presiding Bishop
1833	Troy, NY	Elijah Hedding
1834	Plattsburgh, NY	Elijah Hedding
1835	Albany, NY	John Emory
1836	Pawlet, VT	Beverly Waugh
1837	Troy, NY	Elijah Hedding
1838	Keeseville, NY	Thomas Morris
1839	Schenectady, NY	Elijah Hedding
1840	Middlebury, VT	Robert Roberts
1841	Albany, NY	Joshua Soule
1842	Burlington, VT	Elijah Hedding
1843	Troy, NY	Beverly Waugh
1844	West Poultney, VT	Leonidas Hamline
1845	Schenectady, NY	Elijah Hedding
1846	Keeseville, NY	Edmund Janes
1847	Albany, NY	Thomas Morris
1848	Troy, NY	Leonidas Hamline
1849	Sandy Hill, NY	Leonidas Hamline
1850	Saratoga, NY	Thomas Morris
1851	North Adams, MA	Edmund Janes
1852	Plattsburgh, NY	Edmund Janes
1853	Schenectady, NY	Beverly Waugh
1854	Albany, NY	Edmund Janes
1855	Troy, NY	Matthew Simpson
1856	Burlington, VT	Thomas Morris
1857	Pittsfield, MA	Osman Baker
1858	Middlebury, VT	Edward Ames

1859	Saratoga, NY	Edmund Janes
1860	Lansingburgh, NY	Osman Baker
1861	Albany, NY	Edward Ames
1862	Troy, NY	Levi Scott
1863	Fort Edward, NY	Osman Baker
1864	Amsterdam, NY	Matthew Simpson
1865	Plattsburgh, NY	Calvin Kingsley
1866	Cambridge, NY	Edmund Janes
1867	Pittsfield, MA	David Clark
1868	Albany, NY	Levi Scott
1869	West Troy, NY	Calvin Kingsley
1870	Burlington, VT	Edward Ames
1871	Troy, NY	Levi Scott
1872	Saratoga, NY	Edmund Janes
1873	Gloversville, NY	Jesse Peck
1874	Schenectady, NY	Randolph Foster
1875	Glens Falls, NY	Edward Ames
1876	Albany, NY	Levi Scott
1877	Plattsburgh, NY	Randolph Foster
1878	Lansingburgh, NY	Gilbert Haven
1879	Bennington, VT	William Harris
1880	Burlington, VT	Jesse Peck
1881	Glens Falls, NY	Isaac Wiley
1882	Troy, NY	Matthew Simpson
1883	Gloversville, NY	Henry Warren
1884	Amsterdam, NY	Edward Andrews
1885	Saratoga, NY	Thomas Bowman
1886	Pittsfield, MA	Stephen Merrill
1887	Saratoga, NY	William Harris
1888	Troy, NY	Cyrus Foss
1889	Saratoga, NY	Edward Andrews
1890	Saratoga, NY	John Newman
1891	Johnstown, NY	John Hurst
1892	Plattsburgh, NY	Randolph Foster
1893	Albany, NY	Isaac Joyce
1894	Cohoes, NY	Henry Warren
1895	Saratoga, NY	John Walden

1896	Gloversville, NY	Charles Fowler
1897	Schenectady, NY	William Ninde
1898	Saratoga, NY	Willard Mallalieu
1899	Burlington, VT	Daniel Goodsell
1900	Troy, NY	Stephen Merrill
1901	Saratoga, NY	John Hurst
1902	Saratoga, NY	James FitzGerald
1903	Saratoga, NY	Charles McCabe
1904	Gloversville, NY	Earl Cranston
1905	Saratoga, NY	Henry Warren
1906	Saratoga, NY	David Moore
1907	Saratoga, NY	Alpheus Wilson
1908	Saratoga, NY	William Burt
1909	Gloversville, NY	Joseph Berry
1910	Saratoga, NY	Robert McIntyre
1911	Saratoga, NY	Earl Warren
1912	Saratoga, NY	John Hamilton
1913	Saratoga, NY	Alpheus Wilson
1914	Saratoga, NY	Frederick Leete
1915	Saratoga, NY	William Quayle
1916	Saratoga, NY	Theodore Henderson
1917	Saratoga, NY	William Burt
1918	Gloversville, NY	Wilbur Thirkield
1919	Saratoga Springs, NY	William Burt
1920	Saratoga Springs, NY	William Burt
1921	Saratoga Springs, NY	William Burt
1922	Schenectady, NY	William Burt
1923	Glens Falls, NY	William Burt
1924	Troy, NY	William Burt
1925	North Adams, MA	Adna Leonard
1926	Albany, NY	Charles Locke
1927	Albany, NY	Adna Leonard
1928	Saratoga Springs, NY	Charles Mead
1929	Pittsfield, MA	Edwin Hughes
1930	Saratoga Springs, NY	Adna Leonard
1931	Gloversville, NY	William McDowell
1932	Saratoga Springs, NY	Adna Leonard

Year	Location	Presiding Bishop
1933	Lake Placid, NY	Francis McConnell
1934	Saratoga Springs, NY	Francis McConnell
1935	Troy, NY	Ernest Waldorf
1936	Saratoga Springs, NY	Francis McConnell
1937	Saratoga Springs, NY	Francis McConnell
1938	Saratoga Springs, NY	Angie Smith
1939	Saratoga Springs, NY	Francis McConnell

Methodist Church 1939–1940

Year	Location	Presiding Bishop
1939 Sp	Glens Falls, NY	Francis McConnell
1940	Saratoga Springs, NY	Francis McConnell

Sp = Special Session

Vermont Conference
Methodist Episcopal Church 1845–1939

Year	Location—all in Vermont	Presiding Bishop
1845	Rochester	Edmund Janes
1846	Springfield	Beverly Waugh
1847	Irasburg	Elijah Hedding
1848	Barre	Elijah Hedding
1849	Peacham	Leonidas Hamline
1850	Bradford	Thomas Morris
1851	Woodstock	Edmund Janes
1852	Northfield	Levi Scott
1853	Saint Johnsbury Center	Beverly Waugh
1854	Putney	Edmund Janes
1855	Plainfield	Edward Ames
1856	Newbury	Osmon Baker
1857	Brattleboro	Beverly Waugh
1858	Montpelier	Osmon Baker
1859	Barton	Matthew Simpson
1860	Springfield	Edmund Janes
1861	Barre	Levi Scott

1862	Northfield	Osmon Baker
1863	Saint Albans	Matthew Simpson
1864	Saint Johnsbury	Edmund Janes
1865	Bradford	David Clark
1866	Montpelier	Matthew Simpson
1867	Newbury	Levi Scott
1868	Swanton	Edward Ames
1869	Waterbury	Edward Thompson
1870	Springfield	Levi Simpson
1871	Northfield	Edmund Janes
1872	Chelsea	Edward Ames
1873	Richford	Edmund Janes
1874	Danville	Jesse Peck
1875	Bellows Falls	Gilbert Haven
1876	Saint Johnsbury	Edward Ames
1877	Barre	Randolph Foster
1878	Woodstock	Gilbert Haven
1879	Swanton	William Harris
1880	Barton Landing	Isaac Wiley
1881	Bradford	Edward Andrews
1882	Ludlow	Stephen Merrill
1883	Saint Albans	William Harris
1884	Montpelier	Edward Andrews
1885	Bellows Falls	Thomas Bowman
1886	Chelsea	John Hurst
1887	Saint Johnsbury	John Walden
1888	West Randolph	Randolph Foster
1889	Morrisville	William Ninde
1890	Brattleboro	Edward Andrews
1891	Northfield	Willard Mallalieu
1892	Montpelier	Edward Andrews
1893	Barton	Isaac Joyce
1894	Bradford	Henry Warren
1895	Waterbury	Cyrus Foss
1896	Barre	Charles Fowler
1897	Barre	John Walden
1898	Springfield	John Vincent

1899	Newport	Willard Mallalieu
1900	Bellows Falls	Stephen Merrill
1901	Lyndonville	Earl Cranston
1902	Saint Albans	Daniel Goodsell
1903	Northfield	Henry Warren
1904	Montpelier	Charles Fowler
1905	Enosburg Falls	David Moore
1906	Morrisville	John Hamilton
1907	Saint Johnsbury	Joseph Berry
1908	Barre	Earl Cranston
1909	Hardwick	Daniel Goodsell
1910	Island Pond	Robert McIntyre
1911	Waterbury	Thomas Neely
1912	Newport	Edwin Hughes
1913	Richford	Theodore Henderson
1914	Hardwick	Frederick Leete
1915	Brattleboro	Richard Cooke
1916	Montpelier	Franklin Hamilton
1917	Newport	Franklin Hamilton
1918	Saint Johnsbury	Edwin Hughes
1919	Saint Albans	Frederick Leete
1920	Springfield	Homer Stuntz
1921	Barre	Edwin Hughes
1922	White River Junction	Francis McConnell
1923	Barton	Edwin Hughes
1924	Bellows Falls	Charles Mead
1925	Richford	William Anderson
1926	Brattleboro	Charles Burns
1927	Enosburg Falls	Harry Smith
1928	Montpelier	William Anderson
1929	Saint Johnsbury	William Anderson
1930	Ludlow	John Robinson
1931	Orleans	Frederick Keeney
1932	Waterbury	William Anderson
1933	Saint Albans	Charles Burns
1934	Barre	Charles Burns
1935	Springfield	Wallace Brown

1936	Newport	Charles Burns
1937	Saint Johnsbury	G. Bromley Oxnam
1938	Saint Albans	Herbert Welch
1939	Barre	Charles Flint

Methodist Church 1939–1940

Year	Location	Presiding Bishop
1940	Montpelier	G. Bromley Oxnam
1940 Cl	Waterbury	Francis McConnell

Cl = Closing Session

United Troy Conference
Methodist Church 1941–1967

Year	Location	Presiding Bishop
1941 Se	Glens Falls , NY	Francis McConnell
1942	Saratoga Springs, NY	Francis McConnell
1943	Saratoga Springs, NY	James Straughn
1944	Saratoga Springs, NY	Francis McConnell
1944 Sp	Lake Placid, NY	G. Bromley Oxnam
1945	Albany, NY	G. Bromley Oxnam
1945 Se	Glens Falls, NY	G. Bromley Oxnam
1946	Saratoga Springs, NY	G. Bromley Oxnam
1947	Saratoga Springs, NY	G. Bromley Oxnam
1948	Saratoga Springs, NY	G. Bromley Oxnam
1948 Sp	Albany, NY	G. Bromley Oxnam
1949	Saratoga Springs, NY	G. Bromley Oxnam
1950	Albany, NY	G. Bromley Oxnam
1951	Saratoga Springs, NY	Walter Ledden
1952	Lake Placid, NY	G. Bromley Oxnam
1953	Troy, NY	Fredrick Newell
1954	Saratoga Springs, NY	Fredrick Newell
1955	Pittsfield, MA	Fredrick Newell
1956	Schenectady, NY	Fredrick Newell
1957	Glens Falls, NY	Fredrick Newell

1958	Albany, NY	Fred Corson
1959	Burlington, VT	Fredrick Newell
1960	Gloversville, NY	Fredrick Newell
1961	Saratoga Springs, NY	Lloyd C. Wicke
1962	Schenectady, NY	Lloyd C. Wicke
1963	Lake Placid, NY	Lloyd C. Wicke
1964	Albany, NY	Lloyd C. Wicke
1965	Gloversville, NY	Lloyd C. Wicke
1966	Burlington, VT	Lloyd C. Wicke
1966 Sp	Saratoga Springs, NY	Lloyd C. Wicke
1967	Lake Placid, NY	Lloyd C. Wicke

Se = Second Session   Sp = Special Session

The United Methodist Church 1968–2010

Year	Location	Presiding Bishop
1968	Poultney, VT	Lloyd C. Wicke
1969	Poultney, VT	Lloyd C. Wicke
1970	Poultney, VT	Lloyd C. Wicke
1971	Poultney, VT	Lloyd C. Wicke
1971 Sp	Queensbury, NY	Lloyd C. Wicke
1972	Poultney, VT	Lloyd C. Wicke
1973	Poultney, VT	W. Ralph Ward, Jr.
1974	Poultney, VT	W. Ralph Ward, Jr.
1975	Poultney, VT	W. Ralph Ward, Jr.
1976	Poultney, VT	W. Ralph Ward, Jr.
1977	Poultney, VT	W. Ralph Ward, Jr.
1978	Poultney, VT	W. Ralph Ward, Jr.
1978	Glens Falls, NY	W. Ralph Ward, Jr.
1979	Poultney, VT	W. Ralph Ward, Jr.
1980	Poultney, VT	W. Ralph Ward, Jr.
1981	Poultney, VT	Roy C. Nichols
1982	Poultney, VT	Roy C. Nichols
1983	Poultney, VT	Roy C. Nichols
1984	Poultney, VT	Roy C. Nichols
1985	Winooski, VT	C. Dale White
1986	Poultney, VT	C. Dale White
1987	Poultney, VT	C. Dale White

1988	Poultney, VT	C. Dale White
1989	Troy, NY	C. Dale White
1990	Poultney, VT	C. Dale White
1991	Poultney, VT	James K. Mathews
1991 Sp	Hudson Falls, NY	James K. Mathews
1992	Poultney, VT	James K. Mathews
1993	Poultney. VT	William B. Grove
1994	Poultney, VT	William B. Grove
1995	Castleton, VT	William B. Grove
1996	Poultney, VT	William B. Grove
1997	Poultney, VT	Susan M. Morrison
1998	Poultney, VT	Susan M. Morrison
1998 Sp	Glens Falls, NY	Susan M. Morrison
1999	Poultney, VT	Susan M. Morrison
2000	Poultney, VT	Susan M. Morrison
2001	Saratoga Springs, NY	Susan M. Morrison
2002	Burlington, VT	Susan M. Morrison
2003	Burlington, VT	Susan M. Morrison
2004	Saratoga Springs, NY	Susan M. Morrison
2005	Saratoga Springs, NY	Susan M. Morrison
2006	Burlington, VT	Susan M. Morrison
2007	Burlington, VT	Susan W. Hassinger
2007 Sp	Poultney, VT	F. Herbert Skeete
2008	Saratoga Springs, NY	Susan W. Hassinger
2009	Saratoga Springs, NY	Susan W. Hassinger
2010 Cy	Saratoga Springs, NY	Susan W. Hassinger
2010 Re	Glens Falls, NY	Susan W. Hassinger
2010	Glens Falls, NY	Susan W. Hassinger

Sp = Special Session   Cy = Clergy Session   Re = Retiree Recognition

Upper New York Conference

Year	Location	Presiding Bishop
2010	Syracuse, NY	Marcus Matthews
2010	Albany, NY	Marcus Matthews

Appendix I

Closed and Merged Churches

While it is easy enough to provide a list of currently active churches in Troy Conference, it is beyond our resources to create a complete list of closed churches. First, it is impossible to identify all the places in which Methodist societies became churches because some of those locations were never recorded in the conference journals. Second, early records of the circuit riders are largely non-existent. Third, the names of some individual churches changed due to mergers, relocations, changes in community name, or for no clear reason. Fourth, early non-church sources focus on congregations existing only at a specific point in time. Fifth, records that should have been put into the care of the Commission on Archives and History have frequently not been forwarded. Sixth, what might have been remembered in other ways is fragmentary at best and difficult to locate. Seventh, some churches merged, united, or otherwise altered their identities. They have not always been identified afterward as closed.

Having said all that, what follows is an attempt to be as complete as possible. In 1986, *A Spreading Flame: The Stories of the Churches of Troy Annual Conference* by Charles and Ouida Schwartz included a list that was as accurate as the authors could make it. Karen Staulters, the present Troy Conference archivist, has supplemented the earlier research to bring it up to date adding, where possible, the date of the church's closing.

The tradition in Troy Conference is to distinguish the state where a church is located only as needed for clarification or when the same community name appears in each state. With our churches now going into two different conferences, that approach may not be adequate. Therefore, we have tried to include the state where the closed church was located. A few churches have been closed and then reopened before being closed again. In those cases more than one date may be given.

Adamsville, NY
Addison, VT
Adirondack Mission, NY
Akin, NY
Albany, NY
    Arbor Hill
    Ash Grove (M)
    Benjamin Street
    Bethel
    Broadway
    Central Avenue
    Division Street
    Ferry Street Station (M)
    First (M) – 1964
    Free Central
    Garrettson Station
    Grace (M)
    Hudson Street
    Italian Work
    Lydius Street, Free Church
    Mount Zion – 1923
    Saint Luke's (M) – 1980
    Washington Street
    West Station
Albia, NY
Alburgh, VT
Altona, NY – 1898
Amity, NY
Amsden, VT
Amsterdam, NY
    East Main Street – 1847
    Elizabeth Street
    Forest Street (M)
Argusville, NY – 1913
Arlington, VT
Ascutneyville, VT
Athens, VT
Athol, NY – 1964

Barnard, VT
Barnet, VT
Barnumtown, VT
Barre, VT, Italian Mission
Barton Hill, VT
Barton Landing, VT
Batchellerville, NY
Batestown Mission, NY
Bath-on-Hudson, NY
Battenville, NY – 1950
Bedford, NY
Beecher Falls, VT
Beekmantown, NY
Belcher, NY – 1948
Bellows Falls, VT – 1977
Belvidere, VT
Bennett Station, NY – 1869
Benson, NY – 1931
Benson, VT
Berkshire, VT
Berlin, VT
Berne, NY – 1903
Bethel Lympus, VT
Bethlehem, NY – 1881
Bleecker Mission, NY
Boltonville, VT
Boston, NY
Bowdishville, NY
Braintree, VT
Bridgewater, VT
Bridport, VT – 1919
Brighton, NY – 1927
Brookfield, VT
Brookfield, NY
Brookline, VT
Brookview, NY – 1962
Brownington Center, VT
Brunswick Center, NY

Brunswick, NY – 1898
Burke, VT
Burlington, VT, Pine Street
Burtonville, NY – 1998
Buskirk, NY – 1962

Cadyville, NY
Calais, VT
Cambridge Valley, NY
Cambridge, VT
Cambridgeport, NY
Canaan, VT
Cannon's Corners, NY
Carleston, VT – 1906
Cedar River, NY
Center Valley, NY – 1922
Centerville, VT
Chapel and Glass House, NY
Charlotte, VT – 1903
Charlton, NY – 1906
Chazy, NY (M) – 1970
Chester, VT
Christian Hill, NY
Churubusco, NY – 1940
Clarendon, VT
Clark's Chapel, NY – 1932
Clarksville, NY – 1958
Cobleskill Center, NY
Coeyman's Patent, NY
Cohoes, NY
    First (M) – 2005
    French Mission
    Saint James (M) – 2005
    Two Rivers of Peace – 2009
Colchester, VT
Collinsville, NY – 1949
Columbia, NY
Conklingville, NY – 1922
Cooksborough, NY – 1906
Coons, NY – 1921
Copperfield, VT
Copperas Hill, VT
Corinth Corners, NY – 1967
Cornwall, VT
Cotton Hill, NY

Coventry Center, VT
Coventry, VT – 1920
Craftsbury, VT – 1999
Cranberry Creek, NY – 1930
Creek Center, NY
Crescent, NY (M) – 1957
Cuttingsville, VT – 1951

Damon's Crossing, VT
Danby Corners, VT
Danby, VT
Day, NY – 1919
Denton's Corners, NY
Derby, VT – 1991
Dewey's Bridge, NY
Dog River, NY
Dorset, VT
Dover, VT
Dresden, NY
Duanesburg, NY

East Albany, VT
East Athens, VT
East Barnard, VT
East Beekmantown, NY – 1965
East Bennington, VT
East Berkshire, VT
East Brunswick, NY – 1940
East Burke, VT
East Cambridge, VT
East Charlestown, VT – 1913
East Cobleskill, NY – 1848
East Corinth, VT – 1938
East Dorset, VT
East Dover, VT
East Elmore, VT
East Galway, NY – 1890
East Glover, VT
East Hebron, NY – 1920
East Line, NY
East Lyndon, VT – 1970
East Monkton, VT
East Nassau, NY
East Pittsford, VT – 1949
East Pittstown, NY – 1940

East Poestenkill, NY – 1940
East Saint Johnsbury, VT
East Sand Lake, NY
East Walden, VT
East Warren, VT
East Wells, VT – 1923
East Whitehall, NY – 1970
Eden, VT – 1940
Edinburgh Hill, NY – 1909
Elizabethtown, NY – 1946, 1955
Ely, VT
Ephratah, NY – 1994
Evansville, VT
Evarts, VT

Factory Point, VT
Fairfield, VT
Fairhaven, VT, Welsh Mission
Fairlee, VT – 1998
Farlin, NY
Fayston, VT
Felchville, VT – 1947
Fitzdale, VT
Flackville, NY
Florida, NY
Fort Edward, NY – 1986
Fort Hunter NY – 1999
Fort Johnson, NY (M)
Franklin, NY
Franklinton, NY – 1981

Garfield, NY
Garoga, NY – 1970
Gaskill, VT
Gaysville, VT – 1938
Glens Falls, NY, West Mountain
Glover, VT
Goshen, VT
Gouldsville, VT
Granby, VT
Granville, VT – 1926, 1996
Green River, VT
Green Street, VT
Greenfield, NY – 1998
Grooms, NY (M) – 1957

Guilderland, NY – 1944
Guildhall, VT – 1938
Guilford, VT

Hagaman's Mills, NY
Hague, NY
Halfmoon, NY
Hampton, NY – 1937
Hancock/Granville, VT – 1996
Hart's Falls, NY
Hartford, VT
Hartland, VT – 1950
Heath, VT
Hebron, NY
Hillview, NY
Hinsdale, VT
Hoag's Corners, NY – 1959
Hoosick Falls, NY – 1951
Hoosick, NY
Hope, NY – 1938
Horntonville, VT
Hyde Park, VT

Igerna, NY
Irasburg, VT – 2006
Island Pond, VT – 1938

Jacksonville, VT – 1913
Jamaica, VT
Jay, NY (M) – 1970
Jay, VT – 1913
Jessup's Landing, NY

Keene, NY – 2009
Kenyontown, NY
Ketchum's Corners, NY – 1943
Kinderhook, NY – 1959
King Church, NY
Kingsboro, NY
Kingsbury Street, NY
Kirby, VT
Knowersville, NY – 1923
Knox, NY – 1934, 1940

Lamoilleville, VT

Lansingburgh, NY, Hedding
Leicester, VT – 1898
Lemington, VT
Lewiston, VT
Lewistown, NY
Little White Creek, NY
Londonderry, VT
Loon Lake, NY
Lowell, VT
Lyndon, VT – 1949, 1970

Mad River, VT
Maltaville, NY
Manchester, VT – 1940
Mariaville, NY – 1870
Marlboro, VT
McIndoes Falls, VT
Mechanicsville, VT
Meco, NY
Merrillsville, NY – 1958
Middlefield, NY
Middletown, VT – 1936
Millville, NY
Miltonboro, VT – 1936
Minerva, NY
Mineville, NY – 1941
Morgan, VT – 1999
Morristown Corners, VT
Mount Holly, VT

Nelliston, NY – 1938, 1958
New Haven, VT
New Lebanon, NY – 1872
New Salem, NY
New Scotland, NY
Newark, VT
Newbury Center, VT
Newbury, VT
Newfane, VT
Newtown, NY (M) – 1957
North Albany, VT
North Bennington, VT, Hinsdillville
    – 1944
North Bolton, VT
North Cambridge, VT

North Church, NY
North Concord, VT – 1938
North Danville, VT – 1922
North Easton, NY
North Elba, NY (M)
North Fairfax, VT – 1918
North Fairfield, VT
North Greenwich, NY
North Hartland, VT – 1997
North Hoosick, NY – 2010
North Hudson Mission, NY – 1919,
    1931, 1959
North Hyde Park, VT
North Johnsburg, NY
North Londonderry, VT
North Pittstown, NY
North Pownal, VT
North Troy, VT
North Wardsboro, VT
North Whitecreek, NY
North Wolcott, VT – 1987
Norwich, VT
Noyesville, VT

Olcut, NY
Old Chatham, NY (M) – 1960
Olmsteadville, NY – 1976
Orange, VT
Orwell, VT – 1861
Osborn's Bridge, NY – 1928,
    1930, 1943

Panton, VT
Pattens Mills, NY
Pawlet Community Church, VT –
    2006
Peacham, VT
Perkinsville, VT
Perry's Mills, NY (M) – 1969
Peru, NY – 1944
Pine Lake, NY
Piseco, NY
Pittsfield, MA
Pittsford, VT – 2001

Pleasant Square Mission, NY –
    1875
Pleasant Valley, VT
Point Au Roche, NY – 1948
Port Henry, NY – 1994
Post Mills, VT
Potter Hill, NY - 1990
Putney, VT – 1998

Quaker Street, NY
Quechee Village, VT - 1908

Randolph Center, VT – 1960
Raymertown, NY
Reading, VT
Redford, NY – 1950
Reidsville, NY – 1956
Rensselaerville, NY – 1903
Reynolds Corners, NY – 1848
Riverside (Riparious), NY
Riverton, VT - 2010
Rockingham, VT
Rockton, NY
Rockwood (Garoga), NY – 1942,
    1970, 1974
Rogersfield, NY
Root, NY – 1874
Rotterdam Junction, NY – 2008
Rotterdam, NY
Rouses Point, NY (M) – 1969
Royalton, VT
Rural Grove, NY – 1910
Rutland Center, VT

Sadawga, VT
Saint Johnsbury Center, VT
Salem, VT
Salisbury, VT
Salt Springville, NY
Sand Lake, NY – 1940
Saranac River Mission, NY
Schaghticoke Hill, NY - 1931
Schaghticoke Junction, NY
Schaghticoke, NY – 1960
Schenectady, NY

Grace – 1996
Parker's Corners – 1943
Saint Timothy's – 1954
Union Street (M)
Schoharie, NY – 1937
Schuyler Falls, NY – 1992
Sciota, NY (reopened)
Seward, NY – 1938
Sharon, NY
Sheffield, VT – 1999
Sheldon Springs, VT
Shoreham, NY
Shoreham, VT
Sloansville, NY (M)
Sodom, NY
South Albany, NY
South Albany, VT – 1964
South Alburg, VT – 1997
South Berne, NY
South Cabot, VT
South Cambridge, VT
South Chittenden, VT
South Franklin, VT
South Hill, VT
South Londonderry, VT
South Plattsburgh, NY – 1958
South Remington
South Richford, VT
South Schroon, NY
South Troy, VT
South Victory, VT
South Walden, VT – 1997
South Wallingford, VT
South Woodbury, VT
Sprakers Basin, NY
Sprout Brook, NY (M) – 1974
Stamford, VT – 1961
Standish, NY
Stannard, VT
Starksboro, VT – 1909, 1952
State Road, NY
Stillwater, NY – 1952
Stockbridge, VT
Stony Brook, VT
Stony Creek, NY – 2005

Stowe, VT
Street Road, NY
Stuyvesant Falls, NY – 1919
Stuyvesant Landing, NY – 1869
Stuyvesant, NY
Sudbury, VT
Sutton, VT

Tahaws, NY – 1964
Thurman, NY
Tomhannock, NY – 2010
Topsham, VT
Townsend, VT
Tribe's Hill, NY – 1881
Trout Lake, NY – 1917
Troy, NY
    North Mission
    First Avenue-State Street (M) – 1966
    Grace
    Hedding
    Lansingburgh – 2007
    Levings (M)
    Memorial (M) – 1997
    North Second Street
    Ohio Street
    Saint Marks (M) – 1970
    Saint Titus - 1934
    Third Street Mission
    Third Street – 1923
    Trinity (M) – 1966
    Vail Avenue
Troy, VT
Tunbridge, VT

Underhill Center, VT – 1949, 1976
Union Village, VT - 1874
Upper Jay, NY – 2009

Valatie, NY
Valcour, NY – 1846
Vermontville, NY
Vernon, VT
Vershire, VT
Victory, VT – 1865

Wadham's Mills, NY – 1960
Waitsfield, VT – 1998
Walden, VT – 1997 (reopened 1998)
Wallingford, VT
Warren, VT
Washington, VT – 1881
Waterford, VT
Watervliet, NY
    First (M) – 1997
    Third Avenue – (M)
Weatherfield Center, VT
Weathersfield, VT
Welsh Hollow, VT
West Amsterdam, NY
West Beekmantown, NY – 1941
West Berkshire, VT
West Berlin, VT – 1928
West Berne, NY – 1954
West Bolton, VT
West Bradford, VT – 1946
West Brookfield, VT
West Bush, NY – 1923
West Center, VT
West Chazy, NY (M) – 1941, 1969
West Concord, VT
West Cornwall, VT – 1920
West Crescent, NY (M) – 1957
West Dorset, VT
West Dover, VT
West Fairlee, VT
West Ferrisburgh, VT
West Galway, NY
West Glover, VT
West Grafton, NY
West Granville, NY
West Groton, VT
West Haven, VT
West Hebron, NY
West Lebanon, NY – 1930
West Newbury, VT
West Norwich, VT
West Peru, NY
West Plattsburgh, NY

West Randolph, VT
West Richmondville, NY
West Roxbury, VT – 1956
West Rutland, VT – 1919
West Salisbury, VT – 1957
West Township, NY – 1956
West Troy, NY
    First Avenue
    Third Avenue
West Wheelock, VT
Westfield, VT – 1914
Westford, VT – 2006
Westmore, VT
Weston Island, VT
Westville, NY – 1944
Weybridge, VT – 1925

Whallonsburg, NY – 1994
Wheelerville, NY – 1930
Wheelock, VT
Whiting, VT
Whitingham, NY
Whitingham, VT
Wilder, VT – 1960
Williamsville, VT – 2002
Wilmington, NY (M) – 1970
Wilson Hollow, NY
Wilton, NY (M) – 1965
Winhall, VT
Woodstock, VT – 1930
Worchester, VT
Wright's Mills, VT

(M) - Merged with another church

Churches held for property reasons:

Keene, NY
Rotterdam Junction, NY
Sciota, NY
Thurman, NY
Upper Jay, NY

Index

(Does not include chapter 8, charts, or appendices)

Vision Team, 85
VISN, 266f
Vogel, Fred, 162
Voland, Ann and George, 189
Volunteers in Mission, 18, 116-131, 138, 212, 219
Voorheesville, 32

W

Waitsfield, VT, 117
Walk to Emmaus, 93-98
Ward, Bishop W. Ralph, 192
Warner, Charles, 155
Warner, Kelly, 62
Washbourne, Kay, 276
Washburn, Donald, 27f
Waterfield, Don, 74
Waterford, 104, 174
Watrous, Donald, 268
Web site, 268
Webb, Mary Berry, 65
Webb, Captain Thomas, 1
Welch, Betty, 21
Wells, VT, 2
Wesley District, 48, 49
Wesley Nursing Home, 109, 111-116
Wesley, John, 1, 2, 47, 67, 79, 81, 151, 262, 278
Wesleyan quadrilateral, 38
West Camden, 2
West Sand Lake, 3, 174
Westport, 117
Whatcoat, Bishop Richard, 151
White privilege, 8, 12, 14, 16, 18
White, Bishop C. Dale, 80, 94, 110, 218, 265, 273
Whitingham, 3
Wicke, Bishop Lloyd C., 190
Wihakowi, 216f
Williston, VT, 32, 271
Wilton, 31, 100
Windsor, VT, 3
Wolcott, VT, 4, 9, 11, 259, 260
Woman's Society of Christian

Service, 6
Woodbury, VT, 209
Woodman, William, 74
World Service, 133-136
Wright, Franklyn, 163
Wrigley, Kevin, 193
Wusterbarth, Harold, 135
Wyoming Conference, 270, 280, 284-287

Y

YAC (Youth Annual Conference, Youth Autumn Celebration), 271, 275
Yoon, Tae-Hun, 20, 26
Youth Ministries, Council on, 64, 272-276, 284

Z

Zittel, Barbara, 62
Zitterling, Rick, 278